W9-AQO-603

STUART AND GEORGIAN MOMENTS

Published under the auspices of
The 17th and 18th Centuries Studies Group
University of California, Los Angeles

Publications of
The 17th and 18th Centuries Studies Group, UCLA

1.

Seventeenth-Century Imagery: Essays on Uses of
Figurative Language from Donne to Farquhar
Edited by Earl Miner

2.

England in the Restoration and Early Eighteenth Century
Essays on Culture and Society
Edited by H. T. Swedenberg, Jr.

3.

Stuart and Georgian Moments: Clark Library Seminar Papers
on Seventeenth and Eighteenth Century English Literature
Edited by Earl Miner

STUART AND GEORGIAN MOMENTS

CLARK LIBRARY SEMINAR PAPERS ON
SEVENTEENTH AND EIGHTEENTH CENTURY
ENGLISH LITERATURE

EDITED BY EARL MINER

1972
UNIVERSITY OF CALIFORNIA PRESS
Berkeley • Los Angeles • London

820.9
M664 a

For
Lawrence Clark Powell
from his fortunate friends

Foreword

The 17th and 18th Centuries Studies Group has been founded at the University of California, Los Angeles, with the aim of bringing together students of various disciplines to advance understanding of the lives and the culture of peoples during a crucial period of human experience. To this end the group has undertaken a variety of enterprises (with the support of the Chancellor and the deans at UCLA), including teaching programs, conferences, and symposia designed to cross departmental lines. The aim is to foster studies involving numerous disciplines and to encourage participation by other universities in the United States and abroad. One such enterprise is the publication of a series of books covering a wide spectrum of interests and attracting contributors in various fields.

The group hopes to draw upon the libraries, talents, and resources of one university in a way that will engage the efforts and be worthy of the attention of a more than local fraternity of scholars. Individual volumes are planned to pursue a variety of topics. We welcome comments and suggestions from scholars interested in these two centuries and hope that our endeavors will stimulate comparable study and activity at other universities.

Maximillian E. Novak
Chairman, The 17th and 18th
Centuries Studies Group, UCLA

Preface

The dozen essays reprinted here by the 17th and 18th Centuries Studies Group, University of California, Los Angeles, have been chosen from among the papers read at invitational Saturday seminars at the William Andrews Clark Memorial Library and originally published in pamphlet form. The principle of selection excluded not only the many papers on subjects not literary but also literary papers that did not deal with the literature of the period here defined. A number of the essays included have proved so popular that they have long since been out of print, and the stock of other pamphlets is nearly exhausted. In addition to the scholarly purpose of republishing these papers as a collection, the 17th and 18th Centuries Studies Group welcomes the opportunity to honor one of its greatest benefactors, Dr. Lawrence Clark Powell. In his capacity as director of the Clark Library and as university librarian, Mr. Powell built up UCLA holdings, on a qualitative as well as a quantitative basis, during difficult as well as some more affluent years. As a lover of company as well as of books, he also initiated the Clark Library Saturday seminars. This subject has been enlarged upon in the sketch of Lawrence Clark Powell contributed to this volume by his successor, Robert Vosper. Few universities have been fortunate enough to enjoy the services of two librarians of such eminence in succession, and it is fitting that in honoring one the other should participate.

Anyone who knows the former librarian of UCLA must be

keenly aware that his achievements are extraordinarily varied.
He is an author—probably a more prolific one than any of his
professorial colleagues—and an autobiographer. He has a deep
love of California and, indeed, of the entire southwestern
United States. Certainly the literary and artistic life of the
Los Angeles area during the past three or four decades would
have been sorely impoverished without his achievements and
those of his large circle of gifted friends. Without his puckish
wit and his conviviality, many a bright day would have been
lost. Without his desire to assist that natural inclination of
rare books to move to southern California, the libraries of
UCLA would not be so outstanding in quality and number of
books as they are. Feeling strongly that the books should be
got to UCLA, and then that students and faculty should be
got to the books, he sealed, if he did not begin, the tradition
of UCLA as a place with efficient and hospitable libraries.
Small wonder that he should have implemented his desire to
bring people together to talk about books and ideas by in-
venting one of the most agreeable forms of doing so, the Clark
Saturday seminars.

About two weeks before a seminar Saturday one receives in
the mail a handsome invitation designed and printed by William Cheney, one of the country's foremost designers of printing. One arrives at the Clark Library about ten o'clock in the
morning. The entrance to the library is suitably modest, and
the grounds of the estate, which cover a city block, are en-
closed by brick walls. Inside, the formal arrangement of the
garden struggles with profusion: the strife of art and nature,
as the seventeenth century put it. Such poets as Andrew
Marvell would also have recognized the brick-walled garden
as a *hortus conclusus*, both literally and emblematically a place
for the contemplative soul. Since Los Angeles is a garden in
the desert (as well as many other things), the plants on the
Clark grounds come from many places. There are box and

yew from England, a stunning example of the Brazilian jac-
aranda, many varieties of the Australian eugenia or bush
cherry, a splendid tall specimen of the kauri pine from New
Zealand, and an imposing Moreton Bay fig, also from the anti-
podes. The devotee of the Clark Library will find many
smaller shrubs, such as the camellia and the agapanthus (both
blue and white), and will know that along the walk of the
eastern formal garden there is a myrtle hedge of uncommon
fragrance. Again in Renaissance and seventeenth-century
terms, it is a *locus amoenus*, an earthly paradise, especially
during times of noise or of busy, interruptive annoy on the
UCLA campus.

Before going to the library building, one parks his car in an
area adjoining the old carriage house used by the Clark family.
Presently it serves as the gardeners' toolshed, provides quarters for Mr. Cheney, and houses a couple who maintain
residence at the Clark. The home of the Clark family was a
rather plain brick dwelling whose interior was enhanced by
lovely wood paneling. The first reaction of everybody who
came to the library was that the Clark house should be re-
furnished and brought back to life, but over the years disuse
and termites had reduced it to a somewhat Dickensian rick-
etiness, perhaps like that of Miss Havisham's house in *Great
Expectations*, and recently it was demolished.

As one enters for the Saturday seminar, one heads by instinct for the parterre, where the Clark staff is busy welcoming
guests with goodwill, coffee, and cakes. Usually those among
the coffee drinkers who have come from England are busy
entreating the sun, as Dr. Johnson put it, while the southern
Californians are seeking the shade. The guests vary, depending on the subject of the seminar, but one will meet wives and
husbands from different branches of the University of California and from other colleges and universities in the area.
One is always happy to see again friends from the Huntington

Library in San Marino, including both staff members and visiting scholars who are using the facilities of that great library and enjoying its handsome grounds. Almost always there are guests—booksellers, printers, lawyers, other professional and artistic people—whom one can most simply describe as friends of the Clark Library or of its director.

At about eleven o'clock the librarian of the Clark begins to urge the seminar members into the drawing room of this baroque building, which is constructed of travertine and brick on the outside and of wood and marble on the inside. The drawing room is designed after an Italian baroque council chamber. In its ceiling and at one end are pictures illustrative of Dryden's *All for Love,* with smaller inset pictures illustrating stories in Ovid's *Metamorphoses* chosen from those translated by Dryden. At the other end is a fresco illustrating Shakespeare's *Antony and Cleopatra.* The abundance of pink and brown flesh on ceiling and walls may startle visitors who are not familiar with baroque painting, and perhaps even some of those who are, but the decoration is genuinely baroque, or neobaroque, in spirit, a form of the preposterous that wins one's affection. On the walls hang portraits of the library's donor and his first librarian, along with portraits of literary worthies. Dryden smiles with enigmatic detachment; Pope and Cibber avoid each other's gaze; Tom Killigrew, got up in silks, is accompanied by a dog; Nat. Lee's arms cross, his eyes dart, and his whole countenance reveals a heart pierced by unspeakable tragedy.

After the introductions the first speaker reads his paper, and the moderator leads the audience in raising questions or making comments about the topic of the morning. The morning discussion is followed by an alfresco buffet lunch, and at about one-thirty the audience reconvenes in the drawing room for the second paper and the second period of discussion. The seminar is over around three o'clock, and the automobiles begin to leave the grounds, their drivers assisted by the gardeners and the maintenance men of the Clark Library.

Not everybody leaves the Clark after the seminar. Some stay on, and there are always a few who earlier in the day slip downstairs to the working part of the library while other people are chatting or strolling. What these assiduous spirits are after one can never tell for certain. Perhaps they are Dickensian scholars, for the Clark boasts an extraordinary collection of Dickens published in the original parts, along with other Victorians, especially the Pre-Raphaelites. The Clark's collection of fine printing represents, in addition to the Kelmscott Press, the Cuala Press, and hence includes a Yeats collection; it also offers what is almost a historical survey of the best printing in California. Or the busy scholar may be consulting the Clark's holdings in Montana history, since the family fortune came from that state and the elder Mr. Clark played a major role in early Montana politics. It is more likely, however, that so inquiring a soul will be consulting letters and other materials of Oscar Wilde or Eric Gill, or that he is interested in other similar individual collections. It is most likely, however, that he is looking for something listed in Donald Wing's *Short-Title Cataloge*, or for something published in the ensuing fifty years, because it is in the period from 1640 to 1750 that the special strength of the Clark Library lies. Books, pamphlets, and broadsides from the Civil War period, from the Restoration, and from the age of Pope make up the basic holdings. Science, theology (with many "A Sermon Preach'd"), music, history, editions of the classics, and, above all, literature are heavily represented. The Clark possesses about a quarter of the 80,000 to 90,000 items listed by Wing; it also has a number of titles that are not so listed. All titles are cross-listed with the holdings of the Huntington Library. These two great southern California libraries together probably have all but several dozen Restoration plays. The Clark also boasts one of the eight best Milton collections in the country (even without the items held at the Research Library on the UCLA campus). Mr. Clark, a gentleman collector, was free to buy what he thought he ought to—of course he had to have a Shakespeare first folio and a few quartos—or simply what he himself wanted to own. Since he enjoyed Chaucer, the Clark has a surprising strength in early editions. For what reason I do not know, Mr. Clark built his main collection around the author who remains its center, the admirer of Shakespeare, Chaucer, and Milton, the father of English criticism, John Dryden.

It has often puzzled me that most of the outstanding students of Dryden during the past century have not been English, or if English, have left England. Scots, Australians, and above all North Americans predominate. Sir Walter Scott and James Russell Lowell were Dryden's two greatest nineteenth-century critics, and in the twentieth century the revival of critical interest on the part of T. S. Eliot and Mark Van Doren consisted in writing Scott and Lowell large. Whatever Mr. Clark's reason, it is a fascinating fact that the inheritor of an American fortune should not have gone off to Europe in the approved Jamesian fashion, but instead have stayed home in a formal garden, supported the Los Angeles Symphony almost by himself (legend has it that he was sometimes allowed to play with the second violins), and collected the works of Dryden. With his collection and the endowment to enlarge it, the Clark Library has naturally become the center for the study of Dryden, and in particular for the California Edition started some years ago by the late Edward Niles Hooker and by H. T. Swedenberg. Over the years, Dryden and Milton have frequently been the focus of UCLA seminars taught in the north room of the Clark, though I well remember teaching the metaphysical poets there and noticing one student with Donne's *Poems* of 1633 spread in her lap. Mr.

Clark would be pleased to know that his books are used so extensively, by students as well as by established scholars. I have observed, over many years of university teaching, that a graduate student who has held an actual seventeenth-century edition in his or her hand is thereafter set apart from the less fortunate ones who have access only to anthologies, modern-spelling texts, or paperbacks.

All of us who are familiar with the Clark Library, and who are fortunate enough to have its relatively small holdings fall into our areas of interest, have been served by a staff unmatched, at least in my experience, for kindliness and helpfulness. All of us have acknowledged their assistance in our books. They and I know how much we owe to Lawrence Clark Powell. It is always a better day for Larry's having been by. We hope that he will accept this tribute as it is meant: a gift to him of something that is his own from people who claim him as their own. I speak of these things in the plural because his friends are many.

I acknowledge the permission to reprint freely given by the authors of the papers collected in this volume or, for the much lamented Herbert Davis, by Mrs. Davis. And although he is always the first to help and the last to be thanked, I am grateful to William E. Conway, librarian of the Clark Library, for carefully inspecting the front matter of this book and for helping to prepare copy for the printer. Miss Susan McCloskey deserves my thanks for using part of her Christmas vacation to help prepare the index.

E. M.

Los Angeles
Summer, 1971

Contributors

Don Cameron Allen is Professor Emeritus of The Johns Hopkins University. His paper was presented in 1964 and published the following year.

Bertrand H. Bronson is Professor Emeritus of the University of California, Berkeley. He presented his paper in 1953. It was published the following year and has long been out of print in the Clark series.

The late Herbert Davis was at one time President of Smith College; he later returned to Oxford and held a chair in bibliography. He was Clark Library Senior Fellow in 1966, and his paper was given and published in that year.

Irvin Ehrenpreis is Professor of English at the University of Virginia. He presented his paper in 1969, and it was published the same year.

Robert Halsband is Professor of English at the University of California, Riverside, and he delivered his paper on the same rainy Saturday that Irvin Ehrenpreis gave his.

Leon Howard is Professor Emeritus of the University of California, Los Angeles. He read his paper in 1958, and it was published in 1959.

Maximillian E. Novak is Professor of English at the University of California, Los Angeles. He spoke on the same day as Herbert Davis.

James E. Phillips is Professor of English at the University of California, Los Angeles. He spoke on the same day as Bertrand H. Bronson and later was the first person to give a second paper in the Clark seminar series.

James Sutherland is now retired from the Lord Northcliffe chair of Modern English Literature at University College, London. He was Clark Senior Fellow in 1962–63 and has been a welcome visitor to UCLA on several occasions. The paper he gave in 1956 was published the next year.

H. T. Swedenberg, Jr., is Professor of English at the University of California, Los Angeles, and General Editor of the California Edition of *The Works of John Dryden*. He was the inaugural Clark Professor and held the post from 1969 to 1971. His paper was given and published in 1967.

Robert Vosper is University Librarian at the University of California, Los Angeles, Director of the Clark Library, Professor of Library Service, and sometime President of the American Library Association.

Charles E. Ward is Professor Emeritus of Duke University. He was Clark Senior Fellow in 1967. He spoke on the same day as H. T. Swedenberg, Jr.

Ian Watt is Professor of English and Chairman of the Department at Stanford University. He spoke on the same occasion as James Sutherland.

Contents

L. C. P. and the Clark

By ROBERT VOSPER

Lawrence Clark Powell's appointment by President Robert Gordon Sproul in 1944 as both director of the William Andrews Clark Memorial Library and UCLA's university librarian gave practical administrative assurance that the Clark would be neither an effete and isolated rare book library nor a privileged and specialist faculty enclave, but rather an integral part of library support to the overall UCLA academic program. This administrative style, which persists today, sets the Clark apart from the other separately housed great rare book libraries in the country. It has been an important factor in fostering the Clark's ever increasing scholarly vitality and its interaction with the parent campus, despite the ten-mile physical separation.

Moreover, this successful interactive arrangement, it needs be said, has been but just recognition of the foresight and faith inherent in the generous decision by William Andrews Clark, Jr., in 1926 to leave the Clark, together with a solid endowment, to the then callow "Southern Branch" of the University of California. In the tradition of many other notable American collectors, Mr. Clark might well have opted for a completely separate establishment, or at least have hedged his gift with tight administrative limitations. The library actually came to UCLA upon Mr. Clark's death in 1934, whereupon Mr. Clark's librarian, Miss Cora E. Sanders, was asked to stay on as the university's curator, a position she held until her retirement at the end of 1943.

On becoming director in 1944, Mr. Powell took public stock of the situation by editing the *Report of the First Decade, 1934–1944*, containing descriptive articles about major aspects of the collections by faculty and staff experts, together with a short history of the founding of the library. This useful pattern was followed by the *Report of the Second Decade, 1945–1955*, consisting of Mr. Powell's single essay on the development of Clark Library collections and services during the initial ten years of his directorship. In the *Report of the Third Decade, 1956–1966*, which rounded out his career as director, Mr. Powell returned most effectively to the symposium pattern of the first report of 1944. In that sequence of reports we have an evolving picture of the Clark Library and of Mr. Powell's influence on its program.

In a further and more dramatic effort to make the Clark Library better known to the public community, for whom the university holds the library in trust, the new director instituted in the summer of 1945 an annual Founder's Day program. That first occasion brought two thousand visitors to enjoy the Clark Library and its landscaped grounds where an eighteenth-century musicale was presented on a Sunday afternoon. In subsequent years these gala affairs delighted visitors with outdoor presentations of English country dances, ballad opera, and other programs related to the Clark Library collections.

During Mr. Powell's directorship, several continuing scholarly activities were undertaken in order to relate the Clark more centrally to the academic programs of UCLA. Beginning in 1945 an annual fellowship has been offered to a UCLA graduate student working on a dissertation based primarily on the collections at the Clark. In 1952 the Department of English was invited by Mr. Powell to bring together a group of faculty and graduate students from UCLA and elsewhere to participate in a one-day seminar session. Presented only once annually in the initial years, these invitational Saturday seminar programs have multiplied over the years and become an admired Clark Library trademark. The two formal papers presented at each session have regularly been published and thus made widely available to the world of scholarship. The seminars have ranged across bibliographical, scientific, literary, and musical themes. Since several of the early ones are now out of print, it was Professor Miner's happy thought to reprint this group as a fitting recognition of Mr. Powell's singular contribution to Clark scholarship.

In 1961–62 Professor William Haller of Columbia University was invited to spend four months in residence at the Clark, as a Senior Research Fellow. Among his successors have been such eminent figures as James Sutherland of London, Herbert Davis and H. R. Trevor-Roper of Oxford, and Samuel Holt Monk of Minnesota. A further step was taken in the summer of 1965 with the institution of an annual six-week postdoctoral program, by which a distinguished senior scholar is brought into association with six younger scholars selected by national competition from among those who are within five years of having received the doctorate. The seminar group ·focuses on a broad theme in which Clark holdings are strong, such as Milton studies or seventeenth-century English music, with each member of the seminar pursuing his own research on some aspect of the broad subject. Such individual work is enriched in a congenial setting by an unusual opportunity for a genuine company of scholars to inform and criticize one another's efforts.

The fruitfulness of these several scholarly programs was made evident when the 1971 summer postdoctoral seminar, on Mid-Seventeenth Century Poetry, Exclusive of Milton, was led by Professor Philip R. Wikelund of Indiana, who in 1946-47 had been the second Clark Library Graduate Fellow while completing his dissertation at UCLA.

When it became clear, soon after his coming to the Clark, that the collections would shortly outgrow available space, Mr. Powell had the happy thought of developing an underground addition to provide needed space without altering the architectural charm of the building. The first such addition, finished in 1951, was completely successful, and a second was under construction when Mr. Powell retired. By then the number of books and manuscripts, which had stood at about 18,000 when the library became the charge of the university, had grown to nearly 75,000.

The library's growth during Mr. Powell's directorship was dependent to a remarkable extent on his personal knowledge of the Clark collections and of the book trade, as well as on his enthusiasm for bringing the two together. He personally read catalogues and meticulously leafed through each incoming book. This special bibliographical skill flowered during 1951-52 when he was in England on a Guggenheim Fellowship. As a result of his bookish explorations that year more than 7,500 books and pamphlets, together with 265 manuscripts, were added to the Clark's collections. A significant component of these additions was the 1,400 volumes of the Harmsworth Collection of Protestant Theology, purchased en bloc by private treaty from the dealer, H. W. Edwards, who was handling the sale. The story of that coup is recorded in a typically charming Powell essay, "To Newbury to Buy an Old Book." During 1951-52 Mr. Powell became a familiar figure among the British book trade, as he moved with assurance from one shop to another, bringing with him as an essential tool a carefully annotated copy of Donald Wing's great catalogue, in proof-sheet form.

This warmhearted and precise involvement with the Clark's acquisitions program and its academic activities has not only enriched the world of scholarship and UCLA in particular; it has assured Lawrence Clark Powell of a circle of friendship and admiration extending widely among the scholars and scholarly booksellers of this country and Great Britain.

Poetry and Music in the Seventeenth Century

By JAMES E. PHILLIPS

L ET ME PLEAD at the outset that you interpret very
literally the subtitle given by the Steering Committee to my remarks: "discussion opened by . . . ." The relations of poetry and
music obviously comprise a large subject involving numerous
subordinate areas of special and often technical knowledge.
Neither my own qualifications nor the time allotted me would
permit even the most superficial survey of the whole field. My
own interest is, I fear, a particularly narrow one—statements on
the relationship of poetry and music by seventeenth-century
theorists. But like most of the theorists whom I propose to discuss, I shall probably touch in vague and abstract fashion on a
number of aspects of poetry and music. And since there is here
present more than one highly qualified authority on each of
these aspects, I rest in the hope that the most rewarding part of
this seminar will be an ensuing discussion period which the *New
Yorker* might label, Department of Correction, Amplification,
and Abuse.

Perhaps at the start I should describe in rather broad terms
the aspect of the relationship of poetry and music in seventeenth-
century England that I should like to talk about this morning.

1

I think that anyone who reads the literary and music theorists of the late sixteenth and the seventeenth centuries will be struck by the persistence with which these theorists clung to an ideal concept of the proper union of poetry and music. They readily admitted the history, the nobility, and the future possibilities of each art separately. But they seemed to regard the combination of the two as an independent art, and—in the opinion of some theorists, at least—as an art superior to either of the component two. The concept was often expressed in the formula, "poetry plus melody equals music"; and in this inclusive and—as the Renaissance liked to think—classical sense of the term, music came to have an aesthetic and a system of rules of its own. By these standards, melody was considered to be governed by the words, or was—in the parlance of the theorists—the handmaiden of poetry. But the theorists were firm in their belief that poetry without music and music without poetry were equally inferior to a proper combination of the two.

This is the concept of the union of poetry and music which I should like to discuss now in more detail, first by describing the origin and the persistence of the ideal itself in the writings of Renaissance theorists, and then by commenting briefly on some of the devices and techniques prescribed by these writers for attaining the ideal in practice.

The origins of the concept in the musical humanism and the poetical experiments of mid-sixteenth century Continental academies have been so thoroughly described by D. P. Walker in a series of articles in the *Musical Review,* and by Frances Yates, in *The French Academies of the Sixteenth Century,* that I perhaps need do little more than summarize their findings here.

Two academies in particular were important for their activities in focusing the interest of sixteenth-century humanism on the problems of music and poetry: Jean de Baïf's *Académie de Poésie et de Musique,* instituted by royal decree in France, and the Florentine *Camerata,* in which Giovanni De'Bardi was the

principal figure. These academicians were impressed at the outset by the remarkable "effects" attributed to music by classical
authority—Orpheus's power over the world of nature, Timotheus's influence on the passions of Alexander, and a host of
others collected in that rich storehouse of musical "effects" stories, the *Vita Pythagoras* of Iamblichus. And being Christian humanists, they linked with these stories the biblical accounts of
similar effects of music, such as David's curing of Saul.

Observing that the sixteenth-century music that they knew—
elaborately polyphonic music in the medieval tradition, that
buried words in contrapuntal intricacies—was achieving no such
effects as these, the academicians concluded that music had lost
something since antiquity—namely, the proper relation of words
and notes. They read that Plato disapproved of the two arts,
poetry and music, being separated, and that Plutarch implied
throughout his essay *De Musica* that music and poetry are in-
distinguishable. They noted further that the first musicians were
also poets, and that Orpheus, Timotheus, and David alike
achieved their effects by words as well as by music. Latter-day
victims of the revival of recorder playing may be pleased to be
reminded that John Case, an English musical humanist, noted
in *The Praise of Musicke* (1586) that Minerva gave up playing
the recorder not because, as some thought, it puffed out her
cheeks in unattractive fashion, but "as Aristotle rather thought,
because the playing on a Recorder doth neither avail the mind,
not help knowledge anything at all." The music alone, that is,
could not produce the admired classical "effects."

But the academicians also found philosophical as well as historical authority for their conviction that neither poetry nor
music alone could accomplish the effects achieved by the two in
proper combination. In this respect, they took their lead from
the Neoplatonism of Ficino, where the combination of poetry
and music is identified with the *furor poëticus,* the first of those
intuitive or "enthusiastic" stages in which the human soul, after

its thorough discipline in all the separate arts, begins its ascent back to the original One. Or, as Tyard, one of the French academicians, put it much more concretely, "The lowest point which the soul, in falling here below, has reached is the body, to which she is so firmly attached ... that the superior part is stunned and astonished by its fall, and the inferior part agitated and full of perturbations, whence arises a horrible discord and disorder.... She seems incapable of any just action unless, by some means, this dreadful discord is transformed into a gentle symphony, and this impertinent disorder reduced to a measured equality, well ordered and ordained. And to do this is a peculiar duty of Poetic enthusiasm *(furor poëticus)* ... by the well-accorded diversity of musical accords, chasing away the dissonant discords, and finally reducing the disorder to a certain equality, well and proportionately measured, and ordered in the gracious and grave facility of verses regulated by the careful observance of number and measure" (Yates, p. 80). That is to say, as the tones allay and order the passions, the poetry in the same instant directs the reason, and as a result, the soul is elevated a step further in its progress to perfection.

Such speculation by the academicians inevitably led, finally, to the conclusion that only in the exact union of words and music could the moral "effects" described by classical and biblical authorities be achieved. In the words of the Statutes of de Baïf's *Académie de Poésie et de Musique,* "In order to bring back into use music in its perfection which is to represent words in singing completed by sounds, harmony and melody, consisting in the choice and regulation of voices, sounds, and well harmonised accords, so as to produce the effect which the sense of the words requires, either lowering or raising or otherwise influencing the spirits, thus renewing the ancient fashion of composing measured verses to which are accommodated tunes likewise measured in accordance with metric art ... we have agreed to form an Academy" (Yates, p. 23). A similar conclusion, in terms of basic principle, had been reached in the Florentine *Camerata,* where Vincenzo Galileo, father of the astronomer, attacked "modern music"—i.e., medieval polyphony—because by obscuring the words with musical ornamentation and elaboration for the sake of the music itself, it neglected the "parte piu nobile importante e principale della musica, che sono i concetti dell'animo espressi col mezzo delle parole," and where Caccini later argued for "quella maniera cotanto lodata da Platone e altri Filosofi che affermarono la music altro non essere, che la fauella, e'l rithmo, e il suono per vltimo, e non per lo contrario, à volere quei mirabili effetti, che ammirano gli Scrittori, e che non poteuano farsi per il contrappunto nelle moderne musiche" (Pattison, *Music and Poetry of the English Renaissance,* pp. 126, 127).

Such was the ideal of the relationship between music and poetry formulated by the "musical humanists." Its principal implications as to the relative functions of the two arts in combination are probably clear. The power of music alone over the passions was not denied, nor the power of poetry alone over the reason, or intellect. But to achieve the remarkable "effects" described in antiquity and in scripture, the two arts must be combined in an art higher than either of its components. In this combination, music clearly becomes the hand maiden to poetry; the handling of the tones, which will govern the passions, must be controlled by words, which will direct the intellect. Milton later was to recognize the humanists' basic identification of the arts when he wrote of poetry and music:

> Blest pair of Sirens, pledges of Heav'ns joy,
> Sphear-born harmonious Sisters, Voice and Verse,
> Wed your divine sounds, and mixt power employ....

But Milton was also to recognize the implications of this theory—the subservience of music to poetry—when he praised his musical collaborator Henry Lawes, who "First taught our English Music how to Span Words with just note and accent."

In fact, Milton was to exploit all aspects of the ideal union recommended by the musical humanists in what may have been a mild family argument. For in the Latin poem *Ad Patrem* he sought to justify to his musical father his own choice of a poetic career, by what amounts to a concise statement of the fundamental position of the academicians: "In fine," he says, in Professor Frank Patterson's translation, "what avails the empty modulations of the voice, when devoid of words and their meaning and of rhythmical language? Such a melody befits the choruses of the woods, not Orpheus, who checked the course of streams and added ears to the oaks by his poetry, not by his lyre, and by his singing reduced to tears the ghosts of the dead. It is from song that he has this glory. Do not, I beg, continue to think lightly of the holy Muses, nor regard as useless and poor those through whose boon you yourself skilfully adjust a thousand sounds to fitting rhythms, and, expert in varying your melodious voice by a thousand tuneful changes, may justly be heir to Arion's name. If it has been your fate to beget in me a poet, why do you think it strange if, being so closely united by the precious tie of blood, we pursue kindred art and related interests? Phoebus himself, in his desire to divide himself between two persons, gave one-half to me and the other half to my sire, and thus we, father and son, possess the divided deity."

Milton's echoes of the academicians' concept of poetry and music are not without precedent or sequent in seventeenth-century England. I should like to defer a necessary consideration of the techniques by which the academicians hoped to attain their ideal until after some account of the ideal itself as it persistently continued to underlie theoretical discussions of the relations of poetry and music in England to the end of the seventeenth century.

I cannot describe the way in which the humanists' conception of the "union of music and poetry" reached England because—quite frankly—I do not know. But the similarity of arguments and authorities between continental theorists and theorists in sixteenth- and seventeenth-century England leaves little doubt that the ideal was shared by both. One is tempted to speculate that the "Areopagus" of Sidney and Spenser, which took over so many of the literary theories of the French academicians, also took over their views on the relationship of music and poetry. The Englishmen leave few clues on the subject, although it is perhaps worth noting, as Miss Yates does, that Sidney in the *Defense* describes poetry as suitable for music, observes that the ancient quantitative verse is more adaptable to music than modern accentual verse, and in his own experiments with quantitative verse in the *Arcadia,* introduces each song with some indication of the instrument suitable to accompany it—all directly in line with de Baïf's injunctions about the classical relation of poetry and music. But on all these points, I can only offer speculation.

When we turn to the musical theorists in England, however, we are on surer ground. John Case's *Praise of Musicke* in 1586, for example, cites the same authorities and employs the same arguments as the academicians to proclaim the supremacy of the union of poetry and music. Case applies the principle in particular to a defense of music in the church, and quoting Athanasius, argues that "To sing Psalmes artificially is not to make a shew of cunning Musick, but an argument, that the cogitations of our mindes do aptly agree with our musicke ... for ... they that sing so, as the melody of wordes with the quantitie of them, may agree with the harmony of the spirit, bee those which sing with the tung and with understanding also. ... For the soule being intentive to the wordes doeth forgette the affections and perturbations: & being made mery with the pleasant sound is brought to a sense and feeling of Christ, and most excellent and heavenly cogitations." Case differs from the academicians in defending "artificial"—i.e., elaborately contrapuntal—music in setting words, rather than insisting on the strict tying of notes in all voices to particular syllables. In this respect he probably reveals the lingering influence of the medieval musical tradition. But on the fundamental necessity for union of the arts to achieve the highest effects, he is in complete agreement with continental theorists.

Thomas Morley's *A Plain and Easy Introduction to Practical Music* (1597) is neither very plain nor very easy, but it *is* practical, and only incidentally concerned with theory. Morley's directions show little of the academic influence, but that his practice was based on the assumption that the union of poetry and music is the highest art, and that it is the duty of music to be controlled by the words is indicated when he concludes that a composer, by observing Morley's rules, "shall have a perfect agreement and, as it were, an harmonical consent betwixt the matter and the music, and likewise you shall be perfectly understood of the auditor what you sing, which is one of the highest degrees of praise which a musician in dittying can attain unto or wish for." Campion took the same position, but perhaps with greater awareness of the arguments of the musical humanists, for he acknowledges the strict joining of notes and syllable quantities in classical poetry as his model when, as he put it in his celebrated statement, he "chiefly aimed to couple my words and notes lovingly together."

A remarkable exposition of the doctrine of union is Charles Butler's *The Principles of Musick* (1636), which John Playford later in the century extensively plagiarized for his popular *Brief Introduction to the Skill of Musick* (1662), and which Hawkins, in the eighteenth century, praised as learned and valuable. The treatise is printed with the curious and confusing phonetic spelling which Butler advocated, and which gives his seventeenth-century prose a slight Brooklynese flavor. But it is perhaps worth noting that experiments with phonetic spelling were part of the academicians' effort to restore the exact classical relation of notes and words.

Music, as Butler discusses it in every aspect, clearly means to him melody plus poetry. He has little to say about instrumental music except insofar as it supports the word. For like most of his predecessors and contemporaries in the field of musical theory, he believes, as he puts it [in modified spelling], that "the Voice, which is the work of Nature, doth far exceed all these works of Art." Hence he arrives at his fundamental conception of music and poetry combined as the highest art. "Good Voices alone," he writes, "sounding only the Notes, are sufficient by their Melody and Harmoni, to delight the ear: but being furnished with some laudable Ditti, they become yet more excellent.... This numerous Ditti, or Rhyme, applyed to the Note, the Philosopher equalizes to the Melodi itself, for Resembling and Mooving manners and affections.... And afterward hee makes it a part of Music, shewing that Music is made as well by Poesi as by Melodi.... And therefore it is, that the most powerful Musicians (such as were Orpheus and Arion: yea such as was that Divine Psalmist) were also Poets. And such should our Musicians bee, if they will be complete."

Butler's statement may be taken, I think, as fairly representative of the fundamental attitude toward music that prevailed among seventeenth-century theorists. This is not to say, of course, that they disparaged or neglected music as a separate art. Thomas Mace, in his *Musick's Monument* (1676), waxes rhapsodic about the independent influence of melodic sound and rhythm, but he saves his real enthusiasm for the united arts; thus in describing the use of music in the church he says: "This Organ, when the Psalm was set before the Sermon, being let out, into all its Fulness of Stops, together with the Quire, began the Psalm. But when that Vast-Conchording-Unity of the whole Congregational-Chorus, came (as I may say) Thundering in, even so, as it made the very Ground shake under us; (Oh the unutterable ravishing Soul's delight!) In the which I was so transported, and wrapt up into High Contemplations, that there was no room left in my whole Man, viz., Body, Soul and Spirit, for any thing below Divine and Heavenly Raptures." Such was the attitude, somewhat more moderately expressed, which characterized most of the treatises on music in the century. Thomas Ravenscroft's *Briefe Discourse of the True (but Neglected) Use of Charact'ring* (1614) is an effort to restore music, which he defines as "song and poetry," to its proper function, though perhaps with less regard for the exalted effects of the neoplatonists than for what he calls the "5. usual recreations"—Hunting, Hawking, Dauncing, Drinking, and Enamouring. Christopher Simpson's *Compendium of Practical Musick* (1667), after citing Descartes as his authority on the supremacy of vocal music "because it holds the greatest conformity to our spirits," proceeds to write a technical treatise which clearly keeps the composer in his place: "Your chief endevour," he admonishes, "must be, that your Notes do aptly express the sense and humour of [the Words]." Finally, the same concept and arguments characterize the defense of church music that was the principal theme of a series of St. Cecilia Day sermons preached and published between 1694 and 1697. One of the preachers, Sampson Estwick, concluded his sermon of 1696 with an account of the increase of joy "when melodious Sounds, agreeable to the Matter treated of, give each Word their due force and emphasis, especially when the Composer has an Eye upon the Sense, lays weight upon what is most material, does not clog his Parts with needless Repetitions, but orders his business so, that the Hearer shall be little interrupted, but shall follow him with Ease and Pleasure, whilst he raises your Ideas by a just representation of the Subject that lies before him."

The Rev. Mr. Estwick's remarks in 1696 indicate not only the persistence of the musical humanists' ideal, I believe, but also suggest that the theorists who held to the ideal had definite opinions as to how the perfect union of poetry and music was to be accomplished. I can indicate only a few of the techniques regularly prescribed by seventeenth-century theorists, and these techniques only in broad and general terms. But they may serve to illustrate the ways in which the theorists at least thought that the ideal could be attained and the moral and religious "effects" achieved. Needless to say, in all the techniques prescribed, control of the music by the words, of the emotional by the intellectual, of the passionate by the rational, is the fundamental assumption and the guiding principle.

First of all, the musical humanists insisted on the rule that only one note of music be set to one syllable of a word. They objected strenuously to the medieval inclination—or barbaric practice, as they termed it—to stretch a syllable out over a florid series of different notes. They argued, quite rightly, that such a practice tended to obscure the meaning of the words, and accordingly deprived music of half its proper effect. Such insistence, of course, was not the peculiar innovation of the humanists. Writers on church music, in particular, insisted on the same principle both long before and long after the humanist ideal flourished. Cranmer, for example, declared in 1544: "The song that shall be made for the English service would not be full of notes, but, as near as may be, for every syllable a note, so that it may be sung distinctly and devoutly." But it was the humanists who gave new emphasis to the principle in the interests of securing what they regarded as the effective union of poetry and music. As Miss Yates has pointed out, the academicians took the extreme view, and in their experiments with music and poetry rigidly adhered to the principle of one note per syllable. English theorists adhered to the same rule, if not so strictly. Campion admired the Greeks and Latins for tying notes unexceptionally to syllable quantities, and sought to emulate them. Morley argued that "We must also have a care so to apply the notes to the words as in singing there be no barbarism committed; that is that we cause no syllable which is by nature short be expressed by many notes." And in 1667 Christopher Simpson was arguing, with most of his fellow theorists, that he did not, as he put it, "fancy the setting of many notes to any one syllable, (though much in fashion in former times;) but I would have your Musick to be such, that the words may be plainly understood."

Secondly, in their effort to restore the power of words supported by music, the humanists tended to prefer homophonic to polyphonic settings. Again they were reacting against what they called the barbaric practice of elaborate polyphony in the medieval musical tradition, where each voice not only went its own separate melodic way, but its own rhythmic way as well. Gratifying as the results may have been—and are—musically, they were—and are—admittedly disastrous insofar as understanding of the words is concerned. Four voices singing the same words, but at different times and in different syllabification, are bound to be confusing. Continental academicians reacted against this practice in extreme fashion. In France, de Baïf's academy stressed what they called "rythme d'ensemble," in which each voice sang the same syllable at the same time, albeit on different tones—an emphasis that was to lead to remarkable developments in part-song in seventeenth-century England. In Italy, the academicians tended to stress, for the same ultimate purposes of intelligibility and "effect," a different principle of tying notes to words. As Bruce Pattison puts it, the Camerata went beyond the French academies, and advocated the single melodic line as the only music suitable to enhance the words; if several voices, or voices with instruments, were involved, they played and sang in unison—all producing the same note at the same time on the same syllable. The consequences of this principle for the development of recitative—the *stylo recitativo* of the Lawes brothers, for example—is familiar to all. But, whether in French part-song or in Italian recitative, the reaction of musical humanism against elaborate, word-obscuring polyphony in the interests of securing classical and biblical "effects" is clear.

The influence of such principles in England is perhaps more apparent in the practice of English composers than in the pronouncements of theorists. Among seventeenth-century theorists, at any rate, the humanists' demand for intelligibility in part-writing tended to take the form of protests against the excesses of polyphony rather than of a call for extremely rigid forms of homophony. Charles Butler's attitude in 1636 is perhaps representative, when he gives polyphonic music its due, but places first in his estimation part-song, or what he calls "counterpoint," "when the Notes of all the Parts being of equal time and number, go jointly together." But on the whole, English adherence to the homophonic principle of the humanists is reflected mainly in negative fashion—in strong protests against the unintelligibility of texts set to elaborate polyphonic music. We have already noted the Rev. Mr. Estwick's injunction that a composer "not clog his parts with needless repetition." But perhaps the most vivid assault on polyphonic settings is that of Prynne in his *Histriomastix* (1633), when he protests against such contrapuntal union of words and music as "a whorish harmony to tickle [men's eares], that it may justly seeme not to be a noyse made of men, but rather a bleating of brute beasts; whiles the Coristers ney descant as it were a sort of Colts; others bellowe a tenour, as it were a company of oxen; others barke a counterpoint, as it were a kennel of Dogs; others rore out a treble like a sort of Buls; others grunt out a base as it were a number of Hogs; so that a foule evill-favoured noise is made, but as for the wordes and sentences and the very matter it self, is nothing understanded at all; but the authority and power of judgment is taken away both from the minde and from the eares utterly."

A third technique advocated by the musical humanists of the sixteenth and seventeenth centuries in their effort to achieve the classical effects from the union of music and poetry was strict control of the time and rhythmic values of the notes by the exact time and rhythmic values of the words. Such a principle,

carried to a literal extreme, would—and in some cases did—
preclude the regular two- and three-beat musical measures with
which we are familiar. Rather, the natural quantity and accent
of the words would determine the pattern of long and short
notes—not a predetermined and regular pattern of the musical
rhythm. It was this rhythmic principle in sixteenth- and seventeenth-century music that in the eighteenth century led Dr.
Burney, apparently unaware of the principle involved, to complain about the "false accents of the melody, in which there is so
total a want of rhythm as renders the time extremely difficult to
keep with accuracy and firmness." But the practice deplored by
Dr. Burney exactly conforms to humanistic principles of control
of music by words, even in rhythmic values.

Continental academicians of the sixteenth century were inclined to take this principle quite literally. Jean de Baïf, as Miss
Yates observes, "tried to substitute quantity for accent as the basis
of French verse; his object in doing this was to recover a closer
union between poetry and music (and therefore more powerful
'effects') by making the value of the notes of music correspond
to the quantity of the syllables." In Italy, a similar insistence that
the natural accent or quantity of the syllables govern the value
of the notes was to be another important influence on the development of the declamatory style in music.

English theorists adhered to the same general principle, although they were inclined to treat it less strictly in classical
fashion than did de Baïf and the academicians. Of course,
Campion's celebrated defense of English quantitative verse in
his *Observations in the Art of English Poesy* (1602) is based
largely on the kind of reasoning followed by the academicians.
As he says at the outset of his treatise, "In joining of words to
harmony there is nothing more offensive to the eare then to
place a long sillable with a short note, or a short sillable with a
long note, though in the last the vowell often beares it out. The
world is made by Simmetry and proportion, and is in that re-

spect compared to Musick, and Musick to Poetry.... What Musick can there be where there is no proportion observed?" As Campion himself admits, however, he rarely put this extreme classical theory into practice, but as Pattison points out, his recognition of the dependence of musical rhythm on verbal rhythm probably accounts for some of Campion's loveliest lyric effects.

While English practice in this respect may have varied, subsequent writers on the theory of music and poetry in the seventeenth century clung to the fundamental principle with remarkable tenacity. Ravenscroft, in 1614, urged that composers write airs "not ... for some small tickling of the outward Sence alone, but a great deale more solide, and sweetly united to Number, Measure, and Nature of the Ditty." The same basic assumption underlies Milton's praise of Henry Lawes, for teaching English music "how to Span Word with just note and accent," and Waller's praise of the same composer, who "alone may truly boast That not a syllable is lost." Simpson was underscoring the same principle in 1667 when he admonished would-be composers "not to apply ... any long Note, to a short Syllable; nor a short Note to a Syllable that is long." Sir Hubert Parry has said, in the *Oxford History of Music,* that seventeenth-century songs composed with this principle in mind "appear to be written for amateurs ... with no voice worth considering to recite poems in a melodious recitative, spaced out into periods in conformity with the length of the lines or literary phrases." Such an account may accurately describe the apparent results, but I think that it ignores the serious aesthetic principle that produced these results.

Finally, the theorists of the Renaissance, in discussing the relations of music and poetry, advocated certain general techniques whereby music could be made to enhance the meaning and the coloration of the words. Seventeenth-century English theorists in particular were explicit about these techniques, recommending specific musical effects appropriate to specific words or ideas, and musical modes appropriate to more general literary tones and attitudes. But it should be emphasized that here again (according to the theorists, at any rate) the words were to be the controlling factor of musical melody and color in the ideal union of the arts.

"Word-painting"—that is, the effort to reflect musically the exact meaning and coloration of particular words—had been a prominent feature of both the theory and practice of the English madrigalists. Morley in his *Plain and Easy Introduction* prescribed a whole list of musical devices suitable for enhancing the meaning of specific words and ideas. Continental academicians and musical humanists, on the other hand, were inclined to deplore carrying the practice of "word-painting" by composers to extremes. Especially in the Florentine Camerata, the theorists insisted that on the basis of classical practice the melodic lines of the music should reflect only the natural accent and sound of the words, and some of the practitioners of the theory went so far as to limit the notes used in a song to those within the limited range of the normal speaking voice. In England, Campion probably is echoing something of this humanistic revolt against elaborate word-painting when he ridicules that music where, as he puts it, "the nature of every word is precisely expressed in the note: like the old exploded action in comedies, when if they did pronounce *Memini,* they would point to the hinder part of their heads; if *Video,* put their finger in their eye. But such childish observing of word is altogether ridiculous: and we ought to maintain, as well in notes as in action, a manly carriage; gracing no word, but that which is eminent and emphatical."

But as his last sentence suggests, Campion did not exclude word-painting entirely, nor did subsequent theorists in the seventeenth century. Butler's list of suggestions for word-painting is representative: "A manly, hard, angry, or cruel matter is to be expressed by hard and harsh short tones ... and that with the ordinari and unaltered notes of the scale; but words of effeminate lamentations, sorrowful passions, and complaints, are fitly exprest by the inordinate half-notes (such as are the small keys of the Virginals).... Also, woords importing the circumstances of Time and Place, are to be fitted with Notes agreeable: as those that signifieth running, or speedy motions ... with short Notes, and the contrary with the contrary. Likewise those that signifieth height and ascending, with high notes; and depth or descending, with low." Thomas Mace's *Musick's Monument* in 1676 represents a somewhat different approach to the same problem; the intervals of the 2nd and the 7th, he observes, are "that we call a Dischord in Musick, and is a most Exact, and Lively Simile of the Bad Nature, viz., Perplexity, Vexation, Anxiety, Horrour, Torture, Hell, Devilishness, yea of the Devil itself," whereas conchords—the 3rd, 5th, and unison or octave,—may be employed to express opposite qualities as suggested by the words.

Inevitably associated with discussion of word-painting by the theorists was discussion of the use of the ancient modes in combining poetry with music. In view of the fact that the effect of the musical modes on the passions had been recognized by theorists from Plato onward, it is not surprising to find discussion of the modes prominent in treatises concerned with the union of poetry and music—a union designed to affect the reason and the passions at one and the same moment. Such discussion does indeed appear in practically all the seventeenth-century theorists, although it is not always easy to decide just what the various modes, under their classical names, meant to the theorists by this time. Not even sixteenth-century theorists could agree on the identification of the various modes, so that, as Miss Yates wryly observes, a composer who intended to induce Dorian sobriety and decorum might really, quite against his will, be arousing Phrygian enthusiasm. To complicate matters, from the beginning of the seventeenth century the musical modes themselves were rapidly breaking down under the influence of chromaticism and the development toward modern tonality, or key systems. But whatever they may have meant to individual theorists, the classical names of the modes continued to be employed to designate systems of musical sounds considered capable of producing particular emotional or passionate states.

Not all theorists concerned with the effective union of poetry and music in the seventeenth century would agree with Butler in details, perhaps, but his recommendations represent the general way in which such theorists expected a composer to adapt his musical mode to the requirements of the text. The Dorian mode, he says, is generally set to a Psalm or other pious canticle, the notes answering to the number of syllables, to move sobriety, prudence, modesty, and godliness; the Lydian mode, set to hymns and anthems, with the notes often exceeding the number of syllables, "ravisheth the mind with a kind of ecstasi, lifting it up from the regard of earthly things, unto the desire of celestiall joyz"; the Aeolian "pacifyeth the passions of the mind," the Phrygian "inciteth to arms and activity," and the Ionian is "an effeminate and delicate kind of Music, set unto pleasant songs and sonnets of love, and such like fancies, for honest mirth and delight, chiefly in feasting and other merriments." Butler, like most of the theorists of his century, recognized the independent power of the musical modes over the passions, but like most of his contemporaries, too, he believed that they could exercise their greatest effect only when suitably and appropriately subjoined to poetry.

Such, then, were the principal techniques recommended by theorists of the Renaissance to bring about the remarkable effects considered possible when music and poetry are properly combined. They all add up, it is obvious, to the absolute control of music by the laws of poetry. The practical applications of such a theory in seventeenth-century song, chorus, and opera lie outside my present purpose. But it might be pertinent to suggest that, for the first half of the century, at least, the development in all these applied fields of music and poetry is at least not contrary to the tendency of the theorists. The elaborately polyphonic madrigal gave way to the more verbally intelligible part-song—much to Dr. Fellowes' regret. The single-voiced air, governed in its movement by the meaning of the words, established itself as a principal lyric form. And the brothers Lawes, in writing music for the early forms of English opera, adopted the declamatory style that stemmed directly, as Professor Dent has noted, from the efforts of the academicians to restore the ancient relationship of music and poetry.

But in conclusion, let me hasten to assure the music historians present that I am fully aware that in the latter half of the century music was by no means keeping the subservient place in its union with poetry that the theorists valiantly continued to insist upon. As a rapidly expanding independent art, music was developing laws of rhythm, harmony, and melody of its own. It would not, I believe, be inaccurate to say that while in the earlier part of the century music had been made to follow the laws of poetry, in the latter part, when the arts are combined, poetry is made to follow the laws of music.

Hence it was that, by 1763, Dr. John Brown could publish a *Dissertation on the Rise, Union, and Power, the Progressions, and Corruptions, of Poetry and Music* in which—somewhat regretfully, I think—he not only remarks the end of the humanistic conception of the union and the impossibility of restoring it, but also gives a not-inaccurate summary of what had happened in the meantime to destroy it: "For now instrumental music, having assumed a new and more inviting Form, and being ennobled by the principles of a complex and varied Harmony, was introduced as being of itself a compleat Species, independent of Poetry or Song. This gave it an artificial and laboured Turn; while the composer went in Quest of curious Harmonies, Discords, Resolutions, Fugues, and Canons; and prided himself (like the Poet) in a pompous Display of Art, to the neglect of Expression and true Pathos."

Yet a survey of the theorists shows that the old ideal of the union of the arts died hard. No one makes clearer this survival of the humanistic ideal in the face of growing—and acknowledged—practice to the contrary than John Dryden. Both of the St. Cecilia odes, in 1687 and 1697, are developed in terms of the power of music in the classic tradition. But I venture to suggest that in both, Dryden exalts the saint herself at the end as the symbol of the higher union of poetry and music. The earlier ode ends, it will be recalled:

> Orpheus could lead the savage race;
> And trees unrooted left their place,
>   Sequacious of the lyre;
> But bright Cecilia rais'd the wonder high'r:
> When to her Organ vocal breath was giv'n,
> An angel heard, and straight appear'd,
>   Mistaking earth for heav'n.

"Vocal breath" here may refer, as some commentators on the ode point out, to the wind pumped into the organ's pipes. But Dryden's reference to the elevating power of this "vocal breath" rather suggests to me the "effect" of the union of poetry and music which seventeenth-century theorists regularly referred to in their praise of vocal music. This interpretation of the passage is perhaps supported by the more explicit parallel passage at the culmination of *Alexander's Feast*. After describing Timotheus's marvelous effects with the lyre (but not the voice, it should be noted), Dryden concludes:

> At last, divine Cecilia came,
>   Inventress of the vocal frame;
> The sweet enthusiast, from her sacred store,
>   Enlarged the former narrow bounds,
>   And added length to solemn sounds
> With nature's mother wit, and arts unknown before.

Here the echo of Neoplatonic "enthusiasm" in conjunction with references to the "divine" source of the vocal frame, and to enlarging the powers of purely instrumental music in an art unknown before seems to suggest very strongly that Cecilia's "vocal frame" is the union of poetry and music idealized by Dryden's English contemporaries.

But as a poet often involved in practical efforts to combine his art with music, Dryden was apparently quite aware of the extent to which the laws of music had come to govern the union of the arts in the practice of the late seventeenth century. Because of the demands of music, he writes in the preface to *Albion and Albanius* (1685), the poetry must "please hearing rather than gratify understanding." He has decided that because of its monosyllables, its consonants, and its lack of feminine rhymes, English is not really suited to the equal union of the arts after all. And he concludes with a cry—made bitter, perhaps, by the failure of this opera—that signals the final disillusionment of a musical humanist: "The same reasons which depress thought in an opera have a stronger effect upon the words, . . . for which reason I am often forced to coin new words, revive some that are antiquated, and botch others; as if I had not served out my time in poetry, but was bound apprentice to some doggerel rhymer, who makes songs to tunes, and sings them for a livelihood. It is true, I have not been often put to this drudgery; but where I have, the words will sufficiently show that I was then a slave to the composition, which I will never be again: *it is my part to invent, and the musician's to humor that invention.*"

I have italicized that final statement because therein is contained, I believe, the essence of seventeenth-century theory regarding the relationship of poetry and music.

II

Milton as a Latin Poet

By DON CAMERON ALLEN

THE *Poemata* of Joannis Miltoni Londinensis appeared as the second half of the Poems of 1645. In *The Reason of Church Government*, published four years earlier, these poems are described as trifles composed when their author was not yet twenty or while he was traveling on the Continent after his departure from the university. Although Milton's Italian friends praised them,[1] Latinists beginning with Salmasius[2] and ending with Bishop Charles Wordsworth[3] have had harsh things to say about their syntax and prosody. Modern classicists have been more generous,[4] but none of these poems has been read for its literary merit or been assigned a place in the poetic tradition. To this end I want principally to consider the Fifth Elegy, "In Adventum Veris," written by a boy of twenty, who probably knew Ovid's comparison of the seasons of life to those of the year, and who will shortly complain that his own "late spring no bud or blossom show'th."[5]

The tradition behind this poem begins with Lucretius' pomp when Ver comes forward with Venus while Zephyr and Flora fill the world with color and fragrance.[6] These figures are later joined on occasion by a shepherd poet, Bion's Myrson or Vergil's Moeris, who rejoices that "rosy spring" loiters by the rivers as earth dresses herself in flowers.[7] These rivers flow swollen from

23

the mountain snows when Vergil gives us a glimpse of the
Roman spring in the first *Georgic*.[8] This is the land of "ver ad-
siduum,"[9] of the two harvests, and Vergil, to explain this double
fecundity, uses the old theology that we may hear Earth moan-
ing for the "genitalia semina" when Aether descends to cohabit
with his broad-breasted spouse. This union repeated in the world
of creatures reminds Vergil of the days of creation. "I could
believe at the world's first beginning/ the days that shown
then were not unlike these/ nor was the course of things."[10]
The younger Horace was somewhat sadder and looked through
spring's joys to man's mortality. His poems open on April vistas,
but they are really about the few frail, happy hours before winter
destroys all life. In a familiar one, Death knocks with his "impartial foot" to warn Sestius;[11] in another, Torquatus is informed that the gods may add no tomorrow to our day. "Pulvis
et umbra sumus."[12]

Both moods are common to Ovid. The happy poet of the
Fasti asks Janus why the year does not begin in April, "time's
new season," when "suns are sweet and pilgrim swallows
come."[13] When the swallows really come, Ovid, like Horace,
remembers the tragedy of Philomela and Procne and fears lest
winter return and break the spell of spring.[14] Then on the edge
of April he raises the paean to "the mother of Aeneas, joy of
gods and men." "Formosa Venus formoso tempore digna est."[15]
Venus and Ver are followed by Flora, who tells her story. Once
when she was wandering, Zephyr saw her. "I retired; he pursued; I fled; but he was stronger." Now she dwells in a noble
garden which her husband fills with flowers.[16] The violent union
of Earth and Sky has become an urbane arrangement in an
imperial villa. But Ovid, who would have surpassed both Homer
and Vergil, according to Milton, had he not been exiled, also
suffered in the bitter springs of frozen Tomis.

In lands where the vine grows, the buds push from the shoot, but no
vines grow near the Getic shore. Wherever the tree grows, its branches

bud, but the tree grows far from the coast of the Getes. Now in that land is ease, and the garrulous wars of the wordy Forum are giving place to festivals. Now there is sport with horses, now with light arms, with the ball or the rapidly turning hoop; now youths sleek with slippery oil are bathing tired limbs in the Fountain of the Virgin.... But for me it is only to know snow melted by the spring sun and water not dug from the frozen lake; the sea, too, is not clogged with ice nor as before does the Sauromatian herdsman drive his creaking wagon across the river Ister.[17]

While these Augustan poets were shaping a tradition for the English boy, Meleager of Gadara, writing in Greek, put together a calendar on the coming of spring. The Εἰς τὸ ἔαρ, which fathered poems by Peletier du Mans, de Baïf, Belleau, and Sannazaro before Milton was born, relates the springtime experiences of men as a poet knows them.[18] Winter retreats from the sky; fields laugh in crimson; earth puts on her green crown; the trees are young in leaves; the roses bud and blow. The shepherd's pipe is heard in the hills; sailors make for the sea; and men, binding their heads with ivy, sing the praises of Dionysus. In the air, birds fly, singing in colored flocks: the halcyon on the sea, the swallow about the house, the swan on the stream, the nightingale in the coppice.

> Hence if the tree leafs and the earth greens,
> If the shepherd pipes and the fleecy sheep gambol,
> If birds raise the chorus and bees make honey,
> Should only the poet not sing in spring?[19]

All the traditional metaphors are here, but in addition there is the visible figure of the poet. When creation renews itself shall he alone be silent? It is the same question, inverted into statement, that the boy Milton will phrase in the Fifth Elegy. "Fallor? an et nobis redeunt in carmina vires, / ingeniumque mihi munere veris adest?" But Milton's assertion here may be an abrogation of the lament with which the famous *Pervigilium Veneris* closes.

Greek and Roman responses blend in the *Pervigilium Veneris,*
a hymn for the eve of St. Venus and the rebirth of the world.
"Vere natus orbis est." It is also the season of marriage and
Dione, the pre-Olympian Venus, adorns her throne. Aided by
Favonus and the distillation of stars she calls the roses, "nude
virgins of the morning," into flower while her boy Cupid, naked
and unarmed, wanders among the nymphs. Artemis, of course,
is exiled, but Ceres, Bacchus, and the God of Poets, "poetarum
deus," attend the three-day ceremony where Dione, accompanied by the Graces and nymphs of forest, hill, and springs,
sits in Hybla and gives laws. Those who wait about the goddess
see, as if they were in a great theater, the marriage of Earth and
Sky. "Tomorrow is the day," they are told, "when Aether first
wed," and they watch as he flows into his mighty bride. The
year is quickened by the clouds of spring and flame goes round
the earth to kindle all creatures. But the poet, listening to Philomela and Procne, asks impatiently,

> She sings, we are voiceless. When shall my spring come,
> When shall I be as the swallow, when shall I break silence?
> I have lost the Muse in silence nor does Apollo regard me.[20]

This poem was written sometime between the first and the
fourth centuries; by the fifth century the tone changes.

The "Ver erat" attributed by the seventeenth century to the
sometimes Christian Ausonius is different from the spring
poems of pure pagans and totally different from the "Ver avibus
voces aperit" of Paulinus of Nola. Walking in a garden touched
enough by May's warmth for Venus to be manifest in her symbolic roses, Ausonius sees mortality in the flowers and with
"collige, virgo, rosas" intones the chant against virginity that
was still heard· in Milton's day.[21] St. Paulinus, his devoutly
Christian pupil, has, on the other hand, no objections to virgins.
When he watches the snows melt and the varicolored, multi-
tongued birds return, he sings in honor of his patron, St. Felix.

The soul's winter ends with the God Incarnate, not with the arrival of Ver and Venus; and the poet, liberated by Christian spring, waves his wings and sings.[22] The pagan themes are assumed only to be reshaped, and the tradition of Christian spring is now poetically stated. Writing in the new ambience, Dracontius turns the gardens of Venus and Flora into that of Eden;[23] Venantius Fortunatus, learned in pagan topics,[24] celebrates spring as the Feast of Easter;[25] and Walafrid Strabo makes the resurrection of God, not of God's world, his central theme.[26]

The Latin poets of the Renaissance, jealous as they were of ancient ways, had both thematic modes to choose from and chose from both. Sometimes they do little more than rephrase the songs of Rome. For many Horace is the gifted master. The "De Calendis Aprilibus" of Calcagnini begins with the weaving of violet crowns and the heaping of flowers for the bright day of Venus. "Haec dies nobis Veneris calendas/ candida profert." In time we arrive at the altar of the "obsentum numen."[27] Garlands are also woven and perfumes of India scattered in the first stanzas of Sannazaro's "Kalenda Maii"; then wine smokes in the crystal cup to remind the revelers that "grapes do not grow in Hell's acres" and that "black Death comes while a joke is being told." "Mediis mors venit atra jocis."[28] Marco Antonio Flaminio, best of neo-Latin poets, sees Flora and Zephyr look on as Amaryllis leads her flock to a secret grove, and then he sacrifices a garlanded lamb to Venus.[29] The offering is of no avail, because in two further poems he weighs the joys of spring against the sad absence of his mistress, Lygda.[30] His major poem, "Iam ver floricomum," is darkened with Horatian pessimism. Snows melt, the grass appears, birds sing among the flowers, Venetian sails fill the Adriatic, but the wintered poet sings in weeping and finds rest only in the thought of death. "Soles non aliquo tempore candidi/ sic me perpetua est hiems."[31] Flaminio's contemporary, Fracastorio, draws in his

"Incidens" a series of spring scenes for a memorial pillar. He describes the marriage of Earth and Sky, the spring of the world itself, and the flawless Age of Saturn; he also portrays the spring pastimes and tasks of Italian country life.[32] Other Latin poets celebrated with lesser success the advent of spring,[33] but more pleasing to the boy Milton, perhaps, were the poems of George Buchanan, the "Buchananus noster" of the *Second Defence*.[34]

Buchanan wrote a poem in alcaics and one in elegiacs on spring. The first praises "Holy May Day" and spring as reliques of the Golden Age, which will return when God has purified the world with fire. The elegy begins with a shout, "Festa!" Then Lascivia, Amor, and Indulgentia, celebrants all, are shortly joined by Joy, Cupid, Genius, Pleasure, and the Graces. Once these latter, blander personifications, pleasing to their counterparts in "L'Allegro" and "Il Penseroso," have assembled, the Lady of Cyprus enters. Her yellow hair is woven in a coronet; her fingers are starred with emeralds; her golden palla flows to her feet. She is adorned "as if to be pleasing to her Mars." "Marti seu placitura suo." Earth and its creatures testify, as tradition demands, to her fervent presence and men are urged to be cheerful so that the battle of love "in which many seek to die" may begin. Thus far the poem is a vernal chant in the ritual of Venus, but it is, nonetheless, annotated by the music of dismay. The calm measures swell suddenly as "hard husbands" are required to release their young wives and timid virgins are encouraged to escape their mothers and show their "breasts white as milk." But black death, shadow and dust, the face of winter are thinly masked by May's splendors.

> Gather roses; they perish if you do not.
>   See in this the reflection of life.
> Harsh Boreas destroys the fields' beauty;
>   He fills them with his white frosts,
> Strips leaves from wood, flowers from the garden,
>   Puts reins of ice on the slow river.

> So Time, the deformer, will age you, too;
>   Dry wrinkles will wither your face;
> Your skin will bag; your teeth will rot;
>   Your eyes will redden; and all sweet grace
> Will leave your once so fecund tongue.

Having heard this advice for many centuries, the young do not need the lesson; so the poet turns to old men, his contemporaries, and assumes the cheerful Horatian tone. "While the envious Fates spare us old boys, let us enjoy this season as in youth."[35] The experiences of Buchanan were also shared by the Cambridge undergraduate, who never scorned the wisdom of his great predecessors; yet what he gathered from others, he continually refreshed. By these precocious acts he justified the comment of a seventeenth-century German professor of poetry: "the man," writes Morhof of Kiel, "was apparent in the boy."[36]

The boy Milton wrote three poems on the spring: the Fifth and Seventh Elegies and "Song: On May Morning." The Fifth Elegy seems to stem directly from the poems of his predecessors; the Seventh Elegy, dated "anno aetatis undevigesimo" but thought to be later, appears more original at first reading than the Fifth Elegy which begins with excruciatingly conventional phrases. The return of the perpetual circle of time is recorded; we hear of the fresh Zephyrs, "Zephyros novos," the warmth of spring, "vere tepente," the brief youth of Earth, "induiturque breven Tellus iuventam," and the softly greening fields, "dulce virescit humus." Within twenty lines Philomela, that dusty traveler, returns without Procne and begins to sing "dum silet omne nemus." A year later she will reappear in Milton's first sonnet helping the Hours lead in May by Warbling "at eve when all the woods are still"; and in another year, the "mute Silence" of "Il Penseroso" will "hist along/ 'Less Philomel will deign a song."

After these commonplaces, Milton describes in more mythological detail the alterations of day and night, repeating notions from his earlier prolusion, "Utrum Dies aut Nox praestantior sit." Then as a modest prelude to the passion of Tellus and Phoebus, the traditional spring shepherd, who matches his seven reeds against Phyllis' song later in the poem, jollies the Sungod, implying that like the vigilant poet of the *Pervigilium Veneris* he also has been loveless for the night. The jest is so sharp that Phoebus turns it against Aurora made frustrate by her flaccid spouse Tithonus. Desert the senile couch, says the Sun, "the hunter, Aeolides, stays for you on the green." The goddess is clearly on this occasion not "trickt and frounc't as she was wont/ With the Attic Boy to hunt," her subsequent Miltonic good fortune. She is also unaware that she will take on the role of Ovid's Flora in "L'Allegro" and find herself, thanks to her bad judgment in rollicking with Zephyr on a Maytime bank of violets, apocryphally gravid with Euphrosyne. Carnal playfulness, not unknown to the fallen hero of *Paradise Lost,* is the portion, too, of spring-besotted Jupiter. "Jupiter ipse alto cum coniunge ludit Olympo." Similarly, the Ovidian pursuit of the half-reluctant Flora is rerun when Milton sends Faunus dashing after a slow-footed and anonymous Oread.

But the theme of the Fifth Elegy is not the same as that of *Comus,* and after the adolescent poet has urged Phoebus and Earth to cohabit, he frees earthlings and half-earthlings that they may imitate the example their mother hopes to set them. His line "Matris in exemplum caetera turba ruunt" hints that something like the marriage of Earth and Sky has occurred, but the poem is not very explicit. On the other hand, Cupid, who will have the leading part in Elegy Seven, appears with a torch significantly kindled in Phoebus' fire, with new strings to his bow and points to his arrows. Buchanan, who knew his Horace, also saw him at this paragraph in spring's story, sharpening his darts, retempered "in the Sicilian furnace," on a whetstone red as blood.[37] His luscious mother has hardly any part in Milton's poem, but the boys and girls who attend her church are here and so is Meleager's sailor who sings a new song to the stars and like Arion calls up dolphins as if they were the hounds of spring. Lastly, the venerable gods of venery, who usually appear separately, arrive in a body to do the body's service. Sylvanus, a non-classical "semicaperque deus semideus caper," Maenalian Pan, and Faunus lead the troop through field and thicket to threaten the virtue of practiced fertility goddesses like Ceres and Cybele.

All these incidents are fragments of an honored tradition, and it is interesting to watch the boy Milton fit them together into a new poem. He describes Tellus, for instance, as his masters described Venus and acknowledges the identification with an easily recognized phrase, "cum Paphiis fundit amoma rosis." He remembers then the serious connection of the "diva Sicana" and the "deus Taenarius" with the mythology of spring, and so he opens the door just long enough to let the dank melancholy of Horace mist the lines. Again we see the thin visages of the monarchs in whose sterile garden grow no vines. This poetic experience is hardly ended before Zephyr, henchman of Ver, drops down and shakes his cinnamon-scented wings. This is a new perfume for the West Wind. Does it come from the "Arabum messes" of the superior lines or is it really the phoenix, bird of the sun, fragrant, according to Ausonius[38] and Claudian,[39] with cinnamon that hovers here and settles? If this is the case, the half view of the dead world is lightened by the symbolic creature of resurrection and eternity. But all of these bright fragments are merely ornaments to the wooing of Phoebus by Earth, the radiant myth at the center of the poem.

In the *Theogony,* Hesiod traces the beginning of things to the great union: "Huge Sky came bringing night, and desiring love, embraced Earth and lay on her and stretched out."[40] To these forces Homer gave name and season when in the *Iliad* Zeus clasps his consort in his arms. "And beneath them the divine earth sends forth fresh new grass, and dewy lotus, and crocus, and hyacinth, thick and soft, that raised them aloft from the ground. Therein they lay and were clad with a fair golden cloud, whence fell drops of glittering dew."⁴¹ To these accounts of the hierogamy, Venus, speaking in Aeschylus's *Danaides,* adds her remembrances. "The pure Sky yearns passionately to pierce the Earth and love lays hold on Earth to join in wedlock. The rain falls from the steaming heavens and impregnates earth; and she brings forth the pasturage of sheep and Demeter's gift for mortals and the ripe season of trees."⁴² From these Greek origins came the tradition that the Latins gave to Milton.

But Milton lived in a cold latitude where spring is sun rather than rain; hence, he proposes Phoebus, rather than Aether, as the spouse of Earth. In "On the Morning of Christ's Nativity," written a half year after "In Adventum Veris," Nature wears the drab gown of winter because it is "no season then for her / To wanton with the Sun, her lusty Paramour." But the sun of the elegy is more than sun; it is Phoebus Apollo, the Sungod patron of spring. This is the god whom we meet in the *Aeneid* as he leaves his winter home in Lycia and walks the Cynthian summits, shaping his hair with laurel and binding it with gold while the arrows, the rays of the sun, rattle on his shoulder.⁴³ Claudian, last of the Roman poets, also recounted the journey of the wandering god.

When fair Apollo leaves Delphi's shrine and visits the altars of the north, Castalia's water differ in no wise from those of any common stream, nor the laurel from any common tree; sad and silent is the cave and the shrine without a worshipper. But if Phoebus is there, Phoebus returned from Scythian climes to his Delphic tripod, guiding thither his yoked griffins, the woods, the caves regain their voice, the streams their life. The sacred ripple revisits the face of the waters; a clearer echo resounds from the shrine; and now the inspired rocks tremble to the voice of prophecy.⁴⁴

It is this god, who like the "dea Sicana" spent half a year in cold darkness and took with him music, dancing, and prophecy when he departed; it is this god whom Milton would lure into the bed of Earth.

Because Phoebus Apollo turns the shepherd's jibe against blushing Aurora, Milton, a self-appointed "magister amoris" and warmer of cold beds, recommends to him an amatory exercise. "Earth," he informs the Sungod, "is throwing off her hated age," and fifty lines later he reports that Venus is rejuvenating her ancient flesh. The two ladies are thus made equal; hence, we are not perplexed when Tellus escapes the unflattering Vergilian "magne corpore" and is described as if she were the Cyprian. She bares her voluptuous breast; she is scented with Asian perfumes; she winds flowers in her hair. Her only physical defect is the grotesque "lucus sacer" with which she crowns herself. Phoebus, however, is no Mars. He learns that Earth is eager for his caresses; he is encouraged by compliant putti, "faciles amores"; honied entreaties are conveyed to him; but wanting the vigor of Aether, he holds back. He even seems to have lost the amorous drive that a lover of Daphne, Clymene, Rhodos, Circe, Clytie, and Leucothoe should have. To improve the marital attractiveness of Tellus, Milton remarks that she is not "sine dote," and has already provided her hesitant lover with herbs that help him in his healing. "Alma salutiferum medicos tibi gramen in usus / praebet, et hinc titulos adiuvat ipsa tuos." It is clear that Milton is addressing the father of Aesculapius, who taught Iapyx, Aeneas' physician, "the power of herbs and the art of healing."[45] We can hear him, Milton being absent, speak to Daphne for himself.

By my skill the past, the present, and the future are revealed. Thanks to me the lyre strings thrill with music. My arrow is sure, though there is one surer still, which has wounded my careful heart. The art of medicine is my invention and men the world over give me the name of healer. All the properties of herbs are known to me; but, alas, there are no herbs to cure love, and the skill which helps others cannot help its master.[46]

Not every poet has the audacity to counsel a god in matters of the heart, but Milton was born in London, the city where Venus, as he states in the First Elegy, now lived. Deserting her southern shrines, she had come northward attracted by the beauty of English girls, a beauty which had even brought about the regeneration of that weary womanizer Jupiter. Milton does not inform Charles Diodati, the recipient of the First Elegy, about any English girl in particular; in fact, finding the city uncongenial to a disciple of Phoebus Apollo, he plans to retreat while he has "the indulgence of the blind boy," "pueri indulgentia caeci," and before Amor, employing one of those goddesses with waving, blond hair, catches him in a golden snare. "Aurea quae fallax retiatendit Amor." The danger thus avoided overwhelms this counselor-at-hearts in Elegy Seven.

"L'Allegro" and its companion poem describe Milton's rambles about London and its suburbs. The solitary walker appears first in Elegy One in London and in a suburban grove of elms noble in shade, "suburbani nobilis umbra loci." It was in this grove that he encountered the dazzling but fearsome bands of British maidens. The perambulation of the First Elegy is continued into the Seventh, where, on the first of May, the boy once again saunters through the city and "the pleasing suburban villages." Once again crowds of radiant girls pass, and Milton asks, "Is this where Phoebus gets his rays?" Then, like the poet of the *Vita Nuova,* he sees one girl who far surpasses the others. Love consumes him; he is all flame. "Uror amans intus, flammaque totus eram." He never sees her again, and his plight is hopeless, because he can neither overcome nor obtain his desire. The poem ends; Cupid has had his revenge on Milton, advisor of gods.

The trouble began, Milton tells Venus Amathusia, because he did not learn her laws, was wanting in Paphian fire, and had mocked Cupid, saying to the little bowman,

Go boy and shoot unwarlike doves;
Soft battles suit a tender commander;
Or else triumph elatedly, little one, over sparrows.
These are military honors worthy of you.
But do not try your silly arms on mortals;
Against strong men your quiver has no force.

Now Love, as Ovid, and even George Herbert, knew, was a man of war, a veteran commander, who is justifiably angry when a poet of nineteen proclaims himself among "fortes viri"; hence, when Milton, like the lover of Beatrice, awakens on May Day morning, he finds Eros at his bedside. The god rebukes the poet who is ignorant about his victories over gods and heroes. Orion, Hercules, even thundering Jove have been victims of his fantastic marksmanship. At the top of the casualty list is Phoebus Apollo. In fact, says Cupid, reciting Ovid's "vince Cupidineas pariter Parthasque sagittas,"⁴⁷ the "Parthian horseman is no better shot than I." He informs young Milton, who had already nominated himself in English as the servant of "the Muse of Love," that neither the Muses nor the healing arts of Apollo, the Musagetes, can save him. Perhaps this experience with Cupid really qualified Milton to advise Phoebus Apollo, but he was also simply reliving in 1628 A.D. a love story that had taken place sometime before B.C. 50.

"Daphne, daughter of Peneus," Ovid says surely, "was Phoebus' first love." The tale is familiar. The god, returning from dragon killing, asks Cupid, "lascivus puer," what he is doing with a man's armaments. The bow, he insists, is his personal weapon, and he orders Cupid to be content with his torch and to leave shooting to the experts. But Cupid, who Milton said was "prompter to wrath" because Ovid said he was filled with "savage anger," notches, as he does in the Seventh Elegy, his golden arrow and shoots Apollo. "Tanto minor est tua gloria nostra." Milton had seen a girl who "surpassed all others," and Apollo saw Daphne. Milton, we remember, became all fire;

Apollo burst into blaze. "Sic Deus in flammas abiit; sic pectore toto / uritur." Both loves are hopeless. Milton can only follow in his imagination the girl he will never see again, but is reconciled to Eros in the end and sacrifices at his altar. The luck of Apollo is no better. Daphne pursued is changed into the symbolic laurel and the poet of the gods writes a hymn to his tree. "When the healer was done," says Ovid, "the laurel inclined her newmade branches."[48] The stirring of Apollo's laurel helps us find the true meaning of Milton's Fifth Elegy.

In keeping with Meleager's spring resolve to sing and the complaint about Apollo's desertion voiced by the author of the *Pervigilium Veneris,* Milton expresses, after the opening conventional quatrain, the moving force of genius he feels within. Suddenly the "deus poetarum" is manifest. "Deus ipse venit— video Peneide lauro / implicatos crines—Delius ipse venit." Once again Milton agrees with Ovid. "There is a god in us; we are warmed by his motion which sows seeds of inspiration. Whether I am a poet or sing of holy matters, it is especially fitting that I see the gods' faces."[49] Ovid writes in the age when, if we can believe the "Carmen Saeculare" of Horace, the god and his sister had special honors in the city of Augustus, but Milton's reverend outburst could also have been heard three centuries earlier than then. We could be at Cyrene listening as Callimachus raises the chorus, Callimachus whose "Magnifick Odes and Hymns," Milton wrote, are with those of Pindar "in most things worthy."[50] The bough of laurel trembles; the shrine shakes; "Phoebus knocks at the door with lovely foot." The celebrating poet sees the palm of Delos nod; he hears the swans singing; he sees the bolts and bars draw back of their own accord; and he warns the young men about him. "For Apollo does not appear to all, only to the good; and he who has seen him is truly great but who has not is, indeed, of poor estate."[51] We know the names of some of these "truly great": Hesiod who knew the Muses; Demodocus to whom Apollo gave song; the blindman guest at the divine feast in the first book of the *Iliad;* and Pindar, older than Callimachus, but joined with him in Milton's mind. And Pindar, like Milton, was also present when the god came.

> The fairest choir of Muses sang once in gladness
> While Apollo in their midst with quill of gold
> Chased the notes of the seven tongued lyre
> And led forth holy strains.[52]

It is not then beyond credence that when Apollo appears, the imagination of Milton soars into the liquid sky and passes, free of body, through vagrant clouds. Like Adam who will see the history of man from the "Mount of the Visions of God" or like Christ who will reject the glory of the world from Niphates' height, Milton, disregarding both time and space, visits the haunts of the poets, the homes of the gods, seeing all done on Olympus and all below. "Intuiturque animus toto quid agatur Olympo / nec fugiunt oculos Tartara caeca meos." Shortly before he had this experience, Milton proposed a similar ecstatic journey in his Third Prolusion to his fellow students. He had urged them to fly into the sky, to soar beyond terrestrial limits, to know "those holy minds and intelligences with whom after this you will join in eternal society."[53] Within months he will follow again the stages of this "iter mentis" so attractive to him.

> Such where the deep transported mind may soar
> Above the wheeling poles, and at Heav'n's door
> Look in and see each blissful Deity
> How he before the thunderous throne doth lie,
> Listening to what unshorne Apollo sings
> To th' touch of golden wires, while Hebe bring
> Immortal Nectar to her Kingly Sire:
> Then passing through the Spheres of watchful fire,
> And misty Regions of wide air next under,
> And hills of Snow and lofts of piled Thunder,
> May tell at length how green-ey'd *Neptune* raves,

In Heav'n's defiance mustering all his waves;
Then sing of secret things that come to pass
When Beldam Nature in her cradle was;
And last of Kings and Queens and Heroes old,
Such as the wise *Demodocus* once told
In solemn songs at King Alcinous' feast,
While sad Ulysses' soul and all the rest
Are held with his melodious harmony
In willing chains and sweet captivity.

By the time Milton wrote these lines many saints had made journeys into Christian space; but before they had, Er, son of Armenius, went the pagan course and heard the same sirens,[54] who will "lull the daughters of Necessity" in Milton's "Arcades." The pious Scipio, too, following the lead of his great ancestor's forefinger, looked down from the bourne of souls and saw a universe so vast it beggared the ambition of mortals.[55] For the young Milton, the verses about the Milky Way in the *Metamorphoses* were undoubtedly also impressive. On this bright boulevard, he read, live the important and distinguished gods, whereas the other celestial citizens live in the narrow streets of the stellar Trastevere. "Were I permitted to speak boldly," says Ovid carefully, "I would call this the Palatine district of high Heaven."[56] It is to residential areas of this nature that a poet can ascend when Phoebus Apollo comes down to allow the clear singer to look on his face. "Phoebus gave me," says Horace who knew the Delian well, "the inspiration and the art of song and the name of poet."[57] The nature of this inspiration, Horace's "spiritus," and the praise of its bestower is the true topic of the "In Adventum Veris."

The theme that called forth this elegy is one that had engaged all poets beginning with Plato. In the *Phaedrus* poets are said to be possessed by a Muse-given insanity,[58] and this assumption is confirmed in the *Apology* where it is observed that they can never explain their poems. "There is hardly a person present who would not have talked better about their poetry than poets

do."[59] The whole doctrine of inspiration is voiced in the well-
known conversation with the rhapsodist *Ion*. The poet "does not
sing by art but by divine power," Plato writes, comparing lyric
poets to the Corybantian revellers or to bees, "light and winged
and holy things," who feed in the gardens of the Muses. God
speaks to men through poets, and it is evident "that these beautiful poems are not human, or the work of man but divine and
the work of God; and that poets are the only interpreters of the
gods by whom they are severally possessed."[60] Pindar, who lived
almost a century before Plato, said all of this more tersely: when
the brightness comes and God gives it, there is a shining of light
on men.[61]

Horace's "spiritus" was Θεία δε δυναμις for Plato, but Pindar's
αἴγλα διοσδοτος is closer, perhaps, to what Milton has in mind.
To substantiate this decision we can read the plea of Tellus to
Phoebus which follows that of the advising poet. She requests
Apollo to rest in her cool shades, and assures him that she does
not fear the fate of Phaeton or Semele. It is clear, however, that,
unlike her great classical ancestress, she does not yearn for his
physical embrace. She asks only that he "lay his light on her
breast." "Et gremio lumina pone meo." Within a few lines she
repeats the same prayer: "Cum tu, Phoebe, tuo sapientius uteris
igni, / huc aedes, et gremio lumina pone meo." It is light she
asks, not heat or fire. The poet also prays that the gods remain
in the wood, that Jupiter return with the Golden Age, that
Phoebus Apollo delay his northern journey. It is the poet's right,
as Ovid insisted, to look on the faces of the gods; and it is his
desire that cold sterility, the long dark of nights, the great polar
shadows be slow to come. Within a half year Milton will remember the winter, the night, the shades of Christian December
and the abdication of the pagan god of light. "*Apollo* from his
shrine / Can no more divine / With hollow shriek the steep of
Delphos leaving." But in the Fifth Elegy it is more than the god
whom Milton addresses. It is the power that the god represents

that both he and Tellus supplicate. It is Pindar's αἴγλα διοσδοτος or to dress it in Latin the "lumen divinum." An older Milton will make this plain when he invokes the Muse Urania as now he invokes Phoebus Apollo.

> The Meaning, not the name I call: for thou
> Nor of the Muses nine, nor on the top
> Of old *Olympus* dwell'st, but Heaven born.

When he wrote this, however, he had known the inward blaze of the Heavenly Light.

I have been implying that the "In Adventum Veris" is more a poem on the ecstasy of poetic insight in its apollonian manifestation than on the ancient topic of the annual renewal of earthly life. But the "advent of spring" is not to be read under, for the poem intends to remind us that the force of poetry is also renewed with each generation. Standing on the margin of promised poetic achievement, Milton recognized the eternal revival in himself. Filled with noble plans, he was not ready to settle for anything other than the difficulties of success. He is different in this desire from Propertius visited also by Apollo who criticized his intention to succeed Ennius as an heroic poet. "The meadows are soft over which your little wheels must run," said the unshorn god, "that often your book may be read by some lonely girl waiting for her absent lover."[62] It is enough, says Propertius afterward, "if my writings set boys and girls on fire."[63] The Milton who attempts to reject love in the Seventh Elegy and who rejects both love and these elegies in the Platonically inspired recantation with which the *Poemata* ends, could not be happy with only the affection of Calliope. The brighter hopes of him who wrote the *Culex* at the age of sixteen were more like his. It is possible that he saw a strong similarity between his own plans and those expressed in the *Catalepton*[64] and the *Ciris*,[65] just as he may have found in his own guarded virginity a reflection of Vergil's reputed chastity. But they had other experiences in common, for both had seen Apollo. In the seventh bucolic Phoebus pulls Vergil's ear for prematurely thinking about "kings and battles"; in "Lycidas" the same god pulls the ear of Milton to remind him of the eternity of a poet's glory. By the time that this last pastoral was forced from Milton he had perhaps planned his own "marble temple beside the water" to a greater power than Vergil's Caesar.

These poetic plans, however, did not include further compositions in Latin. With the exception of the "Ode to John Rous" on the loss of the 1645 volume from the Bodleian Library, Milton attempted no Latin verse of consequence after 1646; in fact, with the exception of the "Epitaphium Damonis" of 1640,[66] all of the *Poemata* was done before he was thirty. Other distinguished English poets who had the skill—Abraham Cowley, George Herbert, Andrew Marvell, and Tom May—wrote with both pens for most of their lives. As a consequence, they were read in continental Europe, whereas Milton's great poems had to wait for Latin translation before they could be widely known abroad. Though Milton used the Latin tongue to defend his country and his faith, he turned to his native language when his "celestial patroness" spoke through his lips. He was prompted paradoxically both by a modest sense of his powers and by a proud conviction of his artistic mission. To understand this seeming contradiction, we may hear him speaking in *The Reason of Church Government*.

That if I were certain to write as men buy Leases, for three lives and downward, there ought no regard be sooner had, then to Gods glory by the honour and instruction of my country. For which cause, and not only for that I knew it would be hard to arrive at the second rank among the Latines, I apply'd my selfe to that resolution which *Ariosto* follow'd against the perswasions of *Bembo,* to fix all the industry and art I could unite to the adorning of my native tongue; not to make verbal curiosities the end, that were a toylsom vanity, but to be an interpreter and relater of the best and sagest things among mine own Citizens throughout this Iland in the mother dialect. That what the greatest and choycest wits of

Athens, Rome, or modern *Italy,* and those Hebrews of old did for their country, I in my proportion with this over and above of being a Christian, might doe for mine: not caring to be once named abroad, though perhaps I could attaine to that, but content with these British Ilands as my world."[67]

Notes

[1] *Works* (New York, 1931–38), III, 235–6.

[2] *Responsio* (London, 1660), p. 5; see W. R. Parker, *Milton's Contemporary Reputation* (Columbus, Ohio, 1940), pp. 23, 39, 119.

[3] "Some Faults in Milton's Latin Poetry," *Classical Review*, I (1887), 46–8.

[4] E. K. Rand, "Milton in Rustication," *Studies in Philology*, XIX (1922), 109–35; J. H. Hanford, "Youth of Milton," *Studies in Shakespeare, Milton, and Donne*, Ann Arbor, 1925; D. Bush, *Mythology and the Renaissance Tradition* (New York, 1963), pp. 261–5; W. H. Semple, "The Latin Poems of John Milton," *Bulletin of the John Rylands Library*, XLVI (1963), 217–35; and the prefaces of Walter MacKellar whose *The Latin Poems of John Milton*, New Haven, 1930, is the source of my text.

[5] V, 737–40.

[6] *Idyls*, VI, 11–18.

[7] *Eclogues*, IX, 40–1.

[8] I, 43.

[9] II, 149–50.

[10] II, 336–8.

[11] I *Odes*, 4.

[12] IV, *Odes*, 7; see also IV, 11.

[13] I, 151–7; III, 235–42.

[14] II, 853–6.

[15] IV, 85–132.

[16] V, 183–220.

[17] *Tristia*, III, xii.

[18] *Arcadia*, ed. M. Scherillo (Turin, 1888), pp. 10–13.

[19] *Anthologia Palatina*, IX, 363.

[20] XXII.

[21] *Appendix*, II.

[22] *Carmina*, ed. G. de Hartel (Vienna, 1894), pp. 194–5.

[23] *Carmina*, ed. F. Vollmer (Berlin, 1905), pp. 31–2.

[24] *Opera Poetica*, ed. F. Leo (Berlin, 1881), pp. 124–6.

[25] Pp. 59–60.

[26] *Carmina*, ed. E. Duemmler (Berlin, 1885), pp. 336, 354, 370.

[27] *Antologia della Lirica Latina in Italia nei Secoli XV e XVI*, ed. E. Costa (Citta di Castello, 1888), pp. 85–6.

[28] *Opera Omnia* (Naples, 1732), p. iii.

[29] *Carmina* (Padua, 1743), p. 91.

[30] Pp. 97–8.

[31] Pp. 83–4.

[32] *Opera Omnia* (Venice, 1555), pp. 282v–283v.

[33] Erasmus wrote a long, unpoetic "Certamen ... de Tempore Vernali," *Opera* (Leyden, 1706), VIII, 565–6; there are other poems on the topic in J. C. Scaliger, *Poemata* (s. l., 1600), p. 115; Andrea Dazzi, *Poemata* (Florence, 1549), pp. 112–3; P. Lotichius, *Opera* (Leipzig, 1586), p. 175; J. Cameno, *Libri duo* (Venice, 1570), p. xxxix.

[34] *Works*, VIII, 79.

[35] *Opera Omnia* (Leyden, 1725), II, 415, 304–8.

[36] D. Morhof, *Polyhistor Literarius* (Lubeck, 1732), I, 301–2.

[37] Buchanan, II, 305; Horace II *Odes*, VIII, 14–16.

[38] *Griphus*, 17.

[39] XXII, 421–2.

[40] Lines 176–8; see *Prolusion One*, *Works*, XII, 128.

[41] XIV, 346–51.

[42] Athenaeus, *Deipnosophists*, XIII, 600.

[43] IV, 143–9. Macrobius, writing about 400, informs us that Phoebus and Apollo were the same, *Saturnaliorum libri VII*, I, vii, 13–14; XVIII, 5. His arrows are the sun's rays (I, xvii, 60) and his moderation of the seven strings of the lyre is the equivalent of the sun's dominance of the planets (I, xix, 15). When we visit the palace of Helios in *Metamorphoses*, II, 23–30, Phoebus is surrounded by the hours and seasons and Spring is represented by a young man with a floral crown.

[44] "Sixth Consulship of Honorius," 25–38.

[45] XII, 391–7.

[46] *Metamorphoses*, I, 517–25; see II, 618 and *Tristia*, III, iii, 10.

[47] *Remedia Amoris*, 157.

[48] *Metamorphoses*, I, 452–567.

[49] *Fasti*, VI, 5–8.

[50] *Works*, III, 238.

[51] II, 1–8; one should compare this hymn to Apollo with the so-called Homeric Hymn.

[52] *Nemean*, V, 22–4.

[53] *Works*, XII, 170.

[54] Plato, *Republic*, 614–8.

[55] Cicero, *De Republica,* VI, 9–26.

[56] *Metamorphoses,* I, 163–76.

[57] IV *Odes,* 6, 29–30.

[58] 245, 265.

[59] 22 a–c.

[60] 533–5.

[61] *Pythian,* VIII, 96–7.

[62] III, 3.

[63] III, 9, 45.

[64] XIV, IX.

[65] 92–100.

[66] "Ad Patrem" has sometimes been thought later, but see Douglas Bush, "The Date of Milton's *Ad Patrem,*" *Modern Philology,* LXI (1964), 204–8.

[67] *Works,* III, 236–7.

The Puritans in Old and New England

By LEON HOWARD

I

WHEN I first thought of taking a new look at the Puritans of both Old and New England I already knew something about the complexities of their period and was fully aware of the proverb that "fools rush in where angels fear to tread." But I hoped that by dwelling for a while among the Saints on both sides of the Atlantic I might acquire wisdom. I have. Its essence may be put in the form of a new proverb: When the Saints come marching in, a wise man gets the hell out.

For the Saints—as King Charles I and so many others learned before me—were a troublesome people, unmanageable by the church and state, and also by the historian because of their tendencies to group and ungroup themselves in terms of political and ecclesiastical aims and sectarian doctrines. My only hope was to find some practical device for getting one aspect of the subject under historical control. Since my main interest was neither in the Puritan Revolution in England nor in the American Puritans in isolation, I hit upon the rather obvious method

of looking up the books published by the Americans, collecting
the names of the English writers who sponsored them by writing
introductions, prefaces, and the like, and making a checklist of
their writings in an effort to assemble a body of material which
was sympathetically related and which would thus form a sort
of intellectual raft on which I might float through a sea of revolutionary chaos.

The need for a new look was suggested to me by the apparently paradoxically fact that Independency in church government was a "liberal" movement in England, opposed to a
conservative Presbyterianism and leading to the toleration of
sectarian differences; whereas in America Independency was
conservative from the beginning and became almost completely
reactionary, leading to an active persecution of the sects and
the enforcement of a death penalty against Quakers. An analogy with certain events in the recent World War was readily
apparent: Like some of the European governments who moved
to England during the Nazi invasion, the American "Puritans
in exile" became more conservative as the English "Puritans
of the resistance" became more radical. There were also obvious
analogical explanations for the English radicalism in terms of
the practical necessity of tolerating ideological differences in a
movement directed against a common enemy, the military value
of fanatics, etc. But it seemed to me that there might be some
more positive and perhaps more significant force operating in
America than had yet been identified and defined—something
still to be discovered in the history and literature of early
America which should not be brushed off by the observation
of an interesting analogy.

And so, armed with a list of perhaps a thousand titles, I
descended upon the British Museum and settled myself among
the Thomason Tracts in order to look the situation over. Circumstances prevented me from being as well prepared as I should
have been, from forming as substantial a raft as I would have

preferred to ride upon; and, from time to time, I may have ridden too many odd logs in too many different directions. I must confess that when I looked over my notes in an effort to verify my general drift for this occasion I was a bit surprised and more than a bit doubtful about the wisdom of attempting this premature chart of my course. Yet, since I am supposed to lead a discussion rather than give you the word, I am willing to drift along in the hope that you will find the course suggestive as well as erratic.

II

One of the most ironic facts about the Puritan period was the Saints' own frequent complaints that it was a "name-blasting" age. In the 1640's, as now, the word "Puritan" was a term of opprobrium—"a long-lived murderer," as one reverend gentleman put it, used "to kill sound doctrine, holy life, sobriety, all that is good"—and so loosely used that it signified orthodoxy to an Arminian, sobriety to a drunkard, and a Protestant to a Papist. It was so "poisonous," said another, that it was "not contented to gangrene Religion, Ecclesiastical and Civil policy" but threatened "destruction to all morality" until "even honesty, strictness, and civility itself must become disgraceful." Yet it was so convenient a term that the Saints themselves felt compelled to adopt it with a more specific application, and during the period of the Long Parliament it seems to have been conventional to identify Reformation in England with Puritanism and to recognize three distinct groups of Puritans—"Doctrinal and moral Puritans," "Ecclesiastical Puritans," and "State Puritans."

My concern, in terms of these contemporary distinctions, is with "Ecclesiastical Puritans" who were in the process of becoming "State Puritans." For to the settlers of New England and their English sympathizers the reform of doctrine was an accomplished fact. They dwelt under the Covenant of Grace as expounded by William Perkins and accepted the five points of Calvinism as determined by the Synod of Dort. An acceptance of the Covenant of Grace distinguished them from the Roman Catholics who were held to live under a Covenant of Works. The doctrine involved in this distinction was briefly this: In the beginning God had made a covenant with Adam enabling him to work out his own salvation by obedience to the law. But Adam had disobeyed and thereby condemned his seed to a heritage of total depravity. Mankind still lived under this covenant because the Law was an expression of the will of God, but good works no longer provided a means of salvation and the Roman heresy was to assume they did and thus make men blind to their only hope. This hope was found by the Puritans in the second covenant which God had made with Abraham and fulfilled in Christ. In it He offered by His own free Grace to redeem a select portion of mankind and justify their salvation by the vicarious atonement of Christ. The doctrine of the second Covenant had developed out of Calvinistic theology, and to the Puritans the systematized five points of Calvinism simply clarified man's position under the Covenant by offering a solid doctrine which could be opposed to the inadequate understanding of the Lutherans and the heresies of Arminius. Two of these points stressed the total depravity of mankind and the unconditional election of the chosen few, and the other three maintained that the atonement was indeed limited, that the offer of God's grace was irresistible, and that the selected Saints could not avoid persevering in their sanctity. The Lutheran error and the Arminian heresy, in short, lay in suggesting that men had any natural capacity for achieving grace or any freedom to refuse or accept it.

Now it is true that the Protestant movement as a whole was based upon the substitution of the authority of the Scriptures for the authority of the Church and that the Puritans were firm believers in the progressive unfolding of the full meaning of the Word. For "Truth," as Thomas Hooker observed in this connection, "is the Daughter of time." It is also a matter of fact that the Puritans were committed to an exposition of theological beliefs in terms suitable to the understanding of plain people. But it is a mistake, I think, to find in their refinements of biblical interpretation and in their everyday figures of speech the substance of a theology essentially different from strict Calvinism . I have no wish on this occasion to pick a bone of contention with the author of "The Marrow of Puritan Divinity," but the fact is that I have observed in this particular group no evidence of serious deviation from the doctrines I have just surveyed, either by bargaining with the Lord for their salvation or by demanding it of Him in any legalistic way. On the contrary, Thomas Shepard in New England recognized the dangers of misunderstanding in times of controversy and, as a representative of the legalistic ministers engaged in condemning Anne Hutchinson, preached against the doctrines which have since been attributed to a "federal school of theology." "It is a great plot of Arminians," he said, "to make Christ a means only, to make man a first *Adam;* setting men to work for their living again; for they grant all Grace is lost, all comes from Christ, Christ gives all, and then when we have it use it well, thus you shall have life, else look for death: So 'tis a misery every soul is in." Shepard preached this sermon in June, 1636, and repeated it in May, 1640, and it was published for the benefit of an English public on the eve of the Restoration as a fine example of "the true middle way of the Gospel between the Legalist on the one hand, and the Antinomian (or loose Gospeller) on the other." Shepard's own comment upon such doctrines was: "Men will trade in small wares, rather than live on another's Alms. Do you think the Lord takes it well to make him a Merchant for your ends? Oh no, never look to have communion with him in this way!"

Consequently it seems best to march with the Saints in the direction they themselves thought they were going—away from the controversies over doctrine, which distinguished the sectarians from the Puritans, and into the second stage of reformation which was that of ecclesiastical reform.

III

The earliest Puritans had of necessity attempted reform from within their individual churches and had concentrated their efforts upon such symbolic relics of Roman Catholicism as clerical vestments, set liturgies, and kneeling at the altar for communion. They had no opportunity to reform the government of churches established by law, but when they got such an opportunity—either by exile in Holland or New England or by revolution at home—they immediately took steps to free themselves from the control of an episcopal hierarchy by means of establishing independent churches abroad or by abolishing the hierarchy in England. On such matters as these they were united, and they were also united in their abhorrence of sectarian differences in doctrine which prevented one church from communing with another. They believed in the spiritual existence of one universal mystical church and were ambitious to make their visible churches as pure as any human organization could be made under divine guidance. They had many problems to face, and at least two serious ones were implicit in their reformed doctrine.

First, as Calvinists they were forced to realize that no visible church could be wholly pure in its membership—that the mystery of God's grace would conceal hypocrites among the Saints. Thus they faced the solemn question of whether they should strive for an unattainable ideal or be as realistic as the Scots had been and accept into church fellowship the great body of unsanctified mankind. Second, as dwellers under the Covenant of Grace they were New Testament Christians and never forgot the fact. God's religious and moral law—as exemplified in the two tables of the Ten Commandments—covered all people, wherever expressed; but God's ordinances differed under the two dispensations, and careful distinctions could be made between those that were peculiar to the Jews and those that were proper for Christians. The Old Testament Jewish church had been a "national" church, catholic in its demands for the allegiance of a whole people. The New Testament church of primitive Christians had been a "gathered" church, made up of believers who were confirmed in membership by their belief and voluntarily gathered together in fellowship. The revealed Word, in fact, was neither consistent nor altogether clear in its guidance for the reform of church government. The problem was whether people who genuinely revered the Bible could completely disregard the Old Testament and carry out a major reform entirely under the direction of the New.

The actual solution of these two closely related problems seems to have been dictated almost entirely by circumstances. The Puritans in exile were, by virtue of their voluntary departure from England, members of gathered churches; and those who were led into Holland, where they were tolerated by a government in which they could have no part, avoided any temptation to become State Puritans. A small group of them who returned home in time to take part in the Westminster Assembly of Divines recognized their unique position and used it as an ethical argument to support the reform of church government which they proposed: "We had no new Common-wealths to rear, to frame Church-government unto, whereof any one piece might stand in the others light, to cause the least variation by us from the Puritan pattern," they said; "We had no State ends or Political interests to comply with; no Kingdoms in our eye to subdue unto our mould."

Their opponents, however, refused to accept this argument. "You had new Common-wealths to rear; to frame your Church-

government unto, when you first fell into these principles,"
replied Thomas Edwards; "namely, the new Common-wealth
of *New-England* to frame your Church-government unto, where
some of you were first bound in your thoughts and purposes
(as you well know) and I shall make evident." The justice of
Edward's attribution of a New England political influence upon
the Dissenting Brethren of the Westminster Assembly is doubtful, but it is a matter of fact that Thomas Goodwin and his
associates were the most active advocates of "the New-England
Way" of church government during the revolutionary period
and were largely responsible for the publication of those books,
pamphlets, and letters in which the New England Way was
transformed from a somewhat casual practice into a theory of
government and a pattern of thought which seem to have had
a lasting influence in America, however ineffective the Way
may have been in the England it was partially designed to
influence.

IV

In order to follow the development of the New England
Way we must step backward a decade and a half in time, from
the outbursts of the Westminster Assembly in 1643 to the
establishment of the first Puritan colony at Salem in 1628.

Salem was an experimental colony, organized in anticipa-
tion of the great migration two years later and made up of
more fishermen than Saints. Historians are still debating the
organization of its primitive church and the influences under
which it was formed—whether it owed its peculiarities to the
advice and example of nearby Plymouth or to the principles the
settlers brought with them. I doubt whether the question can
ever be settled, and I also doubt that it is of any serious historical importance. The church was by the very nature of its
existence in exile a gathered church, and its purification from
all ceremonies was an example of the Puritans' normal reac-

tion to freedom. A formal covenant of church fellowship and an ordination of the minister by the congregation may have been practical means of preserving unity in the wilderness and independence from bishops—means to which the settlers resorted under the influence of principles and precedent. But in any event the little church at Salem had neither the position, the power, nor the personalities required to exercise much influence upon their strong-minded proprietors who landed on the shores of Massachusetts Bay in the summer of 1630.

The Saints of the Bay—perhaps two hundred of the thousand souls who disembarked from eleven ships during the first summer of the great migration—came to America for what they called "freedom of ordinances," and their primary concern was for ecclesiastical purity. Yet their leaders were fully aware of the political power which had been exercised against them in England and for safety's sake brought with them the patent which provided for the government of the colony by its proprietors. One of the first acts of the government formed under its provisions—taken a year before the first church building was constructed in Boston—was what we would now call an act of unilateral revision which restricted the franchise to church members. Thus, from 1631 until a new charter was issued after the Restoration, the Massachusetts Bay church was in control of the state, and State Puritanism in the new world took on the peculiar cast which most historians have agreed to call "theocracy."

Yet it seems to me that the term is a misleading one insomuch as it implies that the clergy possessed a political power which was actually kept from them. For the most distinctive—and, to the English and the Scots, the most disturbing—characteristic of the New England Way in church government was its insistence upon keeping the essential power of the church in the hands of the congregation. The congregation called and ordained its ministers—its pastor, teacher, and ruling elders—

and dismissed them at will. The congregation approved or disapproved the admission of each new member and the removal
of any member for any reason. The power of public admonition and of excommunication rested with the congregation
rather than with the ruling elders who might be called upon
to execute it. Since each congregation was independent of every
other, the control of the colony (including the civil franchise)
was vested in small groups of individuals who professed allegiance firmly to God, doubtfully to the king, and not at all
to any kind of ecclesiastical officer. That any considerable community of either Saints or sinners could survive under such a
system of apparently complete independency would seem a
miracle.

That the Bay Colony did survive and flourish as a coherent
community, however, is a fact of history which contains no
record of miracles; and the secret of its survival, I believe, lies
in two peculiarities of the Puritan movement which can be
easily underestimated in our modern concern for the economic
and other material aspects of history. The first of these is
the fact that the Puritan times, as one contemporary observer
pointed out, were "preaching times" in which congregations
were preached into armies and the minister was "both the old
Trumpet of the Law and the new drum of the Gospel." The
preachers believed, as they would have chosen to put it, in
the Sword of the Spirit; for they had achieved their own positions of influence through the power of persuasion, often in
defiance of constituted authority, and those who led the migration to the New World had every reason to assume that
they could maintain an influence in the colony by a purity of
spiritual "gifts" which could not be reflected in political and
eccleciastic institutions.

The second fact is that many leaders of the Reformation had
a faith so absolute that it cannot be exaggerated in the guiding
power of the Scriptures which they believed were literally dic-

tated by the Holy Ghost. In one of the most touchingly intimate of Puritan sermons, "A Childe of Light Walking in
Darkness," Thomas Goodwin refers to men who, "being sometimes led by sense and reason whilst they walk in darkness, . . .
are apt to interpret God's mind toward them rather by his
works and dispensations, which they see and feel, then by his
word, which they are to believe." Even the best of churchmen,
wrote Thomas Hooker from America, "are all but men, and
may err: their judgments are *not the rule,* but must be regulated. Their power is under Christ, only from him, and for
him, wholly to be acted and ordered by the authority in his
Word." "God doth not command such things as are contrary
to his Law, his revealed will, or right reason," declared Samuel
Bolton; "yet he commands such things as are contrary to cor-
rupt reason, and above right reason, and therefore his commands are not to be scanned: it is our reason and the reason
of reasons to obey because God hath commanded." And the
final rule for "a right understanding of Scriptures" offered by
Ralph Venning was: "If Scripture speak it, believe it, though
Reason cannot find out the reason of it." This widespread
belief in the absolute supremacy of biblical law was the prevailing belief among the American Puritans who based their first
attempts at the codification of civil law upon the judicials of
Moses, and, as we shall see later, it provided the basis for their
sincere denial of any affiliation with the independent sects of
England and for their consistent advocacy of the New England
Way as a "middle way" in church government between that
of Presbyterianism and Independency.

But at the moment we must pause and observe that when the
Westminster Assembly met in 1643 the major problem it faced,
as Professor William Haller has so brilliantly demonstrated,
was the problem of discipline. The English preachers were
flaming with enthusiasm. The Scots brought with them the
cold northern light of experience with discipline. The sects

were of course not represented in a body chosen to institu-
tionalize Puritan orthodoxy. Gradually the Scottish experience
and Scottish logic cooled the enthusiasm and began to prevail in planning a national church which would substitute the
authority of an assembly of presbyters for the authority of an
episcopal hierarchy. Only a small group of "dissenting brethren"
stood out consistently against Presbyterianism and advocated
the Congregational or New England Way. They were name-
blasted with charges of radicalism and irresponsibility—justly
so in the minds of their accusers, for rumors were rife in England about dissention in the new world and no one then knew
exactly how the Bay Puritans were handling the problem of
discipline.

V

The most remarkable thing about the problem of discipline
in the New England colony, as we look back over its history,
seems to be that it was not at all anticipated. The earliest settlers,
who had formed seven small communities of Saints by 1632,
had control over their unregenerate servants and artisans and
possessed a land patent which enabled them to discourage the
immigration of the fanatics who were to stir up so much trouble
in England. Their government was vested in the proprietors
who met annually in a "General Court" to elect the governor,
deputy governor, and assistants who served as magistrates and
managers of the colony's or company's affairs. The function of
the Court was poorly defined, but it was primarily concerned
with allotting land and authorizing new churches until necessity
forced it to identify itself as a kind of parliament with the power
to levy assessments upon the towns. It became a representative
body quite casually when the colony became so large as to make
a composite town-meeting impracticable and suggest the convenience of choosing delegates, and for eight years the colony
got along without any formal body of "positive laws."

Quite early the ministers decided that it was against the Word for them to serve in the capacity of magistrates, and a clear distinction grew up between the officers of the church and those of the commonwealth with the former holding an advisory relationship to the latter. The ministers began to meet at regular and frequent intervals for consultation among themselves, and they were, of course, always in close consultation with the magistrates who occupied special seats of honor in their churches. It was an informal government of conscientious men in which the clergy exercised power because they were the keepers of the conscience rather than because they had any civil or ecclesiastical authority. They derived their influence from the respect paid their divinely ordained office and from what was called their "gifts"—that is, their powers of persuasion and their skill in interpreting the Word—and serious disciplinary problems arose only when some of them developed consciences which refused to keep the peace.

The first of these was Roger Williams who arrived in America in February, 1631, and refused to join the church in Boston on the grounds that its members maintained communication with the Church of England and supported the authority of the magistrates in enforcing the first table of the Ten Commandments—particularly the keeping of the Sabbath—which represented religious rather than moral law. He was called and ordained by the church at Salem, however, before the General Court could make known its objections to his ministry; but he remained there for only a short while before joining the Plymouth Colony. In the summer of 1633 he returned to Salem as the lay assistant to its pastor and set the colonial authorities in a dither by writing a treatise denying the legitimacy of their title to lands received under a royal grant, insulting the King, and charging blasphemy against any one who referred to Europe as Christendom. He appeared penitently before the Court, affirmed his loyalty, and offered to have his treatise burned, and in 1634 was again ordained teacher by the Salem church despite the objections of the magistrates. In the autumn he began again teaching the opinions of which he had been repentent in the spring and in April, 1635, was called before the Governor and Assistants and "very clearly confuted" according to the Governor. But he persisted in his opinions and expressed others which opposed the administration of oaths to unregenerate persons and raised objections to praying with them even though they might be members of one's own family.

In the eyes of the Bay colonists, who had consistently opposed separation from the Church of England in principle and whose own unity was a matter of necessity, Williams was becoming a Separate of the worst sort. He was separating religious observances entirely from community and family life. He was called again before the Court in July, charged, and required to give answer at the next meeting. In the meantime pressure was put upon the Salem church by the refusal of an expected grant of land, and Williams himself, in a fit of illness, confirmed the authorities' worst suspicions by writing a letter to his church protesting that he would not communicate with the churches of the Bay nor with his own church unless it also refused communion with them. At the October Court the Reverend Mr. Hooker was chosen to dispute with him but failed to "reduce him from any of his errors," and he was consequently sentenced to banishment for his "divers new and dangerous opinions against the authority of magistrates" and for defaming both the magistrates and the churches.

The second serious case of conscience in New England involved the great John Cotton who crossed the Atlantic in 1633 and to everybody's satisfaction and delight accepted a call to the office of teacher in the Boston church. I say "involved" because the case really centered about Mrs. Anne Hutchinson who followed him over in 1636 and undertook to interpret his sermons to members of the congregation, mostly women, who gathered regularly in groups of sixty or more in her own home. I should like to be particularly kind to Mrs. Hutchinson on this occasion because if it were not for her cousin John we would not have this library in which to gather. Winthrop described her as "a woman of ready wit and bold spirit," and she was to prove exceedingly troublesome because she quite obviously did not inherit that flexibility of conviction which seems to have descended in the paternal line of the Dryden family. She was in fact (and I am sorry to say so in these surroundings) stubbornly opinionated and almost unbelievably outspoken in a community which believed that the Lord had enjoined silence upon the female sex. Unlike Roger Williams, who was simply an extremist, Mrs. Hutchinson was a heretic who held that the Holy Ghost dwelt within a justified person—that is, a Saint—in a state of personal union which gave him spiritual immortality and perhaps some quality of divinity in the flesh. She was also considered an antinomian because she held that saintly behavior was no evidence of saintliness of spirit and thus seemed to be standing out against those laws of God that the Puritans believed a Saint must perforce abide in. Her heresy was almost identical with that which Ralph Waldo Emerson was to preach two hundred years later in his Divinity School Address, and the colonial authorities were evidently afraid that it might lead to the same sort of practical command that Emerson expressed when he told the Harvard graduates to "Cast behind you all conformity and acquaint men at first hand with the deity." At any rate, she was sentenced to banishment in November, 1637, several of her most active followers were disenfranchised, and a considerable number from Boston and five other towns were ordered to deliver up "such guns, pistols, swords, powder, shot, and match" as they should have in their possession and refrain from buying or borrowing any other arms until permitted by the Court. The order cited what had happened in Germany "in former times" and made it clear that John Wheelwright (Mrs. Hutchinson's brother-in-law and most loyal ministerial follower) would not become another John of Leyden nor Boston another Münster.

The whole story is of a fascinating episode in New England history, but I am concerned here with its later effects, and these grew out of the behavior of the Reverend John Cotton. For Cotton, like Williams, had brought with him across the Atlantic a sensitive and somewhat impolitic conscience which he had revealed on public occasions although without any evident desire to create dissent or cause trouble. Mrs. Hutchinson had admired his soul-filling preaching in England, joined his church in America, praised him as the only minister in the Bay who preached the true Covenant of Grace, and professed to infer her doctrines from his sermons. In the early stages of the controversy he stood by her, in opposition to his own pastor and the influential John Winthrop, as an old friend in whom he saw no harm. When matters reached such a state, however, that a formal list of eighty-two "erroneous opinions" was drawn up and the first synod in America was convened to consider them, Cotton had reason to take counsel. After the errors had been condemned, the points of difference between Cotton and the assembled elders were drawn up, reduced in number, and carefully reworded until the entire body were in agreement with the exception of the Reverend John Wheelwright and several lay members from Boston who had already left the assembly. Cotton has been accused of cowardice, hypocrisy, political ambition, and all sorts of other things because of his behavior on this occasion and his participation in the admonition and excommunication of Mrs. Hutchinson afterward; and although I believe that the accusations were unjust I do not want the question of their justice to obscure the effective difference between his case and that of Roger Williams: Cotton submitted his conscience to external discipline and accepted the results. Williams did not.

Now, according to our modern notions, John Cotton's resignation and aboutface is rather scandalous and Williams is the man we are inclined to admire. And it is this that brings me to the crux of what I have to say: We cannot understand the New England Way of church government or the beginning of certain basic differences between American and English patterns of thought until we try to understand what was contained in the Puritan concept of "conscience."

VI

The word "conscience" is a crucial one in Puritan literature because in it were mingled, almost inextricably, two conflicting lines of thought which were the source of infinite confusion. One might be roughly designated Platonic, and the other, even more roughly, realistic. The Platonic concept of conscience may be found in William Perkins who defined it as "a natural power, faculty, or created quality, from which knowledge and judgment proceed as effects." Milton's conception of the "umpire conscience," planted in Adam, belongs in this category, and so does the eighteenth-century conception of an innate "moral sense" which is usually identified with "conscience" in most modern definitions of the word. As an intimate private faculty it could be searched from within by introspection but was not subject to conviction from without by persuasion or authority. The Puritans were able to reconcile it with Calvinistic theology by making a distinction between the natural or sinful and the regenerate conscience, and it is easy to see, I believe, how the introduction of a supernatural quality into the concept could have led to its deification as "the Christ within" or the "inner light" of the Quakers. Roger Williams' outspoken allegiance to this concept of conscience probably explains why he became so sympathetic to the Quakers in his own times and why he has received so much sympathy from our own.

But the Puritans with whom I have been concerned did not use the word "conscience" in any such sense as this. As Calvinists they had no belief in the absolute goodness of any natural faculty, and as realists they were able to observe no marked improvement in their intellectual processes as a result of regeneration. Positive evidence on this matter of course is rare—although there is an abundance of negative evidence— and so I find another of Thomas Goodwin's introspective sermons of unusual psychological interest. Preaching as a regenerate man on "The Vanity of Thoughts," he assumed on faith that "In *Adam* and Christ no thought was misplaced, but though they were as *many* as the *Stars,* yet they walked in their *courses* and kept their ranks." Looking realistically within himself, however, he found a different condition: "But ours, as Meteors, dance up and down in us. And this *disorder* is a *vanity* and a *sin,* be the thought materially never so good." Although there was said to be no other "heart so well headed, nor such a head better hearted amongst the sons of men" in his generation, Goodwin himself was not inclined to depend upon any spontaneous combination of head and heart; for "our thoughts, at best," he said again, "are as wanton Spaniels, who though indeed they go with and accompany their Master and come to their journey's end with him in the end, yet do run after every Bird and wildly pursue every flock of sheep they see." "This foolishness," he continued, "is also seen in that *Independence* in our thoughts, they hanging oft together as ropes of sand; this we see more evidently in dreams: And not only then, but when awake also, and *that,* when we would set ourselves to be most serious, how do our thoughts jangle and ring backward? and as wanton Boys, when they take pens in their hands, scribble broken words that have no dependence. Thus do our thoughts: and if you would but look over the copies thereof, which you write continually, you would find as much nonsense in your thoughts as you find in mad men's speeches.

This madness and distemper is in the mind since the fall (though it appears not in our words, because we are wiser) that if notes were taken of our thoughts, we would find thoughts so vagrant that we know not how they come in, nor whence they came, nor whither they would."

Goodwin's first remedy against the vanity of thoughts was "to get the heart furnished and enriched with a good stock of sanctified and heavenly knowledge in spiritual and heavenly truths"; and I have quoted at length from his description of the raw material on which these truths worked because I think his sermon provides the best available basis for approaching what I have called the more realistic conception of "conscience." The clearest approach to this conception I have found among the English Puritans is in a sermon by the Reverend John Jackson preached at the Spittle before the Lord Mayor of London on Easter Tuesday, 1642, and entitled "The Book of Conscience Opened and Read." In it he asserted "that *Conscience* is not a peculiar and distinct faculty of the soul, as understanding, will and memory, etc., are, but the *soul reflecting and recoiling upon itself.*" "It hath been long said," he admitted in a consideration of the difficulty of his subject, that "Conscience is a *thousand witnesses;* and it's as truly said, Conscience has a thousand definitions and descriptions." But "whosoever understands ... these three English words, a *Law*, a *Witness*, a *Judge*, is in a good way of proficiency to understand the nature and essence of Conscience; for in the execution of these three acts Conscience officiateth and dispatches its whole duty." "Conscience is a *Law* propounding the rule to walk by, a *Witness* to give evidence for matter of fact, and a *Judge* to give sentence according to the evidence."

Jackson tried to absorb the Perkinsonian definition of conscience into his own by admitting that Grace and regeneration could imprint a divine quality of goodness upon the natural conscience, but he was emphatic in his insistence that a good conscience was directed by rule: "let a man acquaint himself thoroughly with that which must be the rule and law of conscience; for it is no matter how strong and active conscience may be if it be not first right informed." Then, "the stronger the better, or otherwise the stronger the worse." As the laws by which conscience could be informed he listed four: (1) "*Divine* law, which is the will of God revealed in Scripture"; (2) "The Law of Nature" or "that natural light and engraffed instinct written in our hearts," which was "a good rule"; (3) "The Law of Nations," which was "likewise binding"; and (4) "*Positive* laws," ecclesiastical or civil, which merely had "*adnate* rather than *connate* power." Granted the rule of Law and the primacy of the revealed Word, "the good eyes and lusty limbs of Conscience" were of great value to the Lord, for "a law without sufficient force to execute it is but a dead letter"—although "force without law is but a riot."

With this background of theoretical discussion we can turn, perhaps with some better understanding, to the notorious controversy between Roger Williams and John Cotton over "the bloody tenent of persecution for conscience's sake"—a controversy which broke out after the calling of the Westminster Assembly of Divines and was strongly influenced by the contemporary situation in England and by the experiences of both men with being called to account for their opinions in New England. The controversy was too long—especially in the details of its charges and countercharges and its relationship to the facts on record—to be reviewed here, and I want to make only two observations upon it. The first is that, as I have already noted, Williams stood on the somewhat Platonic definition of conscience which has prevailed into modern times and thus took a position which is readily comprehensible today. The second is that Cotton stood upon an entirely different definition and thus took a position which I believe is the more significant to our purpose here. For the phrase that John Cotton used over and over again in his defense was that of "conscience rightly informed"—informed, that is, by the Word of God rightly interpreted by the best gifts granted to a community of Saints rather than by the meteoric flash of an individual's own vagrant thoughts. Its significance lies in the fact that it was not a specious evasion of the issue, as many modern readers are inclined to assume, but an expression of fundamental principle which involved a whole theory of government and discipline in church and state.

"We approve no persecution for conscience," Cotton declared in one of his many efforts to summarize the New England position, "neither conscience rightly informed (for that we account the persecution of Christ) nor conscience misinformed with error: unless the error be pernicious, and unless the conscience be convinced of the error and perniciousness thereof so that it may appear the erroneous party suffereth not for his conscience but for his sinning against his conscience." The necessary conviction was not trusted to the vanity of an individual's private thoughts but to the expressable wisdom of judicious experts—the holy members of one's church, or a synod of elders—and was made apparent by formal admonition "once or twice" as the Scriptures had commanded. "Reforming persons," as William Bridge was to observe in England, had to be "self-denying persons": "They must deny their own wits, understandings, reasonings, though they be never so plausible." For the good conscience was one which could bring spaniel thoughts to heel and make them follow a master who was guided to his journey's end by an authoritative interpretation of the divine Word.

The New England effort to achieve discipline within the Congregational Way of church government, in short, had produced what we might now call a theory of judicial review of the individual conscience under the written authority of the Scriptures. This was the essential—but, as a theory of gov-

ernment, still undefined—characteristic of the New England
"Way" between the legislative authority of assemblies which
was characteristic of Presbyterianism and the lack of all authority characteristic of sectarian Independency. And it was the
famed "Middle Way" which the New Englanders and their
English sympathizers tried to urge upon an uncomprehending
mother country throughout the entire period of the Long Parliament and the Commonwealth.

VII

Had the New Englanders been genuine State Puritans—that
is, shrewd and calculating politicians—they would not have
expected comprehension from the mother country. For the
New England Way assumed the existence of a weak state
which would be the instrument of a restricted church—a situation which would lead inevitably to a theocracy unless God's
grace exceeded the munificence of a land which was attracting more settlers for economic than for religious reasons. England, throughout the reign of the Tudors, had been a strong
state in which the church was a national institution and an
instrument of political policy. The New England Way assumed that orthodoxy could be maintained by persuasion and
the removal of stubborn dissenters from the body politic. The
body politic of England was made up of religious dissenters
who had passed beyond the power of persuasion and were
already engaged in a mortal struggle for power. The New
England Way was based upon a belief in the constitutional
authority of the written word, as dictated by the Holy Ghost
and interpreted by skilled divines. England believed in the
authority of principle, precedent, and political power. The importance of this last distinction was recognized by the dissenting brethren of the Westminster Assembly if not by the
New Englanders themselves, for it served as the basis for the
dissenters' refusal to bring the New England Way up for formal

consideration: Since the Assembly had failed to follow Parliament's instructions to seek guidance solely from the Word, they complained, they had no acceptable grounds for the proposals they might submit.

So, England went on its own traditional, experimental way of trial and error, through Presbyterianism and unrestrained Independency and into the restoration of a more tolerable version of the status quo. New England undertook to set an example of Independent self-discipline while its English sympathizers resurrected old letters and published new pamphlets from across the Atlantic and supported them with letters and pamphlets of their own. Despite their steadfast opposition to Presbyterianism, the American Puritans began to find synods both acceptable and useful; and matters of doctrine were entrusted to their care while the spirit of Independency was preserved in church government—formalized, for the first time, in the Cambridge Platform of 1648 which accepted the Westminster Confession of Faith as standard doctrine and offered in return a standard model of Congregational polity. The Ministers and Ruling Elders of the church, put on the defensive by charges of escapism that came from troubled England and genuinely worried by the strife they saw there, became increasingly ruthless in their advice to the Magistrates until immigrating Baptists were whipped on shipboard before they had a chance to disturb the public peace and persistent Quakers were sentenced and put to death. The purity of the church itself was compromised in the Half-Way Covenant of 1656 which provided that baptism was enough to admit members "half-way" into the church and thereby enable them to exercise the civil franchise. Expediency and an aggressive State Puritanism, in short, were taking over the New England reformation; and the guiding principle of the Middle Way was lost sight of before it was ever fully recognized.

VIII

In a fashion, I feel by now that I have drifted far enough to have approached the Enchanted Isles—to have come within sight of something which may be real and may be illusion. Yet I am willing to drop anchor, at the risk of being out of my depth, because I have found that as a scholar I have become less interested in conclusions that can be proved beyond cavil than in more tenuous ones which suggest significant forms and relationships for matters of fact. For at times (as when looking over the latest bibliography of the Modern Language Association) I think that we literary scholars are mostly engaged in piling up busywork which is likely to topple over by its own weight and smother us and perhaps literature itself. We are like the seventeenth-century Saints, doctrinal, academic, and political Puritans engaged in quibbling and quarrelling as we waste the talents and resources that might be especially appropriate to the discovery of more vital matters—those subtle and almost intangible patterns of thought which give a different character to similar ideas and objects of interest as they are found in different civilizations and in different cultural contexts.

So I trust I may be forgiven for suggesting that what I see or think I see in the literature of these early Puritans is a divergence in thought which was to develop into the basic difference between the English and American conception of government as it was gradually taken over by the people and institutionalized in the world's two most stable democratic forms. The English institution is that of authority centered in a legislative assembly controlled only by the unwritten constitutional restraints of principle, precedence, and political prudence. That of the United States is one of a legislative assembly subject to the control of the written word of a constitution judiciously interpreted by a body which has no legislative or magisterial power but which has assumed the supreme power of persuasive authority. Some of the terms I used to describe the early New England system have, I believe, prepared the way for a suggestion of its resemblance to a later political system and have perhaps made the analogy clear.

Because the guiding principle of the New England system was never clearly defined by the men who actually followed it, I am not prepared to suggest that any clear line of descent may be traced from the half-formed ideas of the Puritan fathers to the more fully developed ones held by the founding fathers of the Republic or by the Chief Justice who actually reasoned our Supreme Court into the position of authority once held by the chief ministers of Massachusetts Bay. Nor am I prepared to say whether the most significant activity of a historian should be an investigation of the development of an idea or the investigation of a people's growing willingness to accept it. I can only say, with any degree of certainty, that somewhere and at some time the English and the American way of thinking about discipline and government separated—and that the best place to begin the search for the beginnings of this separation is, perhaps, at the beginning.

IV.

Challenges to Dryden's Biographer

By CHARLES E. WARD

FOR PURPOSES of a more or less orderly exposition of
the challenges to the biographer of John Dryden, I should like
to discuss under several heads what seem to me interesting
aspects of the large problem of bending disparate and sometimes rather intractable materials to the acceptable uses of biographical study. In the order of treatment, but not necessarily
of importance, I shall call them the challenges of fact, of contemporary reference, of interpretation, of selection, and finally
of emphasis.

First, then, to those of fact, without the difficulty and embar-
rassment of definition—perhaps not what the new jargon calls
"true facts," but what we might agree upon as verifiable facts.
In this sense, it is a fact that Dryden was baptized on August 14,
1631: we can cite a church register, the authenticity of which
we are not inclined to question. We accept too, on the authority
of the *Stationers' Register,* the fact that *Amboyna* was registered
in that list on June 26, 1673. And we accept without question
that the Earl of Chesterfield wrote a letter to Dryden on August
10, 1697. Of these kinds of facts we have available hundreds;
they are, I suppose, the bread-and-butter facts upon which any
account of Dryden must be based. They are to be found—if
sought for—in Chancery records, in church and college records,
in wills and probates, in depositions, in Calendar of State Papers
and Treasury Books, in diaries, in Inquisitions Post Mortems, in
letters to and from Dryden, in letters not connected directly
with Dryden, in Term Catalogues.

Another kind of fact—not the "true fact"—is that to be found

73

in Dryden's letters, prefaces, and dedications for which no veri-
fication seems possible but which we are inclined to accept. For
example, when Dryden complains of the effect of an illness at
various times, our tendency, I think, is to accept as fact statements that he is thick of hearing, or that he is left with a cough.
Though we tend, perhaps, to discount the fulsome flattery he is
wont to heap upon some of his patrons, we may still accept in
some dedications comments upon his feelings about poetry and
about his own practice of it. Did he really believe that there was
a God's plenty in Chaucer; was he actually so generous in his
praise of Milton as his published words suggest? Unless we convince ourselves that he was a congenital liar—and I think we
do not—these we also accept as facts even though we have no
ready means of verifying them. Our real problem is not so much
accepting some of them as exercising judgment in the uses to
which we put them, for they are not always significant. It is salu-
tary to recall, with the change of one word, Dryden's statement
to the Earl of Orrery in the dedication to *The Rival Ladies,* in
1664: "For imagination in a poet [read *biographer*] is a faculty
so wild and lawless, that like an high-ranging Spaniel, it must
have clogs tied to it, lest it outrun the judgment."

More troublesome are the "quasi-facts" (as I may term them).
Though they are not very useful to the biographer, yet they, on
occasion, throw a small, indeed at times a very feeble, light upon
a segment of Dryden's life. They are troublesome both because
of their doubtful legitimacy and because, after the decision to
use them has been made, doubts begin to assail one about one's
judgment. Two examples may suffice. In a book on the House
of Blanchard and Child, seventeenth-century goldsmiths and
later bankers, some accounts for the purchase of silver amount-
ing to £86 and extending over a year's time, chiefly in 1669, by
"Mr. Dryden" are included. Though positive identification of
the poet as purchaser is impossible, a "reasonably good case" can
be made that the poet bought the silver. This is how it may be

done: Lady Elizabeth Dryden had, during 1668, received payments for many hundreds of pounds on the Treasury Grant issued to her in 1662; the poet's income from his land and from his successful plays added to his financial well-being. His family was getting settled finally after the return to London, following the enforced retirement to Charlton during the plague. On Christmas Eve, 1668, the first purchase was made from Blanchard's, who were to be Dryden's bankers for many years. Other purchases followed. The case is building up, and at this point I would like to quote from my *Life of John Dryden* (Chapel Hill, 1961, p. 71), "In May, after the birth of Erasmus Henry, they bought two tumblers and six more spoons at £6 11s; later, a small locket for £1 and a ring for £1 5s 6d. (gifts for the baby?)." The parentheses are gratuitous, surely—but useful, perhaps, to establish the quasi-fact. But I doubt that it was worth the bother.

A much less convincing quasi-fact concerns "Mr. Dryden's" purchase at auction, in May and June 1682, of twenty-eight lots of books, many of them on religion. Now, if the poet is to be detected buying books on religion, this time would seem to be the most appropriate. For in May and June of 1682 he was directing his energies to the composition of *Religio Laici*. But did Dryden indeed purchase these books? Beyond the happy coincidence of the auction date and his probable work on *Religio,* there is no real proof for such a purchase. And since the event tells us little or nothing about Dryden, prudence and good judgment probably should have kept it out of the notes (as they indeed kept it out of the text).

In the search for materials, one must cast many nets, and the catch is sometimes awesome, always interesting, and occasionally disquieting. Contemporary references to "Mr. Dryden"— duly noted on 3×5 cards—eventually swell the file boxes. They appear, of course, in many places and in many kinds of manuscript and printed sources: in anonymous doggerel verses, in diaries, in letters; in Aubrey, in Marvell, in Luttrell; in wills; in newssheets; in signed and unsigned published attacks; in signed tributes; in biographical notices and accounts, such as Phillips and Langbaine—almost anywhere, indeed, during a time when people filled an inordinate amount of paper.

Such references, of course, are constantly interesting, often of value, sometimes troublesome, and occasionally quite worthless. The hours vainly spent, for example, in tracing the numerous "Mr. Drydens" in Cornwall could have been used more fruitfully on other matters. But they were there and, therefore, needed to be investigated. And who was the "Mr. Dryden" who spent an evening talking church business with Bishop Nicolson? Could he be the Satanic figure pilloried by the Whig pamphleteers? It proved impossible to connect them, for the godly "Mr. Dryden" appeared to have been domiciled in Cumberland. Was the "Jon Dryden," one of whose letters was once offered for sale at a fancy price by a reputable London dealer as the poet's, our man? No, he appeared to be one of his relatives. The numerous references to John in the wills and testaments of the Pickering and Dryden clans proved troublesome, as did the bewildering variety of spellings for the name, which appeared to have been generally pronounced Drādon. This pronunciation, as is clear, produced some of the phonetic spellings and sent one off on trails—which soon became cold—leading to some *Draytons,* a quite distinct family. A census-taker, who thought he heard *Dayton,* included enough circumstantial description of the poet's household and place of residence to warrant a positive identification. The man no doubt heard—probably from one of the two servant girls—*Draydon.* But what of the "John Dryden" who bought the manor of St. Ives in Huntingdon? He was an attorney.

Eventually, of course, one ought to become cautious. When one encounters the John *Driden* who signed a receipt for £50 received from Secretary Thurloe in October 1657, the Mr. *Drayden* who was on the list of persons to receive "mourning cloth" to wear at Cromwell's funeral in 1658, and the Mr. *Dradon* who at that time walked with Milton, Marvell, and other secretaries for the "French and Latin tongs," one may be hesitant to accept as irrefutable the positive identification of the poet made by Masson and later scholars. The lack of corroborative details or identifying tags remains troublesome, and though we may ask, "Will the real John Dryden please stand up?" we receive only silence. I have been charged with being extremely conservative in this matter, and with being downright inconsistent in my reluctance to accept what seems to many to be an obvious reference to the poet. My candidate for the position—the poet's cousin John *Driden,* who had been graduated from Wadham College in 1655 and whose father, Sir John, was influential in the Interregnum government—has, alas, not generally been accepted.

Unless one wishes to make a biography an allusion book or a source book, one must come to terms with the abundance of references to Dryden which began early in his career and continued to the end of it. The difficulty, I believe, is multifold. The overarching problem remains, of course, that of selection, which must be a consequence of the answers to numerous insistent questions: Where does the reference occur? When does it appear? What are the circumstances and the auspices of its appearance? Who is the witness? How is it to be interpreted in our time? How was it probably interpreted in Dryden's time? How useful or valuable is it?

The first undoubted reference to our Dryden I take to be that in the Conclusion Book of Trinity College under the date of July 19, 1652, a month before his twenty-first birthday.

Agreed then that Dreyden be put out of Comons for a fortnight [sic] at least, that he goe not out of the Colledg during the time aforesaid excepting to Sermons without express leave fro the Master or Vicemaster & that at the end of [that time] he read a confession [*recantation* is lined through] of his crime in the Hall at Dinner

time.... His [*alledged* is lined through] crime was his disobedience
to the Vicemaster & his contumacy in taking of his punishment in-
flicted by him.

As we readily see, this is a remarkable reference, containing
unlimited opportunities for the sensitive, intuitive biographer to
limn a brilliant analysis of the character of this youth who within fifteen years will become poet laureate of England. But before
unleashing all this brilliance, we should recall Dryden's spaniel.
Yet how well one might speculate upon the nature of his *crime;*
upon the sentence of two weeks of somewhat solitary confine-
ment; upon the ignominy of the sentence; he must read not a
recantation of the crime (as perhaps some of the masters wished
to inflict) but a *confession* of it. He had committed what *was* a
crime (not alleged to be); he had been disobedient, but his was
a disobedience compounded by a contemptuous and insolent
spirit. What attractive avenues into the future such a passage
indeed opens up before us! With ease we could no doubt forecast
the dimensions of his self-confidence, the later appearance of his
lampoons and satires, his reluctance to suffer fools gladly, and
so on to the outer limits of our inventiveness. But, alas, as Dryden
said, the imagination must have clogs tied to it.

The authenticity of the citations in the Trinity College Conclusion Book we are not inclined to question. Therefore, when
we read another item, under the date of April 23, 1655, that
places are being held for three bachelors to return to Cambridge,
Dryden among them, until midsummer (should they not return
by that time, then other scholars, already named, shall be elected
into their places, and that one Wilford shall have Dryden's
place), we can feel fairly sure, I think, that Dryden's earlier
difficulties must have been forgiven. Since he had taken his B.A.
in March of 1653/4, it is clear that the college had held a place
open for him for more than a year. Why did he not return?
Since the date of his degree and the date of this notation bracket

pretty well the time of his father's death, in June 1654, a possible reason for failure to take up his place is suggested. Such references as these help, in some measure, to illuminate this portion of his life.

Other references, however, often lack the quality and the value of these. When Pepys early in the 1660's makes an offhand remark that he has seen Dryden, whom he had known at Cambridge, we accept the truth of the reference but note its lack of usefulness. In June 1683, Evelyn records in his diary that he had dined at the Earl of Sunderland's, where, among a distinguished company, was the poet Dryden. This is not an offhand remark, for Dryden is one of a half-dozen persons named. Evelyn, who had known Dryden for years, may be testifying thus to Dryden's access to a certain kind of society. The date reinforces indeed the significance of the reference: his great poems of the preceding eighteen months and his growing reputation seem to have opened doors. Of limited use, to be sure; but such a reference provides a view of the poet not often possible, because of the rarity of this kind of testimony. After the loss of his pensions in 1689, Dryden's grave financial problem is known from many kinds of evidence.

It is obvious, then, that the biographer will seize upon any reference to finances. He will, of course, make what capital he can (as did Dryden) out of the memorial poem called *Eleonora* commissioned for a fee by the Earl of Abingdon in 1691. But what can we do with the document printed by Thorn-Drury recording the gift of £5 to Lady Elizabeth Dryden "in charitye," by Thomas Howard, the son of Sir Robert and, of course, her nephew? Since it was dated (January 16, 1691/2), we will almost certainly try to relate it to the lean days which the poet's family were then enduring. How shall we interpret the phrase "in charitye"? Since we, unhappily, know little about Elizabeth Dryden and probably much less about Thomas Howard, and nothing at all about the family relationships between brother

and sister and nephew, we will probably find it impossible to
discover a meaning for the phrase or to arrive at the real reason
for the gift. The reference, therefore, is of dubious value.

More significant, and quite tantalizing, is another reference
that appeared at nearly the same time—in April of 1692. It is
found in a letter which John Aubrey wrote to Antony Wood:

> I have been here before March but never so much entangled or
> ingaged in business ... and partly in publishing my Booke [his *Mis-
> cellanies*]. I am exceedingly obliged to my old acquaintance Mr. John
> Dreydon for his friendly advice and recommendation. He would have
> had his bookseller print it; but *he* will print only Plays and Romances.
> So I am obliged to do it by subscription.

Added to other evidence of Dryden's helpfulness to friends and
to fellow writers, this enables us to add a dimension to our rather
limited knowledge of his personal relationships. But we also
recall that Aubrey was engaged in writing biographical sketches
of his contemporaries, Dryden among them. Why, we wonder,
did not Aubrey convince "my old acquaintance" that he should
now give him that sketch? We learn from Aubrey's printed
account of Dryden that the poet had agreed to "write it for me
himselfe." It is possible to have a nagging thought that Dryden
did so, but that Aubrey never got around to using it.

Another kind of testimony whose value lies in the witness is
to be found in the minor problem of Dryden's profits from his
translation of Virgil. According to Dryden's contract with Tonson, he would have received about £600, broken down into the
agreed upon £200 for the translation and about £400 from the
sale of both the first subscribers' copies and the second (and less
expensive) edition. But rumor insisted that he had really received at least twice the amount because of gifts from pleased
patrons. The total profits were variously stated. In a document
printed in *Notes and Queries* by John Taylor in 1877, it is alleged
by one James Graham, some years after Dryden's death, that the

poet had told him the amount was £1,400. This figure could be easily discounted as another product of the rumor mill, but when we discover that Graham was the husband of Dorothy Howard, Lady Elizabeth Dryden's niece, it takes on a rather new credibility. We can at least treat it with more respect than we accord the other speculations, for Graham could indeed have received the figure from the poet himself.

The neutral and the laudatory references to Dryden tend to pose fewer difficulties to the biographer, I think, than the depreciatory and the abusive. This is so for several reasons. In the first place, the biographer is predisposed to be the champion of his subject. Indeed, he views, and writes of, him *con amore.* He is therefore conditioned to resist, as with an automatic reflex, any and all attacks upon Dryden's character. His tendency may be to disparage the witness, to try to dismiss the charges (or to explain them away), to ignore them when they become too insistently inconvenient, or to insist upon complete and absolute proof. To maintain a balanced approach, and to exercise his self-conferred mastery of good judgment, become exceedingly difficult. And since the attacks are usually extensive and detailed, they demand more painstaking attention than the simple laudatory or neutral reference. And, of course, the attacker generally is more difficult to identify, for he often writes under an alias or anonymously. The anonymity partly disarms and surely discontents the biographer for the very good reason that he has lost his customary tests for judging the credibility of the witness. For example, the shadowy "R.F." of the *Letter from a Gentleman to the Right Honourable Edward Howard* in 1668 may be very close to Dryden and to the Howard family and therefore so knowledgeable that his statements about Dryden should command our attention and our belief. But when we read that Dryden had been "employed under his father, a zealous Committeeman," we begin to doubt whether R. F. knew at first hand very much about Dryden. The dilemma, however, is clear.

Or to take a more celebrated example: the anonymous *The Medal of John Bayes*. Having reviewed the scholia on this tract, we may indeed become convinced that Shadwell wrote it—or we may not become convinced. In either event, the challenge of its presence does not disappear. If we accept Shadwell's authorship, then a persuasive case can be, and has been, made for the truth or at least the reasonableness of some of the charges and the allegations in that tract. Yet honest doubt may still remain with respect to some of the more outlandish ones: rejection may come more easily than acceptance. Whatever our decision, it will, I think, be colored partly by our knowledge of the witness, Shadwell, of the date of the attack, of the circumstances attendant upon it. We will recall that Shadwell, in Dryden's *Mac Flecknoe,* had been the subject of the most destructively wicked lampoon in the English language, and in the light of this he might be slightly suspect as a thoroughly reliable witness. Furthermore, Shadwell, we remember, was probably the most prominent writer allied to the Whig cause; and *The Medal of John Bayes* appeared in May 1682, in the wake of *Absalom and Achitophel* and *The Medal.* We may also note that Shadwell was hardly unaware of the acute discomfort which these poems induced in the Whigs. We might also decide that he was thoroughly aware that his attack was not an answer to these poems, but a direct attempt to discredit their author. In short, it was a type of political infighting and by all odds not the most effective.

Should we then accept any or all of Shadwell's charges—if they are indeed his? Our knowledge of the time, of the events, and of the participants may dictate a refusal to accept all of them. And if some of them, which? Are we under the necessity, finally, of accepting any or all, unless we can bring irrefutable evidence of their falsity? Must we, indeed, labor to be dull enough to take seriously the obviously ridiculous or to dignify the tendentious; and must we be so prodigal of time as to search diligently into innumerable haystacks to find these needles that may never have existed—under the mistaken notion that the burden of proof lies with us? In any event, it all remains a burden.

The challenge of interpretation, rather than being separate and distinct, is pandemic. Always and everywhere the biographer of Dryden feels the demands of assessment in even the most obviously simple and innocent areas. Much of what I have hitherto said and much of what comes hereafter clearly is concerned in some way with interpretation. In order to illustrate some aspects of this pervasive challenge, I should like to examine several examples. For nearly two centuries it has been well known that facts about Dryden are available in many classes of official records, such as Chancery, the Calendar series, official correspondence, and so on. Clearly these are of great potential value for any account of Dryden's career; yet, once found, they must be understood. Frequently the bare fact does not carry its own interpretation, and therefore its meaning remains all too often obscure. By indirections we find directions out, and sometimes by sheer good luck.

Let us view two examples of facts from the *Calendar of Treasury Books*. In early 1662/63, Elizabeth Howard (before her marriage to Dryden) was granted £3,000 from a grant of £8,000 made to her father, the Earl of Berkshire, by Charles II. Standing thus, the fact is sterile; obviously, we must learn more about the Earl of Berkshire and his family. Search reveals several pieces of pertinent information. Elizabeth was born either in 1636 or in 1638. She was the second daughter of that name, the first having died in 1622. At this time, therefore, she was either twenty-four or twenty-six years of age. Also from other sources, we discover that within the year, she was to marry Dryden (December 1, 1663) with the consent of her father and would be described as a maiden of about twenty-five. Why was she granted £3,000? Her father, we learn (again from other sources), had been prominent and well-to-do in the days of

Charles I, but during the Parliamentary regime he had been subjected to compounding for his estates. By the time of the Restoration, he was so pauperized that he explored every avenue to gain any kind of grant or perquisite as repayment for his loyalty to the Stuarts. In April 1662 he received this grant of £8,000, from which he was to assign the £3,000 to his daughter. Now, in a time of quite early marriages, she was at twenty-five a bit old for marriage. Had a lack of dowry prevented her chances? Was this sum to become her dowry?

To help understand better the meaning of the facts, we are fortunately aided by two letters, one from Dryden and one from Sir Robert Howard to Sir Robert Long—not, to be sure, at this time but four years later. By 1666 no payment—as the official record shows—had been made by the Treasury to either Elizabeth or to her father. At the suggestion of Elizabeth's brother Sir Robert, a Commissioner of the Treasury, the poet and his wife wrote, on August 16, 1666, to thank Long, the Chancellor of the Exchequer, for his original influence in 1662 in convincing the Earl to assign the Patent to her, and to request him to keep what money is now to be paid on it until they come up to town from Charlton, the country place of the Earl, to which they had moved to escape the plague. The other letter, from Howard to Long and dated the day before the Dryden letter, mentions the sum for this first payment on the account—£768 15s. Eventually, by 1669, it is all paid.

In view of the details brought to bear upon the original fact, perhaps we can speculate that the grant was indeed in the nature of a dowry. At any rate, it is now more than a bare fact—indeed, the bare fact of a notation in the Calendar papers led to the charge that Dryden's change of religion about 1685 was part of a venal deal between James II and the poet laureate. It came about as a result of the discovery of the record of Dryden's second pension of £100 as having been granted in 1685–86, that is, upon the accession of James. The isolated reference caused the mischief: a search of the preceding Calendar books reveals the truth, that the added pension of £100 was granted by Charles II on July 2, 1677, more than seven years before James became king.

A second example of this particular kind of problem, which may be solved by recourse to other documents, is to be found in a passage of a letter written by Dryden to Lawrence Hyde, the Earl of Rochester, in 1683. Hyde was then first Lord of the Treasury, and in the letter Dryden begs for his influence to get money, since his pension payments are in arrears. He writes, in part:

I know not whether my Lord Sunderland has interceded with your Lordship for half a yeare of my salary. But I have two other Advocates, my extreame wants, even to arresting & my ill health.

He goes on to say he would plead some merit, that he deserves not to starve, that the King is not dissatisfied with him, and that the Duke of York has often promised his assistance.

Be pleasd [he goes on] to looke on me with an eye of compassion; some small Employment wou'd render my condition easy. Either in the Customs, or the Appeales of the Excise, or some other way; meanes cannot be wanting if you please to have the will.

Now this sounds very much like a plea for a job. Lending credence to such an interpretation was the appointment to the post of Collector of the Customs at the Port of London of another John Dryden. This man—a relative—was sufficiently identified in the official calendar, so that he need not have been confused with the poet. Once we are aware of the existence of numerous "John Drydens," it is possible to be careful. But for too long the poet was said to have been a Collector of Customs—surely one of the oddest cases of presumed moonlighting in English letters. Armed with this knowledge, we can review the letter with a new awareness. When Dryden says that "some small employment would render my condition easy," he means that if Hyde will bestir himself "meanes cannot be wanting" to find money either in the Customs accounts or in the Excise, the surest places for ready money in Charles's government. In short, he is asking for money, not a job; he already has a job, as he more than makes clear when he reminds Hyde that he is "going to write somewhat by his Majesty's command & cannot stirr into the Country for my health and studies, till I secure my family from want." Other examples of this particular kind of challenge abound, but, unhappily, the clarifying pieces of evidence do not always appear, and conjecture, though occasionally useful, will not finally satisfy our need to know. The darkest areas of Dryden's career tend to be as dark now as they were two hundred years ago, and guesses will not do very much to brighten them.

Once the materials of the biography are safely in the file boxes, other challenges of a different kind appear. Two seem to me of paramount importance and difficulty; both depend upon judgment, for both demand choices. One concerns selection, the other, emphasis. About the utilization of much of the available materials on Dryden there can be no question; they must be used, for they are, so to speak, the *materia biographia,* without which the biographer could hardly begin to write. For many others, however, a selective process is demanded. Often the question is not so much *what* to select but *how much.*

For example, Dryden spent most of his working life associated with the theater. His biographer must therefore use material from that part of his life. Here, I think, the question is how much shall he find useful or necessary to include. In general, it might be difficult to justify a complete stage record for each of his plays, which would meticulously include the first performance, the length of the run, the cast of characters, the contemporary comments, favorable and unfavorable, the revivals, and so on. This is properly the work of the editor. To include all of these facts would be to make a dray horse of the biography, which should probably move more nimbly than such freight will allow. Yet the circumstances surrounding some of his plays tell us a good deal about him as a person, about his relationships to his theatrical company and to other persons, and often something about his interests in dramatic form. The unexpected ban of *Cleomenes,* for example, and the protracted negotiations to obtain permission to act it after some months, shed light on Dryden and the conditions under which he sometimes worked. In 1692, such an irritating business helped to reinforce his desire to leave off this way of making a living. But in the following year, 1693, we learn from a letter to Walsh that he has spent a morning rehearsing the actor Doggett in the part he is to act in the poet's last play, *Love Triumphant.* Disgusted with the theater he may have been, but not, obviously, with his function as a conscientious playwright.

Much that he tells us about *Albion and Albanius* ought to be included, for this—along with other knowledge found in official correspondence—gives us a unique view of Dryden's awareness that in cooperation with Betterton and Lewis Grabu he is helping to bring into being an English opera after the continental fashion. But more than this, his foreword allows us to catch sight of Dryden so concerned with the welfare of his actors that he commits himself to extra work so that they will not lose their small wages, and so outraged with the sniping criticism from English composers directed toward the music of his French composer that he castigates the native musicians for their jealousies and writes a feeling defense of the foreigner. This particular work and this moment yield important material, I think, for the continuing exposition of Dryden's character. So, too, may the judicious use of hard-to-come-by materials concerned with his relationship to people. Though we are convinced that his circle of friendships must have been very large, we find surprisingly few contemporary persons who can make significant contributions to our knowledge of Dryden as a social animal. The paucity of such evidence for the kind of man he was among friends induces us, perhaps, to overuse the limited testimony we may garner from a Southerne, a Congreve, or a Walsh. The biographer's selection here is not a matter of choice: the biographer will readily justify his complete use of what is available, even when he may still be sure that part of it is of limited value.

Of that other problem—of emphasis—perhaps little need be said. We may readily enough agree that the biographer should lay the proper stress upon the proper material, without, however, completely agreeing upon what the word "proper" might mean. Being human, the biographer will doubtless be inconsistent at times in choosing *this* or *that* to receive or not to receive the "proper stress." I can think of several reasons why this is so. In some instances, he may equate importance with the difficulty he experienced in gathering this particular material and, therefore, give it undue prominence. Having got together at some expense of money and spirit much information on the Dryden and Pickering families, one may be reluctant to throw away any scrap of it. But to include all of it gives it an emphasis that may be hard to justify, for it may well overvalue what at best is tangential and compromise the needed emphasis upon the poet, who is the important representative of the families involved. That the poet's mother once sued her uncle for the recovery of £1,300 lent to him, or that Honor Driden—the poet's "attractive cousin," as she has been called (on what evidence, one cannot discover)— received a tidy inheritance by the will of her father, Sir John Driden, or that at least four of her older brothers never married, may be, as facts, interesting enough; but to exploit them fully is to let them usurp the attention that ought to be the claim of the poet. That attention may be diverted, indeed, by many kinds of things, facts, events, often against the best efforts of the biographer to reject them. The latent fiction writer which seems to lurk, in varying degrees, somewhere in most biographers may emerge when data are so scarce that they cannot see where the next footnote is coming from. But not often, I think, will they indulge their fancy as did the writer a dozen years ago who began an account of Dryden thus:

In a quiet glade along the banks of the river Nene in Northampton-shire, a boy of about fourteen sits fishing. He is chubby, pink-cheeked, and his auburn hair is close cropped in the Puritan style; there is a slight arrogant lift to his upper lip; his brow is creased with thought beyond his years.

We perhaps ought to be sympathetic with this flight (but firm in our disapproval), for the author was truly baffled by the almost total lack of hard facts. Yet we may be sure that to diva-gate into this kind of fiction, or to supply the lack of facts on Dryden's early years by writing in small the history of West-minster School and Trinity College, Cambridge, or to exposit at length the political and religious controversies of the 1630's and 1640's is to take the attention of the reader away from Dry-den. These techniques are diversionary, and, like the golden apples of Hippomenes cast before Atalanta, they blind us and drive us to temporary defeat in this peculiar race.

Though the challenges are many and of many different kinds, some of them, over the years, are finally met. Unhappily, at the moment, far too many, we may think, remain as intractable as they ever were. We should like to know much more about Dryden's immediate family and his role as husband and father; about his day-to-day relationships with the great number of people we are sure he knew rather intimately; about his religious life and the details of his conversion to Rome; about his un-recovered works, such as his *prosodia* (or the materials he had gathered for it); about his methods of work; about his desire to improve the language and his methods of doing so; about the range and thoroughness of his reading and its eventual impact upon his poetry. These and a host of other questions, we await answers to. And always in the background lurks the constant hope that somewhere well-packed boxes of manuscripts, letters, documents, accounts await discovery by future literary detectives. But even without this hope, we can look to the future with some confidence.

Indeed, we do not need to be endowed with the skills of divination, I think, to know that within a relatively few years (as we measure advances in scholarly knowledge and techniques) new and significant materials for the study of Dryden's life and career will become available. Since I always find a peculiar pleasure in quoting Dryden, I should like to insert here a few sentences from the *Essay of Dramatic Poesy* (written about this time three hundred years ago), slightly rearranged for the present purpose:

> Is it not evident in the last hundred years (when the study of philosophy has been the business of all the Virtuosi in Christendom) that almost a new nature has been revealed to us?—that more errors of the school have been detected, more useful experiments in philosophy have been made, more noble secrets ... discovered, than in all those credulous and doting ages from Aristotle to us? ... It has been observed of arts and sciences that in one and the same century they have arrived to a great perfection; and no wonder, since every age has a kind of Universal genius, which inclines those that live in it to some particular studies: the work then being pushed on by many hands, must of necessity go forward.

That the work goes forward is clearly evident to us who meet today: the work, in truth, is being pushed on by many hands in the creation of the distinguished edition of the poet by our colleagues here. As has happened in the past with other poets, the presence of a great edition is creating a new and vital interest in this poet, who now belatedly begins to receive the attention he has so long deserved. The evidence is indeed so obvious that it hardly needs mention. When Edward Hooker, Thomas Swedenberg, and their colleagues first promulgated the early plans for the California Dryden in the 1930's, some significant studies, of course, had already been made, and others were in gestation. In the second third of the century, we have observed the quickening tempo and we can rejoice in the appearance—almost every year, it seems—of excellent treatments of many aspects of Dryden's career; the work, of necessity, must go forward. Changes in the editorial, biographical, and critical climate surrounding an author will always create new questions and new expectations, and will demand, therefore, a higher level of subtlety and sophistication. And it is this which we now clearly discern.

Are we not, then, amply justified in our belief that in the next third of this century, "almost a new Nature" will be revealed? Can we really doubt that when the tercentenary of Dryden's death arrives in the year 2000, biographical, editorial, and critical studies—honed and sharpened by many hands in our century— will provide such discoveries and insights that Glorious John will at last be seen clearly, and that he will stand as a peer of the very greatest of English poets, where, I believe, he always thought he should stand?

Challenges to Dryden's Editor

By H. T. SWEDENBERG, JR.

IN EXPLORING challenges to Dryden's editor, I am speaking as the General Editor of the California Edition of his works, and I am also drawing upon the experiences of my fellow editors in that venture. Ours is a scholarly sodality of shared problems.

Frequently Dryden is almost as elusive to his editor as he is to his biographer. Speaking of his prose style, Dr. Johnson declared: "He may be thought to mention himself too frequently; but while he forces himself upon our esteem, we cannot refuse him to stand high in his own." I cannot agree that he mentions himself too often; would that he had spoken of his beliefs and experiences more frequently. If so, we should have more guides to the proper explanation of his meaning and implications; and invaluable guides they would be, for my colleagues and I have discovered that we dare not ignore the clues which Dryden drops about his work. When he says that he has proceeded in a certain way or has derived ideas from particular sources, the chances are that he is right. Not always are we able to prove him right, but when we are unsuccessful we retire with the uneasy feeling that more searching will one day turn up what has evaded us.

I could wish also that he had not been so careless with his manuscripts. The editors of Pope and Boswell are embarrassed with a great store of manuscripts, and their burdensome task is to make distinctions and choices among versions and variants. The editors of Dryden are in quite another predicament. Not a single holograph is extant of one of his significant works.

Recently the discovery of one of his manuscripts has been announced. We have had a copy of it in our files at UCLA for
a long time, but we are frankly skeptical that it can be proved
to be in Dryden's hand. What did he do with all those manuscripts? Did Herringman's and Tonson's compositors simply
throw them away, sheet by sheet, as they set type? Or were
they "martyrs of Pies" and relics of an even less elegant use attributed to neglected authors in *MacFlecknoe*? I have a recurring dream fantasy in which I open a croquet box or an ebony
cabinet and find bundle after bundle of Dryden's manuscripts,
including his major plays and poems, and his journal, kept with
detailed frankness from the time he was a pupil at Westminster
under Busby until those last months in the early spring of 1700
when he was surely aware that the weight of mortality lay
heavily upon him. (I should add that there is no evidence that
he kept such a journal. But after all, when I dream, why should
I limit myself?) I turn in the journal to the 1670's and eagerly
scan the leaves to find out precisely when *Mac Flecknoe* was
written and what the ultimate occasion for it was. Then I
wake up.

Until like Adam I awake and find my dream come true, I
shall have to be content with what we have in the works and
in other contemporary material. Indeed, I am not at all confident that Professor Dearing shares my yearning for a cache
of manuscripts, since as textual editor of our edition he often
has enough and more than enough materials and problems to
satisfy even the most avid of textual scholars. I adduce, as a
chilling example, *The Indian Emperour*. Between the first edition of 1667 and Congreve's edition of 1717, there are fourteen
texts which must be taken into account, not to mention the
multiple copies of each which must be examined for press variants: a total of forty copies. In addition, five pertinent manuscripts are involved, two of which are of more than passing
interest. These are the Trinity College and the Douai manu-

scripts. The Trinity one apparently antedates the first quarto and, therefore, demands careful study to determine its status as a possible copy text. Particularly fascinating is the fact that in it the character of the Indian high priest is called Caliban, as he is once also in the first edition. Thereafter, in the first printing, the name tag is simply High Priest. The implications of the name Caliban for the critical interpretation of the play, or a part of it, are obvious; and Professor Loftis has thoroughly canvassed them in our volume which has just now come from the press. The Douai manuscript is not so important, but it has its interest, since the passages in the play reflecting upon Catholicism have been excised. Professor Dearing, with the invaluable assistance of Mrs. Phillips and Miss Dearborn, our editorial assistants, has painstakingly studied all the textual problems, and the result is thirty-six printed pages of collation. As we discussed these matters, I sensed that all concerned developed a strong feeling of empathy for the High Priest, who in the latter part of the play is put on the rack.

Dryden is no less challenging to his literary editor than to his textual editor. Since I am more concerned with literary than with textual commentary, perhaps I may be forgiven for thinking that he is even more demanding in my area of responsibility. Allow me to illustrate. When we were working on *Annus Mirabilis,* I was puzzled by this scientific image:

> Each waxing moon supplied her wat'ry store,
> To swell those tides, which from the line did bear
> Their brim-full vessels to the Belgian shore.

Dryden carefully supplied a side note which reads: "According to their opinion who think that great heap of waters under the line is depress'd into the tides by the moon, towards the pole." Knowing little of oceanography, I began to search the literature of the subject, and I learned a great deal. (Apropos of this, I might observe that Dryden not only challenges his editors, he educates them, too.) But I could find nothing of a theory that lunar pressure at the equator pushes the tides out through the temperate zones into the arctic. I then turned to my friend Professor Dick, a man learned in the history of science, and sought his help. As always, he was generous of his time and assiduous in his search, but he, too, was unable to document Dryden's statement; and we began to wonder whether the poet had picked up some garbled scientific lore in conversation. That side note, however, was so positive that we were uneasy to conclude that it was baseless. Professor Dick then stated our problem in the columns of *Isis* and asked for help. In time we received an answer, which revealed that Descartes was ultimately responsible for the theory woven into the poem and documented with a prose note. It may be that Dryden had learned his science from some of his friends, perhaps from someone in the Royal Society, but wherever he derived his information, he knew what he was talking about.

More recently, Professor Miner and I have been posed a similar problem in a passage toward the end of the second part of *The Hind and the Panther*. Referring to the Battle of Sedgemoor, Dryden wrote:

> Such were the pleasing triumphs of the sky
> For James his late nocturnal victory;
> The pledge of his Almighty Patron's love,
> The fireworks which his angel made above.
> I saw myself the lambent easy light
> Gild the brown horror, and dispel the night.

Sir Walter Scott glossed the passage thus: "Alluding to some extraordinary display of the aurora borealis at the time of the battle of Sedgemoor . . ." Macaulay, as he was wont to do, gilded the celestial display. All very well, but what was his source? He cites the lines from *The Hind and the Panther*. But we can find no contemporary account of the battle which even hints at the northern lights. On the contrary, the blackness of the night and the fog contributed significantly to the defeat of Monmouth's troops. Professor Miner has tentatively suggested a metaphysical explanation, and this may well be correct; but we both believe that it is not beyond conjecture that eventually some simpler answer may be found.

This experience leads me to observe that Dryden's puzzled editor often finds that his brother scholars in history are not very helpful. Several years ago one historian remarked that too many of the studies of the reign of Charles II belong to the mattress-and-chamber-pot school of history. I concur. We have more than God's plenty of that sort of material, and I have long since grown bone weary of the amorous adventures of Rochester, Sedley, Buckingham, Charles, and the rest of that gay mob of gentlemen. I yearn for detailed studies in depth on social and political problems of the Restoration. Another example from a political poem will illustrate why. In the brilliant characterization of Shaftesbury toward the beginning of *Absalom and Achitophel,* we find the following:

> Yet fame deserv'd no enemy can grudge;
> The statesman we abhor, but praise the judge.
> In Israel's court n'er sat an Abbethdin
> With more discerning eyes, or hands more clean;
> Unbrib'd, unsought, the wretched to redress;
> Swift of dispatch, and easy of access.
> O, had he been content to serve the crown,
> With virtues only proper to the gown.

These and six other lines preceding them were omitted in the first edition, and we can only hypothesize why. Were they omitted by mistake or by purpose, or were they not written until the second edition? The question has been discussed in bibliographical as well as critical terms. I think that we might arrive at a more certain answer if we knew just how successful

Shaftesbury was as a judge. He was made Lord Chancellor in November of 1672 and was relieved of his post the following November. Thus he had little time to prove himself. Contemporary estimates, usually written with fierce partisan bias, suggest, as Sir Roger DeCoverley was to say of another matter, that there is much to be said on both sides. *The Compleat Statesman,* a defence of Shaftesbury published in 1683, remarks on his appointment as Lord Chancellor:

Now was the Kings Conscience (as it were) entrusted to his care and management; this was the highest Orb a Subject was capable to move in; but with what Sagacity, Honour and Integrity he acquitted himself in that great Employment, the Transactions of the Court of *Chancery* at that time can best witness. Justice ran in an equal channel, the Cause of the Rich did not swallow up the Rights of the Poor, he that was oppressed found relief, and the Oppressor a Rebuke suitable to his crime; the usual delays of that Court were much abated and all the Transactions thereof were managed with the greatest Judgment and Equity.

On the other side of the political fence, Roger North contended that Shaftesbury was unsuited to his high office and that after a little while he became one of the tamest of judges. Furthermore, he reported that it was said of Shaftesbury's justice that the "Person might be discerned in most of his decrees." Faced with such conflicting testimony, the editor turns to modern scholarship for a resolution. In this instance, he will find that the standard study of Shaftesbury declares that he was indeed an able and an upright judge; and he also discovers that the proof of the assertion is the passage which I have just quoted from *Absalom and Achitophel*. It pleases me to see those finely wrought couplets in print in an important historical monograph, but their presence there comforts me not at all, for with the sight of them I have come full circle in my quest.

Some of you here today may properly raise the question of

why an editor should involve himself in such a search anyway. Is it really of much moment to the reader of Dryden's poem to know whether Shaftesbury was a great Lord Chancellor? I believe that the matter does have relevance to literary response, particularly since the lines are imbedded in a satirical portrait. It has been argued that Dryden inserted them to soften his attack; it has also been argued—with more cogency, I think— that their addition sharpened the thrust of the satire by the use of a well-known rhetorical device, that is, by a show of impartiality. If we could be reasonably sure about the facts of Shaftesbury's tenancy of the Lord Chancellorship, we could furnish data for a firmer critical base. If he was the complete statesman in the law, then the oratorical turn of praise amidst denunciation could hardly be doubted. If he was as crafty in the law as he was in politics, then the passage is an additional maneuver in satiric tactics. If nonactivist Englishmen, that middle group to whom Dryden said he was appealing, had reason to suspect the great Earl's integrity and ability as a judge, then the passage of praise which at first reading seems only that, and which at second reading appears to be a subtle rhetorical device, becomes finally an ironic statement equating the statesman with the justice. It achieves a multilevel ambiguity, and the striving for this I take to be the sole duty of a poet! At least in certain critical quarters, I have been assured that it is.

Another of the satirical portraits in *Absalom and Achitophel* presents a different kind of problem. A large body of contemporary materials about its subject is extant, and the editor must decide, as he must in respect to many other passages in the poem, how much of the available data he may legitimately use. I refer to the account of Shimei, who, you will recall, was Slingsby Bethel, one of the Whig sheriffs of London and Middlesex. Allow me to present to you the real Bethel, a beguilingly solemn rascal. He was an old republican who had resided in Hamburg from 1637 to 1649. Ludlow reported that he was elected a member of the Council of State in January of 1660 and that he was one of those who wanted to raise money for troops to oppose General Monk. In July of 1660, one Robert Long petitioned for the return of his estate, stating that it had passed into the possession of Bethel, "one of the Council of State, to that part of the late Parliament called the Rump, who with others of the Council, abjured and renounced His Majesty and the rest of the royal family, and is otherwise a person of known ill affection to the Government."

Bethel himself in his essay *The Interest of the Princes and States of Europe,* published in 1680 and reprinted in 1681, demonstrated a hostility to monarchy and a true-blue Protestant zeal for nonconformity, or fanaticism, as Dryden was accustomed to call it. In his chapter on France his remarks about Louis XIV and the Estates had unpleasant overtones for the Court party in England and a cautionary warning for the Country party. He declared that the Estates were not likely to meet again, since the King had arrogated all power to himself, and, he continued, "This example may be a caution to all people, who have any priviledges left, to be jealous of them, and careful how they part with them, priviledges not being so easily recovered from Princes, as resigned to them, most of them being like other men, ready to take all they can get, but unwilling to part with anything they can keep." In another passage, also pertinent to *Absalom and Achitophel,* he proclaimed his devotion to the Protestant ethic of work: "There is a kind of Natural unaptness in the Popish Religion to business, whereas, on the contrary, amongst the Reformed, the greater their zeal, the greater is their inclination to Trade and Industry, as holding Idleness unlawful ..."

As a successful man of business and a zealous Protestant, Bethel could claim to speak with some authority on such matters. His activities in government in 1680–81 are, however, even more significant to the editor of Dryden. On Midsummer Day of 1680, Bethel and Henry Cornish, a haberdasher, were elected sheriffs of London and Middlesex. They were objected to because it was claimed that they had not taken the oath or received the sacrament according to law. Another election took place on the fourteenth of July, and again Bethel and Cornish, the candidates of the Country party, won against the Court candidates Ralph Box, a grocer, and Humphrey Nicolson, a merchant tailor. By this time they had qualified according to the Corporation Act. In a letter dated 19 July, Dorothy Sidney, Countess of Sunderland, revealed the tenseness of the occasion:

> At the choosing of the Sheriffs, which are the same again, a loud outcry, 'No Yorkist! no Papist!' thus by hundreds, and one opposed, they beat so that he is very ill, still crying, 'No Yorkist, none of him!' My Lord Russell said he was sorry one of them was chosen, for he was as great a Commonwealth's man as Algernon Sidney.

Russell no doubt referred to Bethel. According to custom, the sheriffs were not sworn in until Michaelmas eve, i.e., September 27. Traditionally they were expected to entertain the aldermen at dinner before the ceremony. The record shows that on the twenty-fifth of September, Cornish complained to the Court of Aldermen about the "untreatableness of his colleague" and asked that he be dismissed. But he was not dismissed, and the dinner was not given. The aldermen refused to go to the Guildhall for the swearing in because they had not been tendered their dinner. This contretemps reflects another element in Bethel's personality, namely, his parsimony.

But before going into that, perhaps in justice to poor Bethel we might recall what an entertainment budget a sheriff of London was expected to maintain from his own funds. A man elected to the office and refusing to serve incurred a fine of £400, unless he could swear that he was worth less than £10,000. We are informed in a contemporary account that a sheriff's table was such "that it is not only open all the year to all comers,

Strangers and others, that are of any Quality, but so well furnished, that it is always fit to receive the greatest Subject of
England, or of other Potentate..." Gilbert Burnet asserted that
a sheriff had to live in such extravagance that it cost a man
about £5,000 to be in office for a year, and he added significantly about the year 1680, "it was proposed that the sheriffs
should be chosen with more care, not so much that they might
keep good tables, as that they should return good juries."

Doubtless, the Whigs were primarily concerned with "good"
juries, that is, Whig juries, but this show of policy did not save
Bethel's reputation for generosity. Roger North said that he
"used to walk about more like a Corncutter than Sheriff of
London. He kept no house, but lived upon Chops; whence it
is proverbial for not feasting, to *Bethel the City.*" The most
telling account of his habits as host comes from Bethel himself.
In February of 1681 he stood for Parliament from Southwark
and was defeated. He believed himself to be the victim of unfair campaign tactics, and so he issued a defense entitled *The
Vindication of Slingsby Bethel Esq.* (1681). If he had been gos-
siped about before in Southwark, now the whole town knew
of the stories against him, for he injudiciously spread them in
detail across the pages of his vindication. We can imagine with
what malicious glee Dryden must have read it.

It was reported, said Bethel, that he was a Papist and that
Dr. Oates knew him to be one; that he had been one of the
judges of Charles I as well as one of the two persons in masks
that assisted at the King's execution. It was also whispered that
while he was at Hamburg at the time of the King's death he
had asserted, "That rather than he should want an Executioner,
I would come thence to perform the Office." Bethel's reply to
this last is ingenuous enough to be worthy of Thomas Shadwell: "I was born a Gentleman, and have had my Education
accordingly, and am too great a Spirit to stoop to an Office of
so base a nature to serve the greatest Prince of State in the

World." As for the idle talk that though a sheriff of London he lived in a garret and kept no house, he replied that he was a single man and did not need a large establishment. For ten years he had taken a house which he rented out except for the garrets, cellars, and one small room on the first floor. If he had been a married man with a family, then of course he would have kept a house and set a table. And, anyway, he held that the customary feasting of the companies is no honor to the sheriffs and is prejudicial to industry.

On the twenty-seventh of June 1681, Bethel and Cornish were rendered thanks by the citizens for the discharge of their duties in the past year and for their "continual provision of faithful and able juries." New sheriffs were elected and took office in September. In November, Luttrell reported that the sheriffs had been ordered to summon a jury to the Guildhall on the twenty-fourth, when it was presumed that the bills against Shaftesbury would be presented. And, of course, they were then presented. I mention these latter events and dates because of the erroneous notion—a notion perpetuated by a distinguished modern historian—that it was Bethel who packed the jury at the trial of Shaftesbury. He had certainly done his part to pack "faithful and able" juries, but he was not in office to insure the choice of the right men for the right verdict for Shaftesbury.

I have done with the telling of some of the facts about Slingsby Bethel, facts which you may have found tedious. If so, I beg pardon. I must confess that for me they have the fascination of historical immediacy, and I must also admit that I belong to that vanishing tribe of literary scholars who find Clio a jade with a siren song.

The data about Bethel are most certainly not poetry, but they may be the stuff of poetry. And so the question is, how do they bear on Shimei? Let us refresh our memories of Bethel under poetic analysis:

Shimei, whose youth did early promise bring
Of zeal to God and hatred to his king,
Did wisely from expensive sins refrain,
And never broke the Sabbath, but for gain;
Nor ever was he known an oath to vent,
Or curse, unless against the government.
Thus heaping wealth, by the most ready way
Among the Jews, which was to cheat and pray,
The city, to reward his pious hate
Against his master, chose him magistrate.
His hand a vare of justice did uphold;
His neck was loaded with a chain of gold.
During his office, treason was no crime;
The sons of Belial had a glorious time;
For Shimei, tho' not prodigal of pelf,
Yet lov'd his wicked neighbor as himself.
When two or more were gather'd to declaim
Against the Monarch of Jerusalem,
Shimei was always in the midst of them;
And if they curs'd the king when he was by,
Would rather curse than break good company.
If any durst his factious friends accuse,
He pack'd a jury of dissenting Jews;
Whose fellow-feeling in the godly cause
Would free the suff'ring saint from human laws.
For laws are only made to punish those
Who serve the king, and to protect his foes.
If any leisure time he had from pow'r,
(Because 'tis sin to misimploy an hour,)
His bus'ness was, by writing, to persuade
That kings were useless, and a clog to trade;
And, that his noble style he might refine,
No Rechabite more shunn'd the fumes of wine.
Chaste were his cellars, and his shrieval board
The grossness of a city feast abhorr'd:
His cooks, with long disuse, their trade forgot;

Cool was his kitchen, tho' his brains were hot.
Such frugal virtue malice may accuse,
But sure 't was necessary to the Jews;
For towns once burnt such magistrates require
As dare not tempt God's providence by fire.
With spiritual food he fed his servants well,
But free from flesh that made the Jews rebel;
And Moses' laws he held in more account,
For forty days of fasting in the mount.

Clearly Dryden has transmuted the base metal of fact and gossip into the gold of witty and heroic satire. The base materials, however, are fundamental to the glittering end product, and some knowledge of them is requisite to a recognition of the alchemical processes by which the poetic mind has converted them. Furthermore, the editor of *Absalom and Achitophel* is constantly reminded that it is not only heroic poetry but also poetic history and that the history as well as the tropes demand his attention. He is challenged to collect the details of history and then he must ponder the extent to which he should burden his reader with them.

Dryden, perhaps no less than Pope, is full of poetic allusions, and tantalizes his editor to uncover and explicate them. In the passage on Shimei, shall he explain the subtly manipulated materials extracted from Scripture? In the line "No Rechabite more shunn'd the fumes of wine," is it enough to gloss *Rechabite* with a reference to the 35th chapter of Jeremiah? Or should some summary account of the Rechabites be written in order to point up Dryden's ironic reversal of the scriptural moral when applied to Shimei? About the "sons of Belial," should the editor rest content with citations from the Old Testament and *Paradise Lost,* or should he quote other seventeenth-century uses, including a sentence from one of Bethel's publications: "I suppose the new Philosophy of Poverty, and the transplantation of all Non-Conformists, called the Sons of Belial,... will

have but few Disciples"? In such instances, he will probably
have to limit himself, if not in the cause of right judgment, then
certainly in recognition of reality and the limitations of space.

But there are other submerged allusions and veiled echoes
that will most surely tempt him to comment, and the temptation may be beyond his powers of resistance. For example, all
students of *Absalom and Achitophel* are aware that the following lines, which come after Shaftesbury's first verbal assault
upon Monmouth and Monmouth's uneasy and weak reply, are
Miltonic:

> Him staggering so when hell's dire agent found,
> While fainting Virtue scarce maintain'd her ground,
> He pours fresh forces in, and thus replies.

This assumption has been a commonplace since Verrall first
related the passage to *Paradise Lost* more than a half-century
ago; that is to say, it is a commonplace to those who have read
Verrall. I find, however, that few people have given their nights
and days to the study of Verrall; and so I, like other editors,
must write a note on the passage to insure that a commonplace
is not metamorphosed into a shining discovery by some unwary
reader. But should I also remark on other, not so obvious Satanic elements in the character of Monmouth? In his answer
to Shaftesbury, Monmouth says:

> Why should I repine at Heaven's decree,
> Which gives me no pretense to royalty?
> Yet O that fate, propitiously inclin'd,
> Had rais'd my birth, or had debas'd my mind.

A little more than a hundred lines later Dryden, as historian-
commentator, returns to the thought and exclaims:

> How happy had he been, if destiny
> Had higher plac'd his birth, or not so high!

Now let us recall Satan's soliloquy at the beginning of Book IV of *Paradise Lost,* particularly the complaint:

> O had his powerful Destiny ordain'd
> Me some inferior Angel, I had stood
> Then happy; no unbounded hope had rais'd
> Ambition.

Here is only one example of many images involving Adam, Satan, and the Second Adam that Dryden wove into an intricate pattern in his poem, and such images seem to demand comment. Even more so does the apparently innocent reference to fame in the account of Monmouth's would-be royal progress to the west:

> From east to west his glories he displays
> And, like the sun, the promis'd land surveys.
> Fame runs before him as the morning star,
> And shouts of joy salute him from afar.

When the account of Fame in the fourth *Aeneid* is recalled, a satiric meaning emerges which is absent before. Here is a part of Dryden's rendering of the passage, in which, it might be observed, there are political nuances not found in the Latin:

> Millions of opening mouths to Fame belong,
> And ev'ry mouth is furnish'd with a tongue,
> And round with listning ears the flying plague is hung.
> She fills the peaceful universe with cries;
> No slumbers ever close her wakeful eyes;
> By day, from lofty tow'rs her head she shews,
> And spreads thro' trembling crowds disastrous news;
> With court informers haunts, and royal spies;
> Things done relates, not done she feigns, and mingles
>   truth with lies.
> Talk is her business, and her chief delight
> To tell of prodigies and cause affright.

In sum, we of the California Dryden are concerned with how much we should put in our commentary and with how we should present it. About the latter question probably we should not fret, since Dr. Johnson has left us explicit directions for writing scholarly notes:

The work is performed, first by railing at the stupidity, negligence, ignorance, and asinine tastelessness of the former editors, and shewing, from all that goes before and all that follows, the inelegance and absurdity of the old reading; then by proposing something which to superficial readers would seem specious, but which the editor rejects with indignation; then by producing the true reading, with a long paraphrase, and concluding with loud acclamations on the discovery, and a sober wish for the advancement and prosperity of genuine criticism.

Dr. Johnson is a lasting palliative for endemic pride, and before him, as before Dryden, we seek to stand in humility. We have no desire to exult over our predecessors; instead, we are grateful for their labors, which have shortened ours. Nor do we want to stand between Dryden and his readers by "refrigerating" their minds with unnecessary notes. For the reader of Shakespeare, Johnson had this advice:

Let him read on through brightness and obscurity, through integrity and corruption; let him preserve his comprehension of the dialogue and the fable. And when the pleasures of novelty have ceased, let him attempt exactness, and read the commentators.

As with Shakespeare, so with Dryden.

VI

Restoration Prose

By JAMES SUTHERLAND

By OFFERING to talk about Restoration prose I realise that I have committed myself to proving that such a thing exists. When we use the term "Restoration comedy" we can count on being more or less understood; we mean, approximately, the comedy of manners as written by Etherege and Wycherley, and a generation later by Congreve, and if we include plays like Dryden's *Marriage à la Mode* and Shadwell's *Squire of Alsatia* and Ravenscroft's *The London Cuckolds* we do not stretch the term to breaking point. But can we talk with the same confidence about "Restoration prose," or are the two words merely a convenient way of referring to the prose that was written in England between 1660 and the closing years of the century? For myself, I believe that there *is* a prose style that is characteristic of the Restoration, and I am going to try, in Walter Pater's words, to "disengage" its special virtue, and note it "as a chemist notes some natural element, for himself and others." I am willing to admit that it is much less easy to disengage the *unique* virtue by which, say, Dryden's prose differs from that of Halifax, or the prose of both those great writers from that of Eachard or Walter Pope; but that in itself seems to be a significant fact, suggesting that there really is a prose

109

style common to the writers of the period, and that this style is the genuine expression of a particular and definite type of culture. If we were to look at any four decades of the nineteenth century, I don't think we should find it nearly so easy to point to "an early Victorian" style, a "mid-Victorian" style, and so on; stylistically, there seems to be little common ground between Macaulay, Carlyle, Ruskin, John Stuart Mill, George Borrow, Dickens, Thackeray, George Eliot, Newman and Sidney Smith.

The prose I have in mind was written to perfection by Dryden and Halifax; with individual variations by such men as Robert South, Bishop Burnet, and Jeremy Collier; by Etherege and Rochester in their letters; with further variations by Roger L'Estrange in his pamphlets and translations; by Walter Pope in his *Life of Seth Ward* and by Robert Wolsey in his Preface to Rochester's *Valentinian;* by Sprat in his *History of the Royal Society* and by Robert Hooke in his *Micrographia;* and by many other minor writers. I do not think I should seriously confuse the issue if I added Cowley in his *Essays* and perhaps Stillingfleet in his *Origines Sacrae.* But I have got to admit that if there *is* such a thing as Restoration prose, not all the writers living in that period wrote it. There are a few of the greatest prose writers of the time whom I obviously cannot possibly include: one of these is John Bunyan, and another is Clarendon, and for various reasons I would exclude Isaac Barrow, the Hon. Robert Boyle, John Evelyn, Richard Baxter, Thomas Rymer, and such eccentrics as Thomas Burnet, the author of *The Sacred Theory of the Earth.* And I don't know what to do with Samuel Pepys. He is, of course, one of the most precious exhibits of the whole period, but a diary written in cipher, and intended for no eye but his own, is obviously outside our terms of reference.

The prose writers I have named as central to our discussion were all influenced by certain historical and sociological conditions which developed after the Restoration. In the first few

years after the return of Charles II there was a tendency to
put the clock back, to restore the *status quo,* to undo all that
had been done during the rule of the saints. This post-war nos-
talgia for the good old days is represented by Clarendon and
the old cavaliers (Bunyan lived in a different world, and doesn't
come in here), and for a short time they seemed to be having
things their own way. But they were swimming against the
tide of progress, and in the end they were bound to give way
to a younger generation. One of the governing factors in the
Restoration period was undoubtedly youth. The King himself
was still a comparatively young man of thirty when he was
restored to the throne, and he brought with him, or attracted
to his court, a group of brilliant young noblemen and gentlemen
whose minds looked forward rather than backward. The accent
was on modernity and youth. London was being modernized
with more commodious houses and wider streets, and after the
Great Fire the rebuilding on modern lines was greatly speeded
up. By 1672 Dryden felt himself entitled to claim in one of his
prologues:

> Our great Metropolis doth farr surpasse,
> What ere is now, & equals all that was;
> Our Witt as far doth forrein wit excell....

New ideas were coming into circulation from the group of
scientists who had started meeting in Oxford during the last
years of the Commonwealth, and who in 1662, in the second
year of the new reign, founded the Royal Society. Trade was
increasing, coffee-houses were springing up all over London,
L'Estrange's *Intelligencer* and *Newes,* followed by the *London
Gazette,* were keeping news in circulation, two theatres were
playing regularly under the patronage of the King and the Duke
of York.

What London now had, to an extent that it never had before,
was a large number of fashionable, and on the whole intelligent,
people living in a recognized Society, very conscious of them-

selves as constituting the polite world—to some extent influenced by the French culture that some of them had experienced in exile and that others had come into contact with during their travels on the continent, but also quite confident that they had a culture of their own, and that it was a really contemporary culture and far in advance of anything that their fathers and grandfathers had known. In earlier generations, it is true, the aristocracy had patronized literature and the arts, and occasionally some gifted member of the class, such as Sir Philip Sidney, had written himself. But what especially marks out the Restoration period—the new factor—is the surprisingly large number of upper-class men and women who wrote with distinction: men like Buckingham, Orrery, Sir Robert Howard, Rochester, Dorset, Mulgrave, Roscommon, Sedley. Writing, both in verse and prose, had become a thing a gentleman might do—indeed, something that he should do. This had never happened before to anything like the same extent, and it has never happened in England since. You will recall that the class in question is the one that Matthew Arnold called "Barbarians," a class marked by "high spirits, choice manners, and distinguished bearing," but also by "an insufficiency of light." It is not easy to account for the sudden appearance in this class of so many "sports," so many gentlemen who wanted to write, and who, as Dryden put it, were "not to be contented with what fortune had done for them, and sit down quietly with their estates." Some of the credit may be given to Charles II, who, if he was too lazy to write himself, could certainly appreciate wit and style in other men, and whom it was therefore a pleasure, as well as a duty, to please. (Charles II was the last English monarch to have an adult taste in literature and the arts; George V collected postage stamps.) In one department of writing especially, the drama, there was a particular obligation on gentlemen to write for the Court, since gentlemen alone were held to have the necessary experience of high society and fashionable life in which contemporary tragedy and comedy dealt. In the literary vacuum that followed the Restoration, the Orrerys and the Howards were therefore busily engaged in turning out new plays for the entertainment of the King and the Court. But a good deal of weight must be given to mere fashion: when a number of prominent persons engage successfully in some activity, more and more people will take it up. To some extent this will account for the mob of Restoration gentlemen who wrote with ease, although it will hardly explain why the proportion of *good* writers in the upper class was at this time so much above normal, and why they were quite unlike the typical young barbarians whom Arnold found to be "so unintelligent, so unapt to perceive how the world is really going."

Whatever the explanation, the important fact remains that Restoration literature was dominated by the aristocracy, who set the tone and exercised a control over the mode of expression. Restoration prose is, in the main, a slightly formalized variation of the conversation of gentlemen. The gentleman converses with ease, and with an absence of emphasis which may at times become a conscious and studied underemphasis, but which is more often a natural expression of his poise and detachment. He is imperturbable; nothing puts him out, or leads him to quicken his pace; indeed, a certain nonchalance and a casual way of making the most devastating observations are characteristic of him, for if he is always polite he is never mealy-mouthed, and has no middle-class inhibitions. He will never betray too great eagerness, or ride his ideas too hard, or insist too absolutely, for that is to be a bore; he will not consciously exploit his personality, or indulge in eccentricity or whimsies, for that is to be selfish, to think too much about himself. On all occasions, like a good host, he will consult the convenience and the pleasure of those he is entertaining; and he will therefore try to express himself clearly and politely and unpedantically, and, if he can manage it, with a witty turn of thought and phrase. He will not dogmatize, or proselytize, or appeal exclusively to the emotions; to do that is the mark of the ignorant zealot and the godly fanatic, of whom no Restoration gentleman wished to be reminded. Carried into prose, these qualities are characteristic of some of the finest writing of the period. I choose two passages from an author whom I consider to be one of the great masters of English prose. The first is taken from a brilliant analysis of Charles II:

> When once an aversion to bear uneasiness taketh place in a man's mind, it doth so check all the passions, that they are dampt into a kind of indifference; they grow faint and languishing, and come to be subordinate to that fundamental maxim, of not purchasing any thing at the price of a difficulty. This made that he had as little eagerness to oblige, as he had to hurt men; the motive of his giving bounties was rather to make men less uneasy to him, than more easy to themselves; and yet no ill-nature all this while. He would slide from an asking face, and could guess very well. It was throwing a man off from his shoulders that leaned upon them with his whole weight; so that the party was not gladder to receive than he was to give.

There you have the easy flow of well-bred conversation, but of course it is conversation a little more studied, a little more precisely controlled than you would naturally expect to hear. The casualness of the tone and the apparent spontaneity of the rhythm should not conceal from us the delicate balance of the thinking. At this precise point in the history of English prose we get what always seems to me the perfect compromise between the formal and the casual, between the foreseen and the fortuitous. "He had as little eagerness to oblige, as he had to hurt men; the motive of his giving bounties was rather to make men less uneasy to him, than more easy to themselves; and yet no ill-nature all this while." If Dr. Johnson had been the writer I feel sure that he would have underlined the contrasting clauses and phrases, and distributed the weight still more evenly: "He had as little eagerness to hurt, as he had willingness to oblige;

nor were his bounties calculated so much to make men less uneasy to him, as designed to make them more easy to themselves." And there Johnson would almost certainly have ended his sentence, omitting the phrase, "and yet no ill-nature all this while," which comes in like an afterthought, and so gives an unstudied air to what might otherwise have seemed too artificial and deliberate an antithesis. The antitheses here are not, of course, stylistic mannerisms of a writer for whom balance and contrast have become almost the only mode of expression; they are the natural utterance of a man who is analysing his impressions carefully. With the next sentence, "He would slide from an asking face, and could guess very well," we have returned to the easy manner of polite conversation; but "slide from" and "asking face" are both expressions of great delicacy and suggestiveness, saying what is to be said with a beautiful economy, and with a hint of visual humour that expresses the detached amusement of a bystander who is missing nothing. I could well imagine, not Johnson, but some imitator of Johnson, thinking that he could improve upon the passage by giving it the pomp of polysyllables, and writing something like this: "He would withdraw by imperceptible gradations from the importunities of solicitation, and had attained to accuracy of conjecture by frequency of experiment." I take it we all prefer the sentence as it was originally written. The writer I have been quoting is, of course, George Savile, Marquess of Halifax, a gentleman born, a man of the world, a wise statesman and counsellor of kings. When I think of the style in which his *Character of King Charles II* is written, I cannot find a better description of it than a line in Wordsworth describing one of his old men: it has "a stately air of mild indifference."

To show that this is not the only way in which he can express himself, let me quote a few sentences from *The Character of a Trimmer,* where he is insisting on the absolute need for an uncorrupted judicature and respect for the laws of the land:

To see the Laws Mangled, disguised, Speak quite another Language than their own, to see them thrown from the Dignity of protecting Mankind, to the disgraceful Office of destroying them; and, nothwithstanding their Innocence in themselves, to be made the worst Instruments that the most refined villany can make use of, will raise Mens Anger above the power of laying it down again, and tempt them to follow the Evil Examples given them of Judging without Hearing, when so provoked by their desire of Revenge. Our Trimmer therefore, as he thinks the Laws are Jewels, so he believes they are no better set, than in the constitution of our English Government, if rightly understood, and carefully preserved.

It would be too great Partiality to say they are perfect or liable to no Objection; such things are not of this world; but if they have more Excellencies and fewer Faults than any other we know, it is enough to recommend them to our Esteem.

In that passage Halifax rises to eloquence, and in the first sentence the rhythm gathers like a long wave before it comes rolling in upon the beach. But even when Halifax grows eloquent he has not forgotten *us,* and he is still addressing himself to our intelligence; he is not preaching at us, and still less is he indulging in some sublime soliloquy which could only embarrass what Dryden called "the best company of both sexes."

Even if we make all due allowance for the unusual number of lords and gentlemen who took to writing in the Restoration period, you may still feel that I have not yet accounted satisfactorily for the fact that almost all the good prose of the period is written in the same polite idiom, even when the writers belong to the middle or even the lower-middle class. The explanation, I suggest, is again to be looked for in the changed social conditions following upon the Restoration. In previous generations Sir Thomas Browne might be writing in a provincial town like Norwich, George Herbert in a remote country rectory, or Robert Burton in an Oxford study. But now London had become, as never before, the one great centre of culture and fashion, to which writers and artists inevitably gravitated. I do not wish to exaggerate the changes that took place after 1660, but the solitary writer, self-reliant, self-pleasing, and self-expressing, had undoubtedly become much less common, and more and more the men of letters were to be found where most of their readers were to be found—in London, sharing gregariously in a common culture and expressing themselves in the polite idiom of the Town.

But were there not plenty of gentlemen in the two famous university cities of Oxford and Cambridge? By your standards and mine, yes; by Restoration standards, no. A "scholar and a gentleman" may be a nineteenth-century or twentieth-century ideal, but in the world of Etherege and Rochester the two terms were scarcely compatible. Dryden, a Trinity man, has many half-contemptuous references to "the lazy gownmen," and he stressed the need to rub off the rust contracted at the universities. Oxford and Cambridge, we might say, were full of potential gentlemen, but they required a lively course of life in town before they could become really fit for polite society. In the aristocratic culture of the Restoration even a little learning was a dangerous thing; a lot of learning was fatal. Erudition, too much conversation with books, too much retirement from society, led to pedantry; and pedantry to the Restoration gentleman was a sort of intellectual body-odour. Some allowance was made to the clergy because as men of religion they had to study divinity and philosophy and the learned languages, but if some of the clergy were gentlemen, it was only in a rather special sense. The most successful preachers in the Church of England were usually men like Robert South, who, though learned enough, was able to conceal his erudition, and who had wit enough to have written a Restoration comedy.

We accordingly find—what is not altogether unknown in the twentieth century—some of the scholars attempting to give an easy and familiar turn to their writing, but only managing to demonstrate how little they have of that well-bred familiarity which was the ideal of the period. Thomas Rymer is one who sometimes tries to be easily colloquial, and John Dennis, in his earlier work, writes at times with the air of a man of fashion; but there is a scholarly awkwardness about both of those writers, something of the exaggerated agility of an elderly bachelor trying to be affable with small children. On the other hand there are university men, such as John Eachard and Walter Pope, who have all the easy elegance and colloquial grace of the best Restoration prose.

As an example of a considerable writer who never really caught the prevailing tone of Restoration prose—and perhaps had no great desire to do so—I quote a few sentences from John Evelyn's *Fumifugium: or The Inconveniencie of the Aer and Smoak of London Dissipated,* dedicated to His Sacred Majesty, Charles II:

> For is there under Heaven such *Coughing* and *Snuffing* to be heard, as in the *London* Churches and Assemblies of People, where the Barking and the Spitting is uncessant and most importunate. What shall I say?
> *Hinc hominum pecudumque Lues.—*
> And what may be the cause of these troublesome effects, but the inspiration of this infernal vapour, accompanying the *Aer,* which first heats and sollicits the *Aspera Arteria,* through one of whose Conduits, partly *Cartilaginous,* and partly *Membranous,* it enters by several branches into the very *Parenchyma,* and substance of the *Lungs,* violating, in this passage, the *Larynx* and *Epiglottis,* together with those multiform and curious Muscles, the immediate and proper instruments of the Voyce, which becoming rough and drye, can neither be contracted, or dilated for the due modulation of the Voyce; so as by some of my Friends (studious in *Musick,* and whereof one is a Doctor of Physick) it has been constantly observ'd that coming out of the *Country* into *London,* They lost *Three whole Notes* in the compasse of their Voice, which they never recover'd again till their retreat . . .

And Evelyn proceeds to another Latin quotation, this time from Cicero. There was always a pomposity about John Evelyn, an air of self-importance and ostentation, a tendency to show off, that separated his writing from the best prose of his own day. His mind and character had been formed before the Restoration, and his scientific interest still further gave his writing a pedantic, and even a pedagogical, tone. In *Fumifugium* it is significant that he remembers from time to time that he is addressing Charles II, and tries to lighten his discourse with a little pleasantry, as when he remarks that the London smoke is death to birds, bees, flowers and fruits "imparting a bitter and ungrateful Tast to those few wretched Fruits, which never arriving to their desired maturity, seem, like the Apples of Sodome, to fall even to dust, when they are but touched." In his lighter moments Evelyn never achieves more than a ponderous jocosity. In his more scientific works like *Sylva,* he feels free to parade his learning, and we find him writing of "the chearful ditties of canorous birds," of "extravagant side branches," "the proper season for interring" (he means planting), "that chearful vehicle light, which the gloomy and torpent north is so many months depriv'd of," "stercoration" for spreading dung, and much else of the same kind. By any standards and in any age John Evelyn must be reckoned a bore: I cannot see why his reputation, or his Diary, or his having been dead for 250 years should prevent me from saying so.

What I am objecting to in Evelyn is personal to him; it has nothing to do with the fact that a good deal of what he wrote was scientific and necessarily technical. I am not going to say much about the scientists now because, for all their importance, they are not quite in the main stream of Restoration prose, and because, after the work of Richard Foster Jones and others, their contribution to the development of English prose is not likely to be underestimated. Not all of the scientists by any means achieved that "close, naked, natural way of writing" which was the expressed ideal of the Royal Society, but some of them did. When we have made all our learned observations on prose style, and examined all the influences and the tendencies, and said what we have to say about the *zeitgeist,* I think

it will be found in the last resort that good writing has a lot
to do with the character of the writer; if he is modest and un-
assuming, if he is intelligent, if he is deeply interested in what
he is doing and is really concerned to let other people know
about it, he will usually write well, or at least decently and in-
offensively, in any period. It is in this way that John Ray writes
in *The Wisdom of God Manifested in the Works of the Creation*.
But a still better writer is Robert Hooke, the author of *Micrographia*. How little he allowed the collective gravity of the Royal
Society to overawe him may be seen from his opening remarks
on the louse-"a creature," he writes, "so officious that 'twill be
known to everyone at one time or other, so busie, and so impu-
dent, that it will be intruding itself in everyone's company, and
so proud and aspiring withall, that it fears not to trample on the
best, and affects nothing so much as a crown, feeds and lives
very high . . . ," and so on. Having permitted himself this sally
Hooke returns to his usual lucid, idiomatic, and evocative description of the object which he has observed under the micro-
scope. Hooke was a natural writer, with none of Evelyn's
ostentation, but with a singularly clear and workmanlike mode
of expression.

I wish I could say the same of that worthy and ingenious
man, the Hon. Robert Boyle. In the history of science Boyle
must always be spoken of with respect, perhaps even with ven-
eration; but as a writer he gives one the impression of living
in a perpetual muddle. He seems to have grudged every moment he had to spend away from his elaboratory, and the
writing down of his discoveries was obviously a labour that
he would gladly have spared himself. Almost every other one
of Boyle's numerous works begins with some sort of apology
to the reader for the careless way in which it has been put together. In the Preface to his *Experiments and Considerations
touching Colours* he tells us that this work was written "by
snatches at several times and places, and (after my manner)

in loose sheets, of which I oftentimes had not all by me that I had already written, when I was writing more". Worse still, when he came to put the book together for the press, he discovered that some of the loose sheets were "very unseasonably wanting," but his avocations prevented him from undertaking any revision, and his weak eyesight made it impossible for him to read the proofs. Indeed, it was only the importunity of the printer that prevailed upon him to sanction publication. As one reads through the six folio volumes of Boyle's Works, one discovers that the *Experiments ... touching Colours* was not an unhappy exception, but rather the rule with him. In publishing *Some Considerations touching the Style of the Holy Scriptures,* he tells us that the work he is now giving the public was reduced from a much larger essay "with a pair of scizzers," but sometimes "the narrownesse of the paper" would not permit him to make all the revisions necessary, and on such occasions he has only "prefix'd a short black line to the incoherent passages, if I found they could not be connected with those whereunto I have joyn'd them." Sometimes he dictated owing to the distemper of his eyes, and indeed much of Boyle's prose reads like the laboured dictation of a man who has no ear for the natural rhythm of a sentence, or the larger movement of a paragraph.

Boyle's writing raises the whole problem of scientific prose. I am not thinking so much of the specialized vocabulary that he was compelled to use, unfamiliar to the general reader in his own day and largely obsolete in ours. I am thinking rather of how, by the very nature of his task, the scientific writer is compelled to express himself in such a way that every possible contingency shall be considered, and every loophole to ambiguity or misunderstanding stopped. Repetition becomes inevitable, and sentence construction is dominated by the need to make a detailed and comprehensive statement. The kind of prose that results from this is the kind that you meet with on

a notice board at the entrance to a public park, in which all
the local by-laws are made clear beyond the possibility of liti-
gation, and every conceivable infringement is taken into account. To show that I am not being unkind to Boyle, let me
quote a single sentence from *The Sceptical Chymist:*

> I will not here debate whether there may not be a multitude of these
> corpuscles, which by reason of their being primary and simple, might
> be called elementary, if several sorts of them should convene to compose
> any body, which are as yet free, and neither as yet contexed and en-
> tangled with primary corpuscles of other kinds, but remains liable to be
> subdued and fashioned by seminal principles, or the like powerful and
> transmuting agent, by whom they may be so connected among them-
> selves, or with the parts of one of the bodies, as to make the compound
> bodies, whose ingredients they are, resoluble into more, or other elements
> then those that chymists have hitherto taken notice of.

What that sentence almost completely lacks is a sense of
direction; the weight is so evenly distributed over the subordinate clauses that everything appears to be equally important,
and the reader is left to work out the meaning by himself.

One interesting writer who was clearly much influenced by
the stylistic recommendations of the Royal Society is Joseph
Glanvill, the intelligent propagandist for the new science. In
his early work, *The Vanity of Dogmatizing* (1661), he writes
often like Sir Thomas Browne, with a bravery of language
which he later almost completely abandoned. He republished
this work in 1665, with some slight revisions; but he finally
put out a much shorter and completely revised edition in 1676.
In its final form the "amplifications and swellings of style"
have almost entirely disappeared: "praeterlapsed ages" have become "past ages", "preponderate much greater magnitudes"
has become "outweigh much heavier bodies," and so on. The
final version is sober, sensible, and lucid, but I confess to a
certain admiration for the splendour and magnificence of the
original work. It must have cost Glanvill some pangs to give

up his noble phrases and resounding periods, for he had indeed great possessions.

In conclusion, I want to return to that conversational idiom in which I see the special virtue of Restoration prose. I do not know if we always realise how often Restoration prose is not only conversational in tone, but actually *is* a sort of conversation with some individual, real or imaginary. One of the most popular of all literary forms in the later seventeenth century was the prose dialogue. It was used for political argument in innumerable pamphlets, and in such periodicals as *Heraclitus Ridens* and L'Estrange's *Observator,* and it was similarly employed by Simon Patrick and many others for religious propaganda. Indeed, the dialogue had become so customary a method of exposition that we even find it used, quaintly enough, to give the current stock prices. I quote from an early Restoration periodical, *The City and Country Mercury. For the Help of Trade and Dealing both in Country and City* (No. 5, June 21–26, 1667). Countryman and Citizen are having their bi-weekly discussion:

Countr. But pray, how goes the Grocer's trade on? for next to the Back we are concern'd for the Belly.

Citiz. It is a hard matter to deal with a Grocer, but I will the best I can inform you. Coarse Barbado's Sugars, formerly sold for thirty five shillings, are now worth forty five shillings the Hundred.

Malaga Raisons rarely to be had.

White Sugars are not yet much risen.

Raisons of the Sun, formerly sold about forty shillings, are now worth fifty shillings.

Currans, formerly sold about three pound, are now at 3l. 10s.

Brandy, at forty five pound the Tun....

Countr. But I pray, how goes Fish?

Citiz. Fish of all sorts are very dear....

When we turn from this humble and practical discourse to the prose of the recognised authors of the period, we find the same tendency to get on easy terms with the reader. It is diffi-

cult to believe that Dryden could ever have expressed himself
stiffly and impersonally in prose, but it is worth pointing out
that the very nature of his discourse encouraged him to de-
velope a prose style that has most of the characteristics of the
spoken voice. The *Essay of Dramatic Poesy* is, of course, actually dialogue, and it is significant how little Dryden's writing
there differs from that of his prefaces and dedicatory epistles.
Those are mostly addressed to individuals, men with whom
Dryden was on terms of friendship, or even intimacy. The
Preface to *Annus Mirabilis* is a letter to his brother-in-law, Sir
Robert Howard; the *Discourse concerning the Original and
Progress of Satire* is addressed to the Earl of Dorset, and so on.
When you are writing to a man you know well, you naturally
fall into an easy and familiar style. When Dryden is not addressing a friend, he still seems to be conscious of a friendly
reader. In *The Defence of an Essay* he has come more than
half way to addressing the reader, for in this argumentative
piece he is putting his own case to an imaginary jury. His Preface to *An Evening's Love* actually begins with the words: "I
had thought, Reader, in this Preface...." After all, a man writing a preface to one of his own plays is fairly well aware of
the sort of people who will be reading it; in Dryden's day they
would be, for the most part, men and women belonging, like
himself, to the comparatively small world of London society
who had already seen his play performed, and who would not
therefore be entire strangers. Dryden can, and apparently does,
visualise his readers, as Addison and Steele in the next generation visualised the readers of the *Tatler* and *Spectator*.

The Restoration writer, at all events, seems to have preferred, whenever possible, to address himself to a reader, actual
or fictitious, when he sat down to write, and to have avoided
the impersonal and *ex cathedra* pronouncement. We find a remarkable number of pamphlets which take the form of "A
Letter from a Gentleman in the Town to his Friend in the

Country." Longer works are sometimes given the same familiar and epistolary form. Thus, when John Eachard writes his well-known enquiry into the condition of the clergy, he does so in a letter to a friend: *The Grounds and Occasions of the Contempt of the Clergy and Religion Enquired into. In a Letter Written to R. L.* Eachard sometimes forgets R. L. for considerable stretches, but sooner or later he will remember him and address him again as "Sir," and the air of familiar discourse is maintained in this way throughout. And Eachard does something else that is characteristic of the Restoration writer. He begins his book with a genial "Preface to the Reader," another device for establishing a friendly atmosphere and enabling the author to write in a pleasantly conversational style. I quote the opening sentences from this Preface:

I Can very easily phansie that many upon the very first sight of the Title will presently imagin, that the Author does either want the great Tithes, lying under the pressure of some pitiful Vicaridge; or that he is much out of humour, and dissatisfied with the present condition of Affairs; or lastly, that he writes to no purpose at all, there having been an abundance of unprofitable Advisers in this kind.

As to my being under some low Church Dispensation, you may know, I write not out of a pinching necessity, or out of any rising Design; you may please to believe, that although I have a most solemn reverence for the Clergy in general, and especially for that of England, yet, for my own part, I must confess to you, I am not of that Holy Employment; and have as little thoughts of being Dean, or Bishop, as they that think so, have hopes of being all Lord Keepers.

The art of being private in public was already well-developed by the end of the seventeenth century—by no one, perhaps, more successfully than Walter Pope in his rambling and digressive but very charming *Life of Seth Ward*. With Walter Pope, however, we have reached a writer who has begun to cultivate his oddities—or, as his own generation would have put it, his maggots; to be whimsical, to exploit his personality; and with him we are perhaps passing into a new age.

Since I have mentioned the whimsical, let me end with a quotation from a book of this period so rare that probably only a few readers know of its existence. It is the work of a determined eccentric, and it oddly anticipates *Tristram Shandy*. "I came peeping into the world..." the author tells us, "as brisk as a little Minew leaps up at a fly in a summer evening; and soon fell a tugging at my nurse's brown breasts, as hard as country fellows do the bell-ropes on a Holy-day." It is an odd, rambling autobiography, and we are not surprised when the author tells us at the beginning of his second volume that his readers "don't know what to make on't. They can neither find beginning nor ending, head nor tail, nor can't for their lives tell what the author would be at, what he drives at or intends in part or whole; what use, what profit, what account it turns to, what 'tis good for." And yet, he reflects, his book is pleasant and diverting "to those who do best understand the whim on't."

The title of this book, which runs to three duodecimo volumes, is *A Voyage Round the World,* and the author is "Don Kainophilus." Don Kainophilus is John Dunton, and this work is a livelier version of the early pages of his *Life and Errors*. It appears to be one of the few books in this period worth having that is not yet in the William Andrews Clark Library.

VII

Some Aspects of Music and Literature in the Eighteeenth Century

By BERTRAND H. BRONSON

IN SETTING OUT, I hope for sympathy when I admit to harboring a virtual conviction that it was not I, but some one (to speak candidly) with a 'dangerous prevalence of the imagination' who consented in my name to address you on the topic announced. I have been looking for this individual for some weeks past, in order either to get him confined before he did further mischief or to beg him to tell me what he had in mind for me to say. But my search has been unsuccessful, and now I must face the music alone, and literally.

Not much in the eighteenth century fails to touch our subject in one way or another. This is the century which Leichtentritt, in his comprehensive survey, *Music, History, and Ideas,* accounts preëminently a musical age: that is, an age which found its supreme and most characteristic expression in music. Of no earlier age in the world's history, he declares, can this be said. Whether in architecture, sculpture, painting, poetry, or philosophy, the earlier past can produce monuments of the very first

magnitude, unsurpassed by anything in the last 250 years. But
with the advent of Bach and Handel, music reached a towering
height which was the undeniable climax of its history of the
previous 2000 years and relative to which, in their own march of
achievement, there were no comparable peaks at this time in the
other arts.

I

Whichever way we turn, while we trace the cultural topog-
raphy of eighteenth-century England,—its ideological or artistic
hills and vales and water-courses, we are within sound of music.
Are we following the antiquarian and historical impulse? There
are for evidence the Three Choirs Festivals, begun in 1724 (and
still continuing); the Academy of Ancient Music, established
1725/26; the Madrigal Society, formed about 1741; the Ancient
Concerts, founded in 1776. There are the two ambitious and
important Histories of Music, by Hawkins and Burney. There
are the ample compendia of earlier cathedral music, anthems
and motets, gathered by Greene and Boyce and Arnold. Are we
observing the powerful and strengthening interest in the earlier
poetry? With it go the abundant fresh settings of Elizabethan
and seventeenth-century lyrics. There is the Shakespearean revival, of which Arne's and Boyce's settings and incidental pieces
are only the most successful musical manifestation among many
attractive things. And still more impressively there stretches the
long line of varied and magnificent settings by Handel of great
English texts: the Bible, Milton, and Dryden foremost among
them.

It is in keeping with an age that thought Man the proper study
of mankind that its major emphasis (and accomplishment) in
music should be dramatic and, in a broad sense, social. As, in
material things, the achievement of the century was not cathe-
drals but dwelling-houses and what went into them and round
them, so its characteristic musical expression was Song, the

matching of words and notes in varying degrees of complexity and employed in all kinds of social ways. Along with the uses of song in the theatre—in opera, ballad-opera, "musical entertainment," and play—go the concerts in the pleasure-gardens, an endless opportunity for the development of talent in the smaller forms, and for the enjoyment of music in a socially informal and *al fresco* setting. Dozens of composers from excellent to indifferent, scores of singers, and absolute shoals of light lyrics were launched at these concerts; the verbal product being gathered and printed from time to time, with or without music, in book and pamphlet form; and the individual songs appearing by thousands on engraved single sheets. Warwick Wroth's vivid work, *The London Pleasure Gardens of the Eighteenth Century,* contains many details of this musical fare, and is doubtless familiarly known. Frank Kidson's and Alfred Moffat's admirably selected and edited *Minstrelsy of England* and *Songs of the Georgian Period* contain several hundred of the songs and you will remember the delightfully printed *Songs of the Gardens,* edited a few years ago by Peter Warlock for the Nonesuch Press, and containing among its two dozen songs pieces by Worgan, Defesch, Festing, Boyce, the two Arnes, and James Hook.

Neither should we forget those other outlets for social music on the semi-professional level, the convivial clubs that were formed for the practice of catches, canons, and glees. Some of these were long-lived: the Noblemen's and Gentlemen's Catch Club, founded in 1761, and still in existence (though but a babe to the Hibernian Catch Club of Dublin, the oldest musical society in Europe, established about 1680 and still alive); the Glee Club, begun 1787; the Concentores Sodales, and doubtless many another, like Goldsmith's Club of Choice Spirits. The best of them, as is well known, offered annual prizes for compositions in these popular forms, and the bulk of their work is to say the least imposing. Thomas Warren, Secretary of the Catch Club, edited 32 volumes of their pieces. Samuel Webbe published nine volumes, James Sibbald four, J. Bland twenty or more volumes of Gentlemen's and Ladies' collections (separately!). *The Apollonian Harmony* of about 1790 has six volumes; Horsley's *Vocal Harmony* contains nine. In addition there are many similar collections of pieces by individual composers— Hayes, Webbe, Callcott, Cooke, J. Stafford Smith, and others.

But on the amateur and popular levels the appetite for song was fed by a constant supply of song-books from beginning to end of the century. Noteworthy at the outset were the successively larger editions of Durfey's *Songs Compleat, Pleasant, and Divertive,* better known as *Pills to Purge Melancholy,* culminating in the six-volume collection of 1719–20. This work may be regarded as almost a national collection of the popular song of that era. It includes favorite pieces by known composers, but in the main it comprises the floating melodies of the second half of the seventeenth century—such things as were familiar and readily available for use with a new topical song or a comic or rowdy ballad or lampoon on politics or fashion—"filthy tunes," as Falstaff called such melodies. The distinction between folk-song and popular song had not yet been conceived, and might have been still harder to draw in that day, because popular music was so much more truly of the people and so much closer to folk-music then than later. But there was a difference, Durfey's tunes often displaying citified, or at least suburban, tricks of modulation, and other self-consciousness less visible in the comparable and contemporary dance-collections of the Playfords. The miscellaneous character of the *Pills* must be emphasized, however, as well as the free and folk-like way in which Durfey pushed his tunes around to accommodate them to the words. The Scottish collections of the same date, Ramsay's *Musick for the Tea-Table Miscellany* and Thomson's *Orpheus Caledonius,* were, as we should expect, more folkish; but the closely subsequent English collections, such as Walsh's and Watts' *Musical Miscellany* in six volumes, cater to a much more sophisticated taste. The long file of ballad-operas in their printed form are of course in themselves little anthologies of popular melody.

Several of the collections of the mid-century display their social character to the eye as well as to the ear. Bickham's *Musical Entertainer,* now a great rarity, offers an engraved scene with each song, 200 in all, and sometimes of considerable historical interest, like those picturing Vauxhall. Another of the same type, but still larger, is *Clio and Euterpe,* 1762, full of pleasant vignettes. In those years, also, pocket-size volumes of words alone were testifying to the passion for song. Some of them were surprisingly full: the three collections called respectively *The Linnet, The Thrush,* and *The Robin* together contain nearly 2000 lyrics, of which the tunes were presumed to be familiar to the purchaser. Toward the end of the century come Ritson's 3-volume collection of *English Songs,* his 2-volume collection of *Scotish Songs,* and his *Ancient Songs;* and, as fitting counterbalance to Durfey at the beginning, the national anthology of Scots song named *The Scots Musical Museum,* again in six volumes. This collection, as is well remembered, is the work for which Burns wrote so many of his deathless songs and for which also he preserved many a lovely folk-tune.

Of most of the collections named, profane love was the commonest theme. But we must not ignore the comparable flood of songs of sacred love current during the second half of the century among the "People called Methodists." Of these Charles Wesley wrote the words of perhaps seven thousand, to be sung to simple and familiar tunes, many of them probably taken from the great ocean of folk-music. It is on account of this outburst that George Sampson in a fine Warton Lecture recently called the Eighteenth Century "The Century of Divine Songs"; and although the phenomenon has been generally neglected in histories of literature and of music, it is obviously of great significance. There are increasing signs that the stature of Charles Wesley as a poet, at least, is gradually becoming recognized.

Throughout these decades, but particularly after 1740, the theorists in aesthetics were busy debating the relations and analogies between music and the other arts, and the specific capabilities and functions of music. Critics like Avison, Brown, Beattie, Webb, and Sir William Jones produced a series of essays that, while they hardly keep abreast of current musical practice, at least offer descriptions of the baroque, and partially organize the attitudes and ideas underlying it. Their treatises have been briefly but competently surveyed by Herbert Schueller in *The Musical Quarterly* for October, 1948. Schueller points out that their discussions mainly revolve about the problems of imitation in music, a subject with a long history, but able still to generate heat; and I shall ask you to spend a little time in considering certain aspects of it, more especially as they bear on the interconnections of music and literature.

II

We are aware that the theory of imitation extends far beyond a single province, and that, not without appeals to the authority of Aristotle, the doctrine was widely held in the eighteenth century that all arts are imitative. For the sake of a suggestive parallel with music, not I hope too far-fetched, we may begin with landscape gardening. This art, so typical of the period, could also be regarded as an art of imitation. For it imitated nature: not by leaving nature alone, but by divining the *meaning* latent in natural phenomena and creatively assisting its quasi-pictorial realization. That meaning, as the century saw it, included, and was incomplete without, references to human life and thought, which added temporal dimensions—remembrance of things past, ideas of antiquity and of classic art, sentiments of mortality and divine hope—to the spatial dimensions that met the eye. Hence the importance of ruins, statues, grottoes, church spires, urns and inscriptions, in Shenstone's conception of the art. These were not merely, as Humphreys so neatly writes, "the punctuation marks in the grammar of natural meaning." Such allusions helped to give definite communicable significance to landscape. The parallel here with music is worth a moment's attention. In both arts the media are possessed of immediate sensuous appeal and rightly managed carry their own inherent patterned validity. But that explicit ideational content which the century demanded of its artifacts has to be borrowed or imported from without. They lend themselves very readily to associations, and in due course with repetitional use a language begins to develop, capable of subtler and subtler refinements of meaning, until (conceivably) the point is reached where the natural or the musical element can state its precisely shaded intention symbolically, without the presence of the interpretative device. Whether the Orientals ever developed the art of landscape to such a degree of ingenuity I do not know, but we all know the "meaning" of a yew-tree or an oak,—if not of a flower in a crannied wall. And we have lately learned that Bach habitually wrote for instruments with an extra-musical implication in mind.

In some sort, of course, the art of the landscape gardeners had already been adumbrated by the landscape poets, selecting and composing the significant items of the natural scene and supplying a meaning:

> See, on the mountain's southern side,
> Where the prospect opens wide,
> Where the evening gilds the tide,
> How close and small the hedges lie!
> What streaks of meadows cross the eye!
> A step methinks may pass the stream,
> So little distant dangers seem;
> So we mistake the future's face,
> Ey'd thro' hope's deluding glass;
> As yon summits soft and fair
> Clad in colours of the air,

> Which, to those who journey near,
> Barren, brown, and rough appear;
> Still we tread the same coarse way:
> The present's still a cloudy day ...
> Thus is nature's vesture wrought
> To instruct our wand'ring thought.

Later generations of nature poets were to drop the explicit gloss (though perhaps not so often as anti-classicists suppose) and it might at first be guessed that they had moved on to that foreseen stage where the natural detail carries a current meaning, like coin of the realm. But the fact is otherwise; for what these later poets are pursuing is not a common but a private meaning. They have a tryst with a secret love, into whose eyes they look for their own image, and who seems to answer their every mood. Autobiography is their métier; they sing themselves. Our present affair, however, is not with novelties of feeling but with conventions of expression,—and more particularly with musical conventions.

In so far as music communicates extra-musical meaning, it, like verbal languages, is a system of aural signs to which in certain contexts particular significance has been attached and which can be combined in a great many meaningful ways. Such a language must depend upon an agreement at least approximate among its users as to sense and modes of employment. In the main, these will be matters of arbitrary convention, like the meaning of words and phrases and the logic of grammar, which have to be painfully learned. The assertion might at first seem to contradict the notion of music as an imitative art; but we shall soon have to discriminate between kinds of imitation. On the primary level, music is of course capable of rudimentary mimicry of certain physical phenomena: sounds animal and human, sounds of water and wind and thunder, sounds of motion. Sounds, the theorists agreed, can be loud or soft, high or low; motions can be continuous or interrupted, even or uneven, swift or slow. Music can reproduce these activities in elementary fashion, and *may* be so understood. But according to 'Hermes' Harris and the Encyclopedists, sound and motion pretty largely comprise the proper limits of musical imitation.

On this basic level, it is interesting to compare Johnson's remarks on Pope's dictum, "The sound must seem an echo to the sense." "This notion of representative metre," writes Johnson,

and the desire of discovering frequent adaptations of the sound to the sense, have produced, in my opinion, many wild conceits and imaginary beauties. All that can furnish this representation are the sounds of the words considered singly, and the time in which they are pronounced. Every language has some words framed to exhibit the noises which they express, as *thump, rattle, growl, hiss.* These, however, are but few, and the poet cannot make them more, nor can they be of any use but when sound is to be mentioned ... The fancied resemblances, I fear, arise sometimes merely from the ambiguity of words; there is supposed to be some relation between a *soft* line and a *soft* couch, or between *hard* syllables and *hard* fortune.

Motion, however, may be in some sort exemplified; and yet it may be suspected that even in such resemblances the mind often governs the ear, and the sounds are estimated by their meanings.... Beauties of this kind are commonly fancied; and when real are technical and nugatory, not to be rejected and not to be solicited.

It will be noticed that Johnson puts poetical imitation exactly where the theorists put musical imitation, with the same limitations to sound and motion. He touches, moreover, on false resemblances arising from the heedless crossing of literal with figurative meanings. By analogy, the point raises consideration of one of the most notorious and widespread kinds of musical imitation. The commonest example is the picturing of high and low by sudden steep ascents and descents in the notes that carry or accompany the words. Baroque composers were far indeed from following Johnson's advice to treat such effects as fortuitous. So long ago as 1597, Thomas Morley had written:

If the subject be light, you must cause your music to go in motions which carry with them a celerity or quickness of time...; if it be lamentable, the note must go in slow and heavy motions... Moreover, you must have a care that when your matter signifieth ascending, high heaven and such like, you make your music ascend: and... where your ditty speaks of descending, lowness, depth, hell and other such, you must make your music descend. For as it will be thought a great absurdity to talk of heaven and point downward to the earth: so it will be counted great incongruity if a musician upon the words *He ascended into heaven* should cause his music to descend.

To be sure, "high" and "low" in music are figurative expressions, but the metaphor in post-classical times seems by the Western world to have been universally understood, and it requires some effort to think it away. In fact, any discussion of music finds it indispensable. But, once having accepted the convention of an "up" and a "down" among musical tones, we can of course extend the figurative analogies at will. Bach uses the device of dropping to the lower bass to suggest Adam's "fall"; and also to indicate night, and darkness, and hell. Handel, in the Cecilia Ode, writes Dryden's phrase, "depth of pains and height of passion" as E to A above, to A at the octave, and back to E, the octave leap coming on the word *height,*—and such was no doubt Dryden's intention. Other instances occur at the line, "What passion cannot Music raise and quell," and again at "wond'ring, on their faces fell To worship."

We are already far enough from the physical correspondences with which we began, and we had best try to see what is happening. Two points are clear. The first is that we should get nowhere in grasping the full intention without the words. In order for the sound to seem an echo to the sense, we must start with the sense. The second point is that we are forced to perform a ratiocinative rather than an intuitive act. There is no need to object to this necessity. It is proper to an honest echo to start from the sense, and it seems a bit perverse of Johnson to complain because he cannot have it the other way round. After all, Pope said "seem," not "be." When Johnson says that "in such resemblances the mind often governs the ear, and the sounds are estimated by their meaning," he is objecting to an axiom. But I must beware of putting more weight on an echo than an echo will bear, and I return to the baroque tonal language.

III

We shall waive for the present any discussion of the question, Whether music *ought* to express any but musical ideas, and agree that for some of the very greatest masters it has in fact done so. It should be profitable to look a little more closely at some of the means employed to that end. For this language is surely related to some of the profoundest and most characteristic elements of the eighteenth-century temper. To keep within bounds, let us draw most of our illustrations from a single masterpiece, Handel's setting of Dryden's *Song for St. Cecilia's Day,* for Soprano and Tenor, Chorus, and Orchestra. Dryden's poem belongs to the year 1687. Handel's work was written and performed in 1739, in an atmosphere of national excitement over the war with Spain, which gave topical significance to the third stanza.

The prevailing tonality of the work is D major, and the spirit of it, over all, is one of confidence and power and trust. The choice of key is of course by no means haphazard. This particular tonality is selected, not because Handel has thought of some musical themes that promise to lie comfortably in the key of D major, but because the dominant mood of Dryden's Ode *means* D major. The tonality could have preceded the formulation of a single phrase of the music in Handel's imagination. Why D major has this significance is not easy to tell, but it is not by Handelian fiat that it does so. Handel is following a tradition that has its origin in mists of cosmological theory:—involving the music of the spheres, planetary influences, the attributes divine and human and affective that were believed to inhere severally in each of the ancient modes. Some of the aura surrounding the medieval modes floated over to influence the baroque feeling for keys. Primarily, however, it is less a matter of feeling than of received doctrine. It has nothing to do with private impressions or sensibilities—as a hyper-sensitive modern with absolute pitch will see the color of old rose when he hears C-sharp minor. On the contrary: this is objective, in that it is determined by the intellect rather than by the sense. It is not a meaning originally inherent in the key, but one that was put there by cogitation. It belongs to the *idea* of the key rather than to the sense-impression:—inevitably so, in an era when pitches were inconstant, and when mean temperament had yet to be firmly established. But by Handel's day the intellectual significance of the keys was sufficiently fixed to enable an emotional meaning to associate itself with the idea. So every fresh authoritative use of a particular tonality within the range of its accepted definitions could serve to confirm and refine and enrich the knowing experience of that tonality.

The tonality established also serves a structural purpose. In the present work, Handel departs from it several times, not in the way of occasional modulations to avoid monotony—though that, too, he does—but in order to change the subject or take up another case. Because Dryden's poem is artfully contrived with provision for musical effects, the tonal architecture is by implication relatively fixed, and this fact, like the designing a house for an owner who knows exactly what he wants, raises special problems in musical tact and logic. Dryden's third, fourth, fifth, and sixth stanzas are deliberately disconnected, describing various passions and the evocative power of several instruments. Handel, besides heightening these contrasts, must give the series a semblance of cohesion, and the sequence of chosen tonalities will be an important aid. Contrast alone in music will not suffice as an organizing principle. If we consider that the pace of the Ode when read is about fifteen times faster than that of Handel's musical utterance, we can realize the much greater need in the latter to establish an underlying unity and to clarify relationships between the parts. Most of this work of tonal, as well as metrical, articulation is naturally brought into sharpest focus at the ends and beginnings of adjacent movements. During these moments we become aware of the subtle way in which two keys can reveal their kinship in the very act of asserting their difference.

Handel begins the Ode with an orchestral overture composed of three short, sharply contrasted movements. The first is *larghetto,* and employs a figure breath-taking in its suggestion of controlled power, a muscular crouch and spring from dominant up to tonic, tonic to third, tonic to fifth, tonic to octave, and back to the starting-point,—each return to the tonic being emphasized by an appoggiatura or turn that seems to establish the foothold more securely. Halfway, the tonality shifts from D major to A major, from which at the end it launches into a fugal *allegro* in D major again. The vigorous drive of this second movement is then quieted into a minuet, and we are ready for the voices. Nothing up to this point is able *by itself* to suggest any extra-musical ideas; and, in fact, all three of these movements are found again in the Fifth Concerto as the opening and closing parts of that work, which belongs to the same year.

Over sustained chords the tenor announces the first lines of the Ode, recitative: "From harmony, from heav'nly harmony This universal frame began." And then, to a tonality dark and continually shifting, no sooner defined than defying definition, come the words, "When Nature underneath a heap Of jarring atoms lay." The orchestra, we begin to notice, is running changes on broken diminished triads, until it occurs to us that here is a continual succession of the most avoided, "most dangerous" interval in music, the dreaded tritone, the "diabolus in musica." "Fa, sol, la, mi" hums Edmund in *Lear,* and we know at once that he is plotting deviltry; and here are mi's contra fa's thick as leaves in Vallombrosa. The churning, yeasty but unassertive, figure continues while the lines are repeated, the melodic line at "could not heave her head" making a futile effort to rise and falling back dejected. Then, imperceptibly, the tonality clears to A major on the words, "The tuneful voice was heard from high," and the voice, unaccompanied, rings out three times on the cry, "Arise," with an interjected trumpet-like echo from the orchestra. Now, suddenly, there is a wild burst of life among the strings, on a disjunctive but energetic figure, as of particles striking together and rebounding chaotically and violently. This ceases, after two bars, as suddenly as it began; and the voice, on a melodic line that arches like a bow, announces,

> Then cold, and hot, and moist, and dry
> In order to their stations leap;

and suddenly again, with the same furious energy, the divided orchestra tosses a leaping figure in sixteenth-notes from one side to the other. We take it at first for more chaos, until we notice what the alternating choirs of high and low had concealed, that the leaping figures are entering at every beat on a perfectly regular and controlled descending scale. After two bars, the chaos returns, to be silenced by the voice repeating its declaration. Thereupon, chaos once more breaks in, but after a bar and a half falls into order as before on the leaping downward scale sequence, and after brief gestures of rebellion at the repeated words, "And music's pow'r obey," the movement is brought to an end with the same demonstration of orderly control:

> Those opposed eyes,
> Which, like the meteors of a troubled heaven,
> Did lately meet in the intestine shock
> And furious close of civil butchery,
> Shall now, in mutual well-beseeming ranks,
> March all one way.

One would surely have thought that so startlingly dramatic a *tour de force* as this would have been acclaimed on every hand. That it has escaped overt notice is proof how far out of the habit we have grown of scrutinizing this music for a kind of meaning which has latterly come to seem almost illegitimate, but which to the makers of it was indigenous to their conceptions. In his *Music in the Baroque Era,* Bukofzer has put the essential point with admirable force (p. 369):

Music reached out from the audible into the inaudible world, it extended without a break from the world of the senses into that of the mind and intellect ... We must recognize the speculative approach as one of the fundamentals of baroque music and baroque art in general without either exaggerating or belittling its importance. If abstract thoughts could be enhanced through poetic form, as we see in the philosophical poetry of the baroque era, then by the same token concrete works of art could be enhanced through abstract thought. Audible form and inaudible order were not mutually exclusive or opposed concepts, as they are today, but complementary aspects of one and the same experience: the unity of sensual and intellectual understanding.

Handel saves the rest of Dryden's first stanza,—appropriately in view of the recapitulative content,—for separate treatment by full chorus and orchestra. The orchestra opens with a syncopated theme of driving, purposeful energy. Incidentally, we may remark that Handel knows better than any one how to use syncopation to suggest eager, anticipatory impatience. With him it never suggests reluctance to go forward or an inclination to walk on the grass. The difference between his use of it and that of some later exponents is the difference between receiving a succession of electric shocks and brushing against India rubber. Handel here keeps his orchestra pressing vigorously ahead; but he spaces out the vocal parts in broad sustained tones, except at the line, "Through all the compass of the notes it ran," where he runs divisions up and down the scale, an octave at a time for the voices and two or more in the strings. The movement ends with unflagging energy, and still in D major. Now is introduced the first structural shift of tonality. Handel with stanza two moves into G major, a key for him of calm confidence, of sunlight and security. The vocal statement is anticipated by a long cantilena for 'cello. The whole movement, which carries all of stanza two, is more of a hymn of praise and thanksgiving for "celestial sound" than of awe for music's power. It is a gently floating, sometimes soaring, meditative *andante* for soprano, in 3/4 time: a long moment of repose in a work full of excitement.

The stanza that follows returns to D major. It makes an obvious bid, with rather obvious effect, for popular applause. The trumpet has rather less solo work than one might have expected, though that is possibly because the instrument has a way of making itself felt as soloist, whatever else is going on. The drums also have less to do than we anticipate. The treatment of the tenor's line, "With shrill notes of anger and mortal alarms," is noteworthy: three descents from A major dominant to tonic on the same pentachord, with a concluding roulade on the last syllable; and above, a true trumpet call—not thematic— on successive triplets at the fifth, octave, and tonic. The movement reaches its climax with repeated cries of "Hark!" and "Charge!" over a drum-roll. The whole stanza is then repeated in compressed form by the full chorus and orchestra.

Handel finds it intolerable to obey Dryden's instructions and pass at once from all this martial excitement to the "soft complaining flute"—an effect which Dryden, aiming only at a striking contrast, did not wish to shun. The reason may lie in the fact that while reading the verses we are mainly conscious of the contrast alone, while in music the order of the contrast becomes much more important. To move from the "big" emotion of war directly into the "little" emotion of hopeless love strikes us as anticlimactic. At least, one may suspect that had the order been reversed there would have been no difficulty. Dryden's trumpet and drum might have been shifted except for the fact that his flute, violin, and organ form an ascending sequence from earthly to heavenly, and so to the day of judgment and the dissolution of the "universal frame." There is thus no other suitable place for stanza three, and Handel respects the given order. He solves the difficulty, at least in part, by inserting an instrumental march in the same key, thereby bringing the martial fever under public, if still martial, control, and at the same time separating the antipathetic stanzas three and four. Even so, were there to be a break in performance, this would be the moment for it:—that is to say, after the March.

For the flute stanza, Handel drops to the relative minor, B minor,—the second extended shift of tonality in the work. This one, like the first, is a leisurely *andante* in 3/4. It is marked by imitative dialogue between the flute and the soprano, the voice assuming an impersonal, instrumental quality, with ornamental trills. Above lutelike "warbling" in the bass accompaniment the word "warbling" is itself extended over six bars of vocalization.

At the violin stanza, there is another change of key, this time to A major. The reasons appear to be intellectual rather than descriptive or impressionistic, and indeed this movement is one of the least pictorial of all. Leichentritt (*Musical Quarterly,* April, 1935) tells us that in his operas Handel is likely to employ G minor when depicting "passionate outbursts of jealous fury." And elsewhere, he uses A major for amorous delight. What motivates the present brilliant and spirited *allegro,* which seems on its face to exhibit no distress commensurate with the anguished words?

It seems clear that the reasons are partly strategic. To follow the pathetic *andante* portraying love-melancholy with another equally poignant minor movement would be ill-advised. No doubt Handel could invigorate the music sufficiently to differentiate the love-madness from the love-sadness. But G minor following upon the heels of B minor obviously would not do in any case: the clash of tonal systems precluded it. E minor would be possible but its connotations were also elegiac. Now, there is no reason why jealous pangs and fury should not be brightly and boldly articulated, and a major key is therefore both permissible and indicated by the context. Because of its tuning, the violin's two most congenial and brightest keys are D major and A major, and of these A major is the more brilliant. This was the moment of all moments in the work for the violin to be displayed. It was not yet time to return to D major, which Handel would need again for his big concluding chorus, and which in any case belonged especially to the trumpet.

Why did Dryden use the term "sharp" in characterizing the violins? If they were sharp in one sense, they were out of tune; and if they were sharp in another, were they not unpleasant in tonal quality? It seems likely that the epithet was due to recent events. When Charles came back from France, he came with a special liking for violins which he insisted should play for his pleasure on most festive occasions and even in church. They had a noticeably brighter tone than the viols, and began everywhere to displace the old-fashioned instruments. One who had the sound of the viols in his ears from childhood would be likely to think the new-fangled violins (only then being brought by N. Amati to their classical perfection of form and tone) too bright by half, however fashionable they might be at Court. The change was familiar to every one in Dryden's generation; and no doubt it was the impact of this recent shift in tonal fashion that lay behind his choice of the term "sharp" to describe the violin timbre, which made them suitable to express jealous pangs and height of passion.

Handel's way of depicting these emotions is entirely symbolic rather than expressive in the modern sense. We have to learn from the words what the intention is, and then listen through the mind's ear. Apart from a conspicuously recurring figure of ascending chromatic notes (which conventionally indicate an-guish), the intensity is signified by long ladder-like passages in sixteenths, all in the violin part except for two elaborate roulades on the accented syllable of "desperation," each three bars long. The texture of this movement is not very different from what one finds in a typical allegro in one of the violin sonatas. It is pure baroque, and as such makes more of a demand today on the listener's enlightened sympathy than any other part of the work. There is a very similar and familiar treatment of Rage in the *Messiah* (Why do the nations) and in Polyphemus' recitative in *Acis and Galatea.*

The *larghetto* which follows, in praise of the "sacred organ," is a hymn of the most ethereal loveliness, certainly the aesthetic climax of the Ode. For the first time the organ plays its compel-ling role, in perfect accord with the words. The movement car-ries Handel's special stamp of grave, lofty serenity, which the world identifies with the *largo* from *Xerxes.* As in the other two slow movements for soprano, the metre is again 3/4, with re-peated chords on the second and third beat of each bar. The shift of tonality from the preceding movement is thrillingly dra-matic, like being lifted to a purer air. F major is the established key for ideas of pastoral and contemplative happiness, and re-mained so throughout the century. Leichentritt reminds us that Beethoven wrote his Pastoral Symphony and "Spring" sonata in this key. For Handel it clearly also carried religious connota-tions, and was pastoral in a double sense. It is not an accident that at the words, "Notes inspiring holy love, Notes that wing their heav'nly ways," we are reminded of the nearly identical musical phrase in the *Messiah,* "He shall feed his flock." There is a momentary disturbance of the mood of rapt contemplation in two bars occurring after the voice has finished: a reference to F minor, like a wisp of cloud crossing the sun, and vanishing.

This divine movement is followed by a short and rhythmically vigorous one in the same tonality, *alla hornpipe;* and that by eight

bars, *largo,* of recitative in A minor. The work then returns to
D major for the final chorus, laid out on massive chorale-like
lines, the soprano solo alternating with the full choir of voices
and strings. At "the last and dreadful hour," the tonality shifts
to D minor, and with "this crumbling pageant" goes into a succession of alien keys, ending on A major. The soprano now enters alone, in D major, rising to high A with the announcement,
"The trumpet shall be heard on high," and holding the high
note for four bars while the trumpet climbs in partial imitation
up to the same note, a second trumpet then joining on a fanfare
below, supported by the whole orchestra and chorus. The last
two lines are treated first canonically by chorus and strings, then
in concert with the whole orchestra; and the work is finished.

IV

We need not labor any longer the importance of tonality in
this world, except to emphasize that it was a component of a
current musical language and, as such, neither had to establish
its significance independently in the individual work, nor was
limited to a personal meaning elaborated by a single composer.
It was rooted in general agreement, and had the strength of
common consent. But it was only one element in this language.
Bukofzer tells us that Andreas Herbst, a mid-seventeenth-century
theorist, distinguishes *verba* and *res,* words and things. The
things meant are states of being, emotional states, like sadness,
as distinct from verbal notions or ideas. The *res* are connected
with specific tonalities, as we see in Handel's practice. But the
translation of ideas or *verba* into music is more complicated.
Ideas were classified as *Motus et Locorum:* words of motion and
place; nouns, verbs; and adverbs of time. To correspond with
these, musical tropes were devised. The system was enlarged and
developed by Johannes Mattheson, the close friend of Handel's
youth. Music, he says, is sound-speech (*Klangrede*) and declares: "It is the ultimate aim of music, by means of the naked

tones and their rhythm, to excite all passions as successfully as the best orator." The purely technical side of music must be understood and employed, but "Descriptio" is the surest and most essential means. The *Affekten,* the Passions, have to be "beschrieben oder gemalet," described or painted.

"Great thoughts," wrote Johnson, "are always general." The fundamental urge of the new classicism was to discover Law, to get beyond the private to the common significance, to escape from the prison of particulars to the freedom of the general, to the realm of great thoughts that embrace man and his place in the universe. Baroque music is but one manifestation of this far-reaching ambition, but it is, I think, a rather neglected one in this view. It was in order to give music a meaning as broad and general as philosophy or literature that the baroque language was developed. The ruling postulates and habits of thought of the age find significant expression here as elsewhere, and instructive analogies and correlations with the literary arts can be discovered. Fundamental agreement as to ends gives rise to analogous conventions among means. Perhaps we can push our exploration of one or two of these conventions a little farther on the less technical side.

Because men wished to understand and rationalize human existence, they needed to objectify the emotional life; and the doctrine known as *Affektenlehre* is a major effort to get the passions out where men can look at them. It is a form of personification, and thus perforce has radical connections with earlier allegorical impulses and with the dominant forms of medieval and renaissance art. The urge to allegory had of course by no means died out in the eighteenth century. The widespread love of personification in the poetry of the age is a notorious manifestation of it; and the allegorical fable in the periodical essays is another. It sometimes appears where we least expect it. One might trace a line through the morality plays back to the medieval literature of personified debate, to the *Roman de la Rose* and beyond, if one were to look for the antecedents of the following paragraph in *Tom Jones* (Bk. VI, ch. 13):

Black George having received the purse [intended by Sophia for Tom], set forward towards the alehouse; but in the way a thought occurred to him, whether he should not detain this money likewise. His conscience, however, immediately started at this suggestion, and began to upbraid him with ingratitude to his benefactor. To this his avarice answered, That his conscience should have considered the matter before, when he deprived poor Jones of his £500. That having quietly acquiesced in what was of so much greater importance, it was absurd, if not downright hypocrisy, to affect any qualms at this trifle. In return to which, Conscience, like a good lawyer, attempted to distinguish between an absolute breach of trust, as here, where the goods were delivered, and a bare concealment of what was found, as in the former case. Avarice presently treated this with ridicule, called it a distinction without a difference, and absolutely insisted that when once all pretensions of honour and virtue were given up in any one instance, (that) there was no precedent for resorting to them upon a second occasion. In short, poor Conscience had certainly been defeated in the argument, had not Fear stept in to her assistance, and very strenuously urged that the real distinction between the two actions, did not lie in the different degrees of honour but of safety: for that the secreting the £500 was a matter of very little hazard; whereas the detaining the sixteen guineas was liable to the utmost danger of discovery. By this friendly aid of Fear, Conscience obtained a complete victory in the mind of Black George, and, after making him a few compliments on his honesty, forced him to deliver the money to Jones.

From his general censure of Fielding, Johnson should have excepted this good-humored dissection of a limed soul, which conforms so closely to Imlac's prescription. It would be too painful to stretch so perfect a confection upon the rack of pedagogical demonstration, but I cannot resist remarking that it is the allegorical machine that has here turned Black George into Everyman. This strikes me as a shining example of benefits forgot by later times—benefits derived from the skillful use of personification, or what I once only half-playfully called the "Abstractive Correlative."

Turning back now to music, we may inquire how the same intention was fulfilled in that medium. How does Handel personify? The process is naturally best seen in his operas, and in this connection I should like to read a few sentences from Leichentritt (*Music, History, and Ideas,* p. 150), who gives much more authority to the answer than I could possibly do. "In Handel's manner of psychological analysis and characterization," he writes,

the systematic, rationalistic spirit of the age is reflected. A character in a Handel opera is expressed musically by the sum of the arias given to him. Each aria reveals a different characteristic. Thus, for instance, in the opera *Alceste,* the heroine, Alcestis, expresses in her [six] arias the various sentiments agitating her in such a manner as to reveal to the listener her individual character ... presenting every emotion in isolation, unmixed, pure, and leaving it to the listener to form an impression of [the] character as a whole. [In Handel's dramatic music] the contest of emotions *in abstracto,* rather than the acting characters, is the central point of interest.

If this be true,—and one's own experience confirms it,—one can easily perceive how closely analogous in this province of his art is Handel's technique to that of the allegorist in verse or prose. It impersonalizes personality by giving the facets of the individual emotional life separate and independent embodiment. The "passions" are objectified in a series of personifications, and thereby we approach 'general and transcendental truths, divested of the minuter discriminations, exhibited in their abstracted and invariable state.' Thus Handel can write—to appropriate the rest of Johnson's statement—"as the interpreter of nature, and the legislator of mankind ... presiding over the thoughts and manners of future generations, as a being superior to time and place."

Even in the Ode, matters are conducted, although (because of

Dryden's libretto) more arbitrarily, according to the same rationalistic ordonnance. Here the passions are represented as absolutes, disconnected or at least separable from men. We may compare the even clearer cases of *Alexander's Feast* and Collins' Ode, *The Passions*. One wonders, parenthetically, whether some lingering vestiges of this ancient mythology survived as genuine belief into the eighteenth century, to give a sense of helpless irresponsibility to persons, whether actual or imagined, in the throes of some emotional seizure. It would go far to explain the actions of Tom Jones in a crisis, or Boswell's fatalistic submission to his fits of Hypochondria, if it were so. Dryden, subscribing for poetic reasons to the ancient doctrine, depicts music's power to raise and subdue any passion at will, like what is delivered of Orpheus. There is a double personification here: the passions are personified, and the musical instruments that serve to rouse them have an autonomous life. This last is a poetical fancy that, so far as I know, has nothing to do with the *Affektenlehre* with which we have been concerned. The theorists were indeed very sceptical about the powers of instruments by themselves to paint the passions meaningfully, unless where words had already given a clue. That particular instruments had associations or affinities with particular moods was not denied; but the potential range of allusion was ordinarily too wide to be of much use. The drum, yes; the sacred organ, yes. The flute and the lute are arbitrary, and the violin is so, too. The trumpet, even in the Ode itself, has very divergent connotations, first as the inciter to battle, and then as the "tuba mirum spargens sonum Per sepulcra regionum." But the essential importance of words in the theory of the passions is reflected in the text of the Ode by being made instrumental to the climax—at least if I understand the climax correctly. For it is when "vocal breath" is added to Cecilia's playing that the angels become confused. [I suppose it is possible to interpret "vocal breath" as the perfecting of the instrument itself by adding a *vox humana* stop.] Thus, it is the marriage of "perfect music unto noble words" that produces the highest, richest musical achievement. There are profound causes for the post-classical, last-minute emergence of pure instrumental music in Western history, to its present position of dominant importance. Never before, probably, has caviar been served as the main course.

We have, of course, not even scratched the surface in describing the intellectual complexities of this baroque language of music. The four levels of meaning in medieval explication are relatively simple, compared to some of Bach's convolutions of significance. The curious may consult Manfred Bukofzer's illuminating essay, "Allegory in Baroque Music" (from which I have drawn facts and illustrations), for a demonstration of five different allegories simultaneously appearing in a single cantata by Bach,—not one of which would be perceptible to the untutored listener at a performance.

V

It is literally shocking to turn from a complexity such as this, involving art and mind and heart in total devotion, to the products of the popular musical genius—the vulgar music in the best sense. There are, of course, scores of levels—the cliffs of Helicon are terraced—from those who, as Burns puts it, "never drank the Muses' stank" upward to where there is an uneasy awareness of what is still above. When, in the famous song in *Semele* (Where'er you walk), Handel subjects the monosyllable "shade" to melismatic treatment, with two rests interrupting its flow, he is describing the spreading umbrage, not unbroken, of the animated trees. When, in Polly's complaint of the "saucy jade" her rival, she sings to Macheath, "How can you see me *made* the scoff of such a gipsy?," treating the monosyllable "made" in nearly identical fashion, we realize what kind of sense the average "sensible" person would probably make out of such artifice.

No doubt, also, the common-sense view had many defenders who happened not to set down their judgment in writing.

One of those who did so—a very distinguished one—had clear reasons for his opinion, and a practised pen. This was John Wesley, who published a pamphlet entitled "Thoughts on the Power of Music." To him, the hint of intellectual appeals in music was at best ridiculous, at worst sinful. His distinctions did not stop half way. It is, he holds, within the power of melody "to raise various passions in the human mind." But harmony, "namely, a contrast of various notes, opposite to and blended with each other," appeals not to the emotions but to the intellect. "What," he writes, "has counterpoint to do with the passions? It is applied to the ear, to the imagination, or internal sense. It no more affects the passions than the judgment." As for instrumental music, "artificial sounds without any words at all," what use does it serve? It has nothing to do with the passions, with the judgment, with reason, or common sense: "All these are utterly excluded by delicate unmeaning sounds." Polyphony? "Appointing different words to be sung by different persons at the same time . . . is glaringly, undeniably contrary to commonsense." Nevertheless, "this astonishing jargon has found a place even in the worship of God. It runs through (O pity! O shame!) the greatest part of even our Church Music! It is found even in the finest of our Anthems and in the most solemn parts of our public worship. Let any impartial, any unprejudiced persons say whether there can be a more direct mocking of God." [Cf. Fred Luke Wiseman, "John Wesley as a Musician," in *Wesley Studies by Various Writers,* pp. 156–160. London, 1903.] Doubtless, Wesley approved of the caveat in one of his brother's hymns:

> Still let us on our guard be found,
> And watch against the power of sound
>   With sacred jealousy,
> Lest haply sense should damp our zeal,
> And music's charms bewitch and steal
>   Our hearts away from Thee.

Nevertheless, John Wesley had every right to consider himself a music-lover. It was owing originally to him that music became an essential element in the Methodist worship. He insisted on the importance of congregational singing; determined what kind of music should be sung, and gave instruction as to when and how it should be sung. He stood for no whining and droning, but ordered his followers to sing out with wholehearted, open-mouthed fervor, and at a good pace. He selected tunes for his own and his brother's hymns, and he assembled and edited a number of hymn-books before the definitive collection of 1780, which has been the heart of all subsequent Methodist hymnals. Musical talent ran in the family, and rose to genius in a later generation.

It is difficult to recover an accurate idea of early Methodist hymnody. In this country, Methodist tune-books dating before 1800 appear to be virtually non-existent. For our information, therefore, we must rely on one or two very brief recent studies and on indirect contemporary testimony. James T. Lightwood has identified the contents of the earliest collection, the so-called "Foundery Tune-Book," of 1736. It contained 42 tunes, of which a third were English, a third were German, and the rest mostly of unknown origin. The German tunes came mostly from Freylinghausen's and Jacobi's song-books of 1705 and 1722, and reflect the profound influence of the Moravians on Wesley. They are mostly chorales. The English sources are miscellaneous and go back as far as Day's and Parker's psalm-books of the 1560's. A few are by known composers: Tallis, Gibbons, Croft, and two or three others, including—rather surprisingly—Handel, whose march in *Richard II* is here adapted and named "Jericho." The authoritative psalm-books are rather lightly drawn upon by Wesley, who was quite willing to reach out in secular directions for a good tune.

The 1742 collection was somewhat larger, and that of 1761, "Select Hymns with Tunes Annext, designed chiefly for the use of the People called Methodists," contains 102 tunes and 133 hymns. Included is Wesley's Grounds of Vocal Music. The hymns are arranged according to metrical pattern. They include most of the 1742 collection, and sixteen tunes written for the Methodists by J. F. Lampe, rather more florid than the others. Nearly half the collection is in triple time; nearly a third in a minor key. The last line or half-line of the hymns frequently repeats as a sort of refrain, and there are four "Hallelujah" refrains; but none of the so-called "Old Methodist Tunes" appears in this book. For a clue we turn elsewhere.

In the autumn of 1766, an attack of the gout took Horace Walpole to Bath, whence he wrote to Chute, on the 10th of October:

> My health advances faster than my amusements. However, I have been at one opera, Mr. Wesley's. They have boys and girls with charming voices, that sing hymns, in parts, to Scotch ballad tunes; but indeed so long, that one would think they were already in eternity, and knew how much time they had before them.

This passage raises questions: Did Wesley, who himself preached on that particular day, approve or merely tolerate the part-singing? Was it canonic, like the "fuguing-tunes" of early American worship, or only SATB harmony? This was the Countess of Huntingdon's chapel, where things were done with more refinement than elsewhere; and Walpole adds in the same letter that he is "glad to see that luxury is creeping in among them before persecution"; so that the music may not have been typical. But what are we to understand by "Scotch ballad tunes"? In Wesley's own hymnals, so far as I can discover, there are no tunes that would be likely to be taken as Scottish folksong, though a few of those from unknown sources appear to have Welsh affiliations. On the other hand, we now know, thanks largely to George Pullen Jackson's researches, that the very stuff out of which the so-called "white spirituals" were made throughout the last century, in New England and the Southeast, was

British traditional folk-music, including a large infusion of Scottish tunes in gapped scales. Baptists and Methodists were the chief disseminators of these songs, and of course the latter have within recent memory always enjoyed a reputation for lyrical enterprise in their worship. A likely inference is that long before the days of Moody and Sankey, and even before the days of Lowell Mason, the Methodists were employing a great many folk-tunes that never got into their hymnals and were never perhaps officially sanctioned. With Wesley's single-minded love of melody, and with his all-powerful approval, Methodism was a singing faith; and the traditional tunes would be the ones that his congregations would have known and loved from childhood. If perhaps he himself would have preferred more discrimination in choosing, his lay-preachers certainly would be hospitable to the use of the people's own music; and Wesley, seeing that it was innocent and apt for the work of God, would not be likely to stop it. There is a familiar story that Charles Wesley, interrupted in his preaching by some rowdy sailors singing "Nancy Dawson," compounded with them by declaring that he liked their tune well, and promising to supply them the next day with some better words to it. In any case, any one who poured out hymns at Charles Wesley's rate of speed would always be bankrupt of fresh tunes, and would welcome them from every quarter. There must have been a natural reluctance to use the same tune again and again, always with a new text; and once a favorite tune and text had become closely united, they would not easily be divorced. The official tune-books were certainly insufficient for the thousands of hymns that Charles Wesley wrote.

Thus it must have happened that Methodism became one of the main disseminating agents of popular melody. At the same time, even on the higher levels there was a growing revulsion from the complexities of the baroque to simpler forms, in every kind of music, vocal or instrumental. The tendency toward the plain, the uncomplicated, the popular, was part of the spirit of the age, and was manifest on the Continent as well as in England. In Germany, for example, Leichentritt can declare (*Music, History, and Ideas,* p. 163), with the exhaustive work of Max Friedlaender to support the statement: "The hundreds of song melodies written at this time ... seem almost primitive in their bare harmony, their intentional lack of all artistic complication. Nevertheless, it was out of their artless style that Schubert's incomparable songs grew in the course of time." The seeds had been sown, and interest in popular balladry and song was springing up everywhere, to lead to Herder and the brothers Grimm, to Percy, Ritson, Scott, and Jamieson. It was, if not inevitable, at least beautifully appropriate that at this historical moment, and no other, Robert Burns should make his appearance.

Burns was one of the few poets who never, or seldom, wrote a lyric without a tune in mind to which it was to go. The consequence of this fact is, of course, that the metrical conditions of his composition were settled in advance. He had no freedom to innovate or to alter the stanzaic pattern during the course of the song; and, if he made any dramatic shift in the tone from one stanza to another, it was almost certain, he could rest assured, to be neutralized in its effect by having to conform to the normative musical statement. For any variety, he would have to rely on the refrain, which to make its due impact would have to be a full-length *burden*—that is, of equivalent length with the stanza proper. Or, if the tune had no such element, it would be less monotonous if it were a double-strain tune, accommodating two quatrains in a single full statement. In another view, these two cases are identical: quatrain plus *burden* equals two-strain tune. Although I have not taken a thorough census, I think it will be found that a large majority of Burns's songs conform to the double pattern, and fill out an eight-phrase tune or its equivalent. The texts that are printed in quatrains must be checked by the tunes themselves unless the number of stanzas is odd; and sometimes the odd stanza will prove to be a *burden* that is intended to be sung after each regular stanza. Indeed, to leaf through the texts of his songs is to realize that they are nearly unthinkable without their tunes. Their verbal patterns, their repeated lines, the frequent incidence of "O" at the end of lines, the undodgeable refrains or choruses: these all presume a musical reference. Let two examples chosen at random stand for all:

> Landlady, count the lawin
> The day is near the dawin,
> Ye're a' blind drunk, boys,
>   And I'm but jolly fou.
>   Hey tutti, taiti,
>   How tutti, taiti—
>   Wha's fou now?

And this:

> My love she's but a lassie yet;
>   My love she's but a lassie yet;
> We'll let her stand a year or twa,
>   She'll no be half sae saucy yet.
> I rue the day I sought her, O;
>   I rue the day I sought her, O;
> Wha gets her needs na say she's woo'd,
>   But he may say he's bought her, O!

This is as much as to say that in sober truth we owe the existence of Burns's lyrics to Scottish folk-music and Burns's familiarity with it. And of course the debt does not stop there. His texts are themselves so interwoven with traditional matter that the more we know of his antecedents, the less sure we become that his part in the most spontaneous and best-loved songs is more than a cleaning-up of the clarty, a filling in of the forgotten, and a civilizing of the ramgunshock—forbye the putting a wheen smeddum in the smeerless.

By its very nature, the folk-tune is better suited to pure lyric than to narrative. The folk-tune is always beginning again, at an unchanging pace, at the same emotional pitch, in unvarying statement. It takes kindly to a series of parallel expressions of an emotion—a single emotion, whether joy or sadness, love or grief—where the element of story is withheld. Narrative asks naturally to vary the pace, to change the pitch, to introduce delays or suspensions or surprises, but always to be going on and never repeating. The effectiveness of the folk-ballad—when it is effective—depends partly on the tension that arises from this opposition, the musical form exerting a steadying and controlling power over the extravagant text. But it was to be expected that sooner or later, as music became less objective and more impressionistic, there would be an attempt to make the musical vehicle reflect more intimately the changes of meaning and mood in the text,—in the smaller forms as in the larger. The solution was not completely attained until the nineteenth-century art song came into being. One answer of the eighteenth century to this problem was the *glee,* which employed a varied succession of short subjects, each one being brought to a cadential pause before the next was taken up. One is tempted to call the glee the poor musician's madrigal; but it took a good musician to write a good glee. Yet another answer, closer to the folk level, is offered by Burns in his so-called "cantata," "The Jolly Beggars." Here the connecting narrative tissue is called "recitative," probably without any expectation of its being actually sung; while musical variety is attained by the introduction of a series of songs, each independent of the others and sung by a different personality.

Burns had of course no way of making the details of his text conform to the details of his musical medium. There is, for example, nothing in the music to which he set his sardonic "Merry hae I been teethin' a heckle" that can bring out or truly express the sense of his words:

> Bitter in dule I licket my winnin's
>   O' marryin' Bess to gie her a slave.
> Blest be the hour she cool'd in her linens,
>   And blythe be the bird that sings on her grave.

Yet there is often a chameleon quality about these Scottish tunes that makes them notably adaptable to different uses. The same air will be mischievous and spirited or pathetic, according to the speed and mood in which it is sung. A good example is "Hey tutti taiti," which we have already noticed as the drinking song, "Landlady count the lawin," and which Burns made world-famous by his words, "Scots wha hae," and to which, later, Lady Nairne wrote her tender "Land of the Leal." The adaptability appears to be especially Scottish, and I suspect that part of the cause lies in the gapped scales so frequently appearing in the music of that country, so uncommon in English folk-music. These are natural bridges from mode to mode; and each pentatonic scale has latent reference to three heptatonic and two hexatonic scales, every one with its own special character and feeling.

VI

By way of conclusion, looking back over the century, we can I think distinguish two phenomena of greatest significance for the vital interconnections of music and literature. The first culminates in the first half, the second in the latter half, of the century. The first is the strenuous and almost successful effort to evolve a language that could convey general and abstract truths with a high degree of objectivity, by means of the mutually interpretative support of which words and tones were capable: a conventional language that, rather than pursuing novelties, relied, as did all classical diction at its best, upon using the accepted modes of expression with deepened awareness, refined sensitivity and precision. The second phenomenon is the part, the multifarious and far-reaching part, played by popular song in the transition from classicism to individualism. The influence of Percy's *Reliques* on the theory and practice of the elder romantic poets has long been acknowledged; but the inseparable role of humble melody in conditioning the formal and stylistic habits of the ballad and of all popular lyric has, I think, been imperfectly recognized. Here, too, but from the opposite direction, a common and universal language is being evolved, not by the cerebration of an aristocratic tradition, but by the gradual and unconscious sifting out of those graces and subtleties that could not be immediately seized and retained by the unforced memory of the people as a whole. Burns's best-loved songs speak to the mind and heart of our common humanity; and it was only, it would seem, by descending to rest for a historical moment "flat on the nether springs" that a new cycle could be begun on a radically different principle, the exploration of individualism.

VIII

The Ironic Tradition in Augustan Prose from Swift to Johnson

By IAN WATT

WHEN THE STEERING COMMITTEE of the Clark Library Seminar honored me with an invitation to initiate a discussion in the general area of eighteenth-century prose it occurred to me that, surprisingly enough, there was one fairly large and reasonably germane topic—that of the tradition of irony in the eighteenth century—which had not, as far as I knew, received any general treatment. It is surely true that in no other period does irony loom so large upon the literary scene: many of the acknowledged masterpieces are ironic both in their basic strategy and their local style—the *Tale of a Tub,* *Gulliver's Travels,* the *Rape of the Lock,* the *Dunciad, The Way of the World,* the *Beggar's Opera;* nor can we look long before finding an important ironical element in many others: the indulgent mockery of the *Spectator* or the *Citizen of the World;* the lofty awareness of the narrow limits placed on man's endeavor in *The Vanity of Human Wishes* and the *Decline and*

161

Fall of the Roman Empire; the comic counterpoint of action and comment in *Tom Jones* and *Tristram Shandy:* similar tonalities are everywhere, from the speculative heights of Berkeley and Hume to the abysses of Grub Street, with all its jaded poems about nymphs and its pamphlet wars between ninnies.

What are the reasons for this virtual omnipresence of irony? How is it connected with the many other characteristics of the period which we have learned so much about in the last few decades? Does it shed any light on the relation of the eighteenth century to what comes before and after, to the Restoration and to Romanticism? These are the directions in which I would like to initiate a few tentative explorations.*

I

There seems no doubt that, as he himself claims in the *Verses* on his own death, Swift inaugurated the ironic tradition in eighteenth-century literature.

> Arbuthnot is no more my Friend,
> Who dares to Irony pretend;
> Which I was born to introduce,
> Refin'd it first, and shew'd its Use.

Swift does not, however, help us very much to understand *how* he refined it. His few remarks about irony—like all those I have come across in other writers of the period—are very casual, and stay well within the classical treatments of irony in Aristotle, Cicero and Quintilian. There is perhaps a little more help—some negative tangential clues at least—to be found in Swift's letter to the *Tatler* on "the continual Corruptions of our English Tongue." There, singling out two of his favorite lexical *bêtes noires,* he writes: "I have done my Utmost for some

---

*I am deeply grateful to Harold D. Kelling, John Loftis and Henry Nash Smith, who read drafts of this paper and made valuable suggestions and criticisms.

Years past to stop the Progress of *Mobb* and *Banter,* but have been plainly borne down by Numbers."

"Mob" and "Banter" are being singled out as vulgar neologisms: but, as notorious recent additions to the speech of the time, they are also significant, I think, of certain new forces in the Augustan scene—forces which help us to isolate some of the elements of Swift's irony, merely because Swift, and his irony, were diametrically opposed to them.

"Mob," of course, was the modish abbreviation of *mobile vulgus:* and Swift objected as much to the thing as he did to the abbreviation. Roger North says in the *Examen* (1740) that the word first appeared, in place of "rabble", when the London crowd became the "beast of burthen" of Shaftesbury and his Green Ribbon Club, which met at the King's Head Tavern, and which is attacked in the Second Part of *Absalom and Achitophel.*

The word was naturalized, according to the *Oxford English Dictionary,* in 1688, the year of the Glorious Revolution: and for the following century most of the great men of letters remained on guard against the mob, against all those who threatened to subvert the established order, whether in politics or in literature or in manners. To say that the Augustans invented the dichotomy of the elite and the mob would obviously be exaggerated; but they certainly conceptualized the distinction and applied it more unremittingly than ever before. The idea seems indeed to have defined their basic conception of their role as writers: they were a small band, a righteous minority, ever battling for truth against every kind of deviation from the norm; against the Dunces and the Foplings and the Virtuosos— almost any page of Swift or Pope will supply confirmation and additions.

Out of this there arose a vision of a double, a divided audience which made irony, in the sense of speaking by contraries, a possible, and almost an obligatory mode of discourse.

The chosen few—the men of wit and judgment and learning—could be assumed to have considerable identity of attitude
and understanding: to them you could speak as subtly and
elliptically as you wished. But to the many, the mob—you obviously couldn't and in any case wouldn't use the same language; in Johnson's delightful phrase, they had "no claim to
the honour of serious confutation." There was, therefore, a
strong pressure towards shaping every element of discourse,
from the single word to the total work, with two different and
opposite categories of people in mind. For example, there were
the people in the largest category, the literary mob, who could
be persuaded that Gulliver was a real person, and they were
provided with the most elementary kind of narrative interest
in the simplest kind of prose—if you played the game well
enough you might even take in an Irish bishop. While those
for whom Swift really wrote were allowed to savor simultaneously, not only the ironical interpretation of the fable—the
book's real meaning—but also the literary skill with which the
less percipient were being hoodwinked. The ironic posture, in
fact, was both a formal expression of the qualitative division in
the reading public, and a flattering reinforcement of the sense
of superiority which animated one part of it.

This separation of the true wits from the mob, incidentally,
had the great advantage of flexibility: in any given context it
was defined merely by the absence or presence of proper standards. So if, for example, the Hanoverian boors and the vulgar
millionaires, along with their political toadies and their poets
laureate, seemed to most people to be the great ones of their
time, Pope could put a brave face on the situation and an-
nounce that "Scribblers or peers alike are mob to me"; Swift
could reserve his choicest scorn for the "better sort of vulgar";
and Fielding could continue the tradition by explaining in *Tom
Jones* that "wherever this word [mob] occurs in our writings,

it intends persons without virtue or sense, in all stations; and many of the highest rank are often meant by it."

The mob, then, was the perfect antitype of proper standards: the more so as, being mobile as well as vulgar, it could naturally represent sentiment, enthusiasm, every kind of fashionable novelty, as opposed to the unchanging norms of nature and tradition espoused by the Augustans. Finally—and perhaps most significantly—the mob, as an ancient symbol of irrational forces, could stand for passion, as against reason.

If "mob" could stand for the complete antithesis to the kind of audience and outlook which Swift esteemed, and thus dictated something of the content and basic strategy of his irony, "banter" helps us, also by contradiction, to describe the tone and the attitude which characterize his ironic technique.

In *A Tale of a Tub,* Swift, after promising us a treatise entitled "A modest Defense of the Proceedings of the *Rabble* in all Ages," turns briefly, in the prefatory "Apology," to the subject of banter. "This Polite Word," he tells us, "was first borrowed from the Bullies in *White-Fryars,* then fell among the Footmen, and at last retired to the Pedants." Swift then goes on to illustrate the difference between "Bantring" and genuine "Productions of Wit" from the works of his antagonist William Wotton: "it is grievous to see him ... going out of his way to be waggish, to tell us of *a Cow that prickt up her Tail,* and in his answer to this Discourse, he says *it is all a Farce and a Ladle.*"

Swift, then, thought of banter as open personal attack cast in the vulgar dialect of the marketplace: both in manner and matter it violated the decorums of social and intellectual refinement. Irony, we can see, is the exact opposite. Its rhetorical aim, perhaps, is the same: to expose your enemy to shame and ridicule; but the game is played in much more seemly fashion. Aristotle had written in the *Rhetoric* that the role of *eiron* befits a gentleman more than that of the buffoon, and the reasons are not far to seek. Irony tends to understatement, to meiosis, which itself insists on the difference of social rank: the mob are little people. And while the gentleman is disposing of his foe by the method of irony, his serenity need never be discomposed, even by laughter: the true gentleman, like Fontenelle, "n'a jamais fait ha ha ha." Whether Swift, as reported, never laughed, we do not know; I think he probably did; but not, certainly, in his prose. Puttenham defined irony as "the dry mock"; and Swift's prose rigidly obeys the code of irony which, like that prescribed for Prussian officers, allows no more than "ein kurzes militarische Lachen"—a single, chilling, "Ha!"

Irony is better suited to the gentleman and the wit than banter in many other ways: it's rude to stick your tongue out in public, whereas, it is the very pink of politeness to praise your enemy with your tongue in your cheek; and this obliquity of insult is, moreover, much more difficult to counter. As Max Beerbohm said long ago of the father of irony, the Socratic method is not a game at which two can play.

Such are some of the ways in which Swift's irony may be seen as the complement of his opposition to mob and banter: and the basic situation I have sketched is closely related to some of the characteristics of his prose style. If a sentence is to be susceptible of two contrary interpretations, the simplest kind of predication will be best: to get the opposite we only have to supply a "not" for the verb, or an antonym for the noun; and it is therefore likely that eighteenth-century irony both required and stimulated the development of a kind of prose perspicuous enough for its double meanings to be sufficiently transparent. Swift's conciseness, his avoidance of adjectival ornament, his subordination of all the rhetorical arts to an easy conveyance of meaning—all these are prerequisites of his irony.

With such a staple established, prose could, of course, become capable of emphasis with much less expenditure of effort; and this, too, is necessary for irony. If we compare Swift's method of emphasis with those of earlier writers, with Lyly or Nashe or Donne or Milton, it is surely apparent that in this case, at least, Henry James's law—"economy of means—economy of effect"—does not apply. Consider, for example, the famous line in the "Digression on Madness": "Last Week I saw a Woman *flay'd,* and you will hardly believe, how much it altered her Person for the worse."

Shocked into a full realization of the inner-outer, appearance-reality dichotomy with the very slightest of verbal pressures from Swift, we cannot withhold from him the honor which Dryden claimed for the true satirist: he is the very Jack Ketch of his art, without rival in making "a malefactor die sweetly." Swift's "you will hardly believe" so casually ranges us with the mob, with those habitually blind both to the realities below the surface of things, and also, perhaps, to the actual cruelties and miseries of this world, however much they may fancy themselves to be "brimful of that *Modern* Charity and Tenderness" ironically alluded to at the end of the "Digression." And, of course, the ominous modulation would lose its effect if we did not know that the pretended author was actually an obtuse spokesman of the mob; or if Swift's prose were not so beautifully lucid, and our attention, occupied by the difficulty of deciphering the sentence's bare meaning, were deflected from its double range of implication.

"Proper words in proper places"—such was no doubt Swift's greatest legacy to eighteenth-century prose. If we look for a more specific indebtedness to Swift's irony in later writers, it seems most obviously to reside in two other characteristics of the passage which are closely connected with its economy of effect.

First, it surely is evident that the device of understatement might formerly have passed unnoticed. In Jacobean prose, for example, the competition for our attention would be much too energetic for the meiosis of "how much her person was altered for the worse" to serve as effective climax: Swift's fastidious

aversion—at once ironic and real—to anything more than a
spare, analytic notation of an effect—requires to be set in much
more equable and unemphatic surroundings if it is to strike
home.

Swift's perfectly controlled lucidity, combined with his habit
of understatement, probably did much to attune the ears of
succeeding generations of readers to similar ironic effects in
later writers: and to the duplicities of calculated hyperbole as
well as of meiosis. When Hume, for example, spoke of the
"hideous hypothesis . . . for which *Spinoza* is so universally
infamous," a good many readers could be expected to see that
the adjectives were ironical: Hume's normally restrained vocabulary being what it is, "hideous" and "infamous" could only be
wanton hyperboles, which the deist minority would delightedly
recognize—and find their pleasure increased by their recognition of the author's straight-faced parody of the overstrained
indignation of the—this time orthodox—mob.

Perhaps the most significant ironical characteristic of Swift's
style, however, is that exemplified in the cool, distant generality
of "how much it altered her person." A degree of abstraction
would seem to be necessary for ironic diction. Partly because the
number of non-abstract nouns which have an opposite is fairly
limited: there is no antonym, as far as I know, for "Ian Watt":
but there is one for "human" or "wisdom," as I am aware.

Even more important, perhaps, and certainly so in the present
case, is the fact that the use of abstract words in itself often
creates an ironical effect: if anyone who knows my proper name
calls me "Professor," I at once suspect him of intending a certain
ironical distancing. So one constantly finds the strong abstract
element in eighteenth-century prose connected with one of the
characteristic features of its irony—the lofty, analytic, and
slightly supercilious command of the entire human scene. When
Shaftesbury, for example, after proclaiming the great benefits
of "raillery"—the banter of the elite—for composing differences

among educated gentlemen, goes on to confess that "the mere Vulgar of Mankind . . . often stand in need of such a rectifying Object as *the Gallows* before their Eyes"—there is surely an implicit social and literary alignment of Shaftesbury with his ideological opposite, Swift. Both, at least, give us a vision conspicuously removed from the ordinary man's concrete apprehensions.

Abstract diction, in fact, has dissolved the terror of the gallows, like the bloodstained agony of the flayed woman, into the metaphysical air; the witty compression of "rectifying object" is a whole world away from the crowds on Tyburn Hill; generality of diction functions as the verbal expression of the vast distance between the wit and the mob.

II

So much for the connection between the opposition to "mob and banter" and some of the essential features of Augustan irony. Before passing to a somewhat more detailed—but necessarily still rather schematic—consideration of three of its constituents which, I think, were both problematic in themselves, and contained the seeds of major literary developments in the tradition of irony, I would like to suggest that what I have already said provides some clues as to the reasons for the difference in tone between Restoration and Augustan literature. Swift's predecessor Samuel Butler, for example, invites the mob as well as the elite to jeer at Sir Hudibras, and his verse aims at stimulating his audience into the loudest possible guffaw. Similarly Dryden—in *Mac Flecknoe* for instance—comes much closer to banter than Pope ever does, and the barrier between himself and his satiric targets is not normally the unsurmountable one of irony: his verse implies that both he and they are human beings, and this is not always the impression we get from Pope. Finally—to take a third example from the domain of literary genre—it is surely the instinctive preference for meiosis over hyperbole which explains why the Augustans were given to mock heroic rather than to travesty.

Looking forward, now, I would like to single out as the first of the problematic elements in Augustan irony the tendency already noted towards general and abstract statement. When Johnson, for example, gave us his immortal definition of gin as "a compendious mode of drunkenness," the context—a serious attack in the *Literary Magazine* (No. 13) on the "enormous and insupportable mischiefs" arising from intemperance— proves that he did not mean to be ironical. "Compendious," like Shaftesbury's "rectifying," is merely an abstract modifier: but taken in conjunction with its concrete referent "gin," the terse abstractness arouses a suspicion of irony, merely because of the absence of the expected moral connotation: compendiousness, which he defined in the *Dictionary* as that "by which time is saved and circuition cut off," is normally a welcome, useful quality, and what approbative connotation exists in the word is therefore somewhat contrary to expectation. But the main reason for our surprise is, I believe, the generality of the diction itself, which involves an absence of the powerful connotations we would normally expect from the referent concerned, an absence which is so conspicuous as to generate irony.

The analytic, generalizing tendency of the eighteenth-century vocabulary may itself be regarded as ironigenic then, as tending to produce irony whether intended or not; partly because it lacks connotation, excludes the normally attendant feelings and evaluations with which its concrete referent is usually associated; and partly because generalized diction has its own kind of connotation, always suggesting a cool, unemotional and hence sceptical evaluation of what it describes.

A passage from Swift's *Letter to a Young Gentleman Lately Enter'd into Holy Orders* may serve to illustrate this tendency: Swift is earnestly advising his charge against attempting to explain the mysteries of the Christian religion: for, he says, with impeccable logic, "If you explain them, they are Mysteries no longer; if you fail, you have laboured to no Purpose." Taken out of context, this could well come from an ironical deist tract; and the effect is heightened when Swift goes on to say "For my part, having considered the Matter impartially, I can see no great Reason which those Gentlemen you call the *Free-Thinkers* can have for their Clamour against Religious Mysteries; since it is plain, they were not invented by the Clergy, to whom they bring no Profit, nor acquire any Honour." I pass over Swift's apparent chagrin that Providence has dealt the Deists all the theological aces, to emphasize how the mere application of rational argument, and the reduction of the essential terms of Christianity to such general abstractions as "mysteries," "profit," "honour," cannot but have a sceptical effect.

A similar tendency—the tendency of the cool absence of connotation, in any discourse concerned with things fraught with emotion, to create a disturbing ironical ripple even where it is not intended—is discernible in Shaftesbury's epithet for God— "the best natur'd One in the World"; and it similarly subverts his own beloved avocation, philosophy, when he asserts that "to Philosophise, in a just Signification, is but to carry Good-Breeding a Step higher." In a sense, then, Swift's refinement of expression and especially his easy manipulation of general terms may have helped—quite unintentionally—to prepare the way for works so totally contrary to Swift's ideas as Hume's essay "Of Miracles" in the *Enquiry Concerning Human Understanding;* Hume's tone, as indeed his logical method, has a very close kinship to Swift's coolly abstract treatment of the Christian mysteries: "So that, upon the whole, we may conclude, that the *Christian Religion* not only was at first attended with miracles, but even at this day cannot be believed by any reasonable person without one."

It would be possible, I think, at this stage, to show how Swift's rather exaggerated belief in the extent to which words, and indeed the human mind, operate, or rather should operate, by means of single, logical meanings—actually extends far beyond the question of diction. If Voltaire—no innocent when it comes to irony—took the *Tale of a Tub* as an attack on religion, it was surely in part because the total effect of allegorical and metaphoric devices can no more be rigidly circumscribed to the single logical effect intended than can that of single words. The analogy of the coats as such is not forgotten once we have discerned its application to factional quarrels in the Church: the prestige of the Church itself is likely to be—no doubt irrationally—diminished by the association. Words, images, the human mind, will not always keep to the single track marked for them by irony, especially when—after a lapse of time—we have only a hazy recollection of a few concrete images divorced from their logical structure: the Bishops had their own kind of alogical wisdom when they feared that the true religion had been besmirched by the company it had been made to keep in the *Tale of a Tub*.

III

The meaning—whether of a single word or of any larger unit of expression—cannot, then, be wholly restricted to the role which it is allotted by the logic of the ironist: and the same difficulty occurs in the case of the largest ironic weapon of all— that of the author's pretended narrator or protagonist—the ironic mask or *persona*.

The use of a fictional *persona* would seem to be a structural necessity in any extensive piece of ironical writing: the actual author must remain invisible, for we would lose our interest in the chase if we could see from the beginning that it was the same man who was running with the mob of hares and hunting with the witty hounds. The ironic *persona* can be on either side: most often he is with the hares, making us see which way the author's hunt is going by speaking or acting the contrary: such is the Grub Street hack who writes the *Tale of a Tub,* for example. But the *persona* can also be a huntsman, as long as he is in disguise: he may speak direct truth, that is, but by some *naïveté,* some Cassandra-like disablement, some apparent inferiority to ourselves as a witness, what he says sounds false, except to the initiated: such, essentially, is the role of the clair-voyant Chinamen, penetrating Persians, and existentialist Abys-sinians who smile at us mockingly from the pages of Goldsmith, Addison, and Johnson; and they are close literary kinsfolk to the King of Brobdingnag, and of the even wiser nags of the Fourth Part.

The use of the *persona* is, of course, a very ancient device; and we must remember that the element of actual pretense was still strong in the eighteenth-century usage of the term irony. Swift, however, is surely unrivalled both in the number of *personae* he adopted, and in the imaginative completeness with which he merged himself into them.

There, I think, is the rub. In many of Swift's satires the *personae* are so convincing that, in addition to our awareness of the two levels of interpretation intended, the fictional world of each *persona* also takes on a reality of its own: the mask looks perfectly lifelike. This, of course, has some great advan-tages: in the *Drapier's Letters,* for example, or the *Modest Pro-posal,* Swift enlists to his purpose the force of the immediate, personal participations and revulsions which are normally either weak or absent in expository prose. But in other circumstances— and we come now to the rub—this surely places a double re-sponsibility on the *persona* which he cannot easily discharge. In so far as he is an ironic device, his effectiveness is directly proportional to the completeness of his disciplined subordina-tion to his creator's purpose; while, *qua* individual character, the *persona* can become living and effective only by transcend-ing the role he is allotted as the vehicle of the transparently dual or multiple presentation of reality which irony requires. This implicit contradiction becomes manifest if the plot re-

quires that the *persona* not only be lifelike, but actually come
to life and be changed by his experiences, just like a real person
or a character in a novel; and I believe that it is this which has
caused the climax of Swift's career as an ironist—the Fourth
Part of *Gulliver*—to tease two centuries of critics: an ironical
fate, be it added, for a writer whose main literary intention
was the enforcement of truths which he believed to be universally available to the common sense of mankind.

I cannot even begin to consider the complex problems which
arise when you have several *personae* engaged in ironic counterpoint, as in *Gulliver's Travels;* nor am I proposing here yet
another solution to the problems offered by the Fourth Part;
I wish only to suggest that such a solution must take account,
not only of the inherent contradictions between the functions
of the ironic *persona* and the fully developed literary character,
but also of the philosophical problem which underlies it—how
to handle the individual-class dichotomy.

One modern tendency in Swift criticism has been to articu-
late the hypothesis of a progressive ironical structure in *Gulliver's Travels* by tracing the developing sequence of the hero's
reactions to his experiences. It seems to me that there are many
difficulties in doing this. Theoretically, for example, it depends
upon the premise that you can have flat and round, static and
developing ironic *personae,* just as you do characters in a novel;
and Part Four seems to me to present undeniable evidence that
the possibilities of combining the effects of character and *persona* are strictly limited; that as readers we cannot, in fact,
maintain the separation between the pretended ironic *persona,*
and the actual suffering person. Swift, I have little doubt, merely
intended Gulliver to exhibit a climactic reaction to a never-
before-glimpsed vision of the squalors of passion—the Yahoos,—
and the splendors of reason—the Houyhnhnms: and the blind-
ing brightness of the vision was to be brought home by making
his *persona* end his days in a comically hyperbolic revulsion

from the actual human scene. But—in the very process of shattering the complacency of the dullest reader—Swift's narrative genius gave the episode a psychological reality so deeply disturbing that many initiated readers find it difficult not to allow their gaze to be deflected from the relentless intellectual pressure of Swift's ironic tenor to the pathos of the fate of its literary vehicle; in so far as Swift made Gulliver convincing as a character, our possession of his logical meaning was necessarily disturbed by our sorrow that a fellow human being, who had, after all, no harm in him, should, as the fruit of his labors in life, have become a candidate for the madhouse.

The duality of *persona-character* is essentially the special case in the field of ironical narrative of the general problem of the duality of general and individual, which is the topic of Swift's famous letter to Pope about *Gulliver's Travels:*

I have ever hated all nations, professions and communities, and all my love is toward individuals; for instance, I hate the tribe of lawyers, but I love Counsellor Such-a-one and Judge Such-a-one; so with physicians— I will not speak of my own trade—soldiers, English, Scotch, French, and the rest. But principally I hate and detest that animal called man, although I heartily love John, Peter, Thomas, and so forth. This is the system upon which I have governed myself many years.

I must confess that, as a commentary on *Gulliver's Travels,* I do not find this by any means self-explanatory or unambiguous. I can share Swift's general feeling only too well; but, at the risk of calling down very varied thunders on my head, I must confess that, judged as a statement of "system" or set of correlated principles, I find the passage hyperbolic, if not ultimately illogical; while as a gloss, I find it mainly helpful as an example of a confusion which rather closely parallels that which I find in Swift's handling of his *persona* in the Fourth Part.

Briefly, Swift seems to be qualifying the blank misanthropy of his preceding assertion that "the chief end I propose to myself in all my labours is to vex the world rather than divert it" by explaining that his reaction to man in his collective aspect is the complete opposite of his reaction to man in his individual aspect. But since the common qualities of "John, Peter, Thomas, and so forth" constitute whatever may be denoted by the collective term "man," it is surely to invert the fallacy of the class to assume that there can actually be any total contradiction between them. It follows, then, that the whole force of Swift's distinction must lie, not in the existent, objective properties of the individual and the group, but in the different ways they are regarded; it is, in fact, all a matter of two opposite ways of looking at what is ultimately the same thing.

This seems to offer a suggestive parallel to the analogous shift in the way we see Gulliver: mainly, and most of the time, he is an ironical *persona*, essentially a general representative of man collectively considered: but in the Fourth Part he becomes man individually considered, with a particular wife and a particular problem; and our feelings change, if not from hate to love as in Swift's letter, at least from amused detachment to a much closer emotional involvement.

Swift's letter seems to me to support this interpretation in another way: for, just as it suggests a tendency—and not, I think, in the interests of paradox alone—to make the dichotomy of the individual and the general more total than it can actually be, so it also exhibits a certain lack of discrimination between the different ways we address ourselves to philosophical and to human objects. Swift's basic paradox depends for its effect on making the words "love" and "hate" antithetic: and so, indeed, they normally are, except perhaps in the abysses of the unconscious. But in the context of the letter, they are antithetic in direction but not in degree, because they apply to rather different levels of feeling: the "hate" that Swift bears to all collectivities must surely be a somewhat abstract, philosophical kind of aversion, since it is directed to an entity which does not exist except in the mind: while the "love" he bears to the individual members of the species is presumably much closer to the realm of passion and emotion, closer to what we normally mean by "love," although it is surely still hyperbolic to talk of love when the circumstances can at best allow a general disposition to be benevolent.

The hyperbole in the use of "love," it is true, disappears if we read "I heartily love John, Peter, Thomas, and so forth" as meaning a finite listing of Swift's actual friends, rather than as an infinite series of individuals considered as such, which the paradox requires for its maximum force: but there remains a lesser hyperbole in the antithetic collocation of *"love"*—of particulars—and *"hate"*—of collectivities; and this alone tends to confirm my previous suggestion about *Gulliver's Travels*. If Swift was prone to apply the same emotional terms to abstract ideas as are applied by most people only to their feelings towards a few individual persons, he may not have foreseen what would happen when, in the Fourth Part, he involved Gulliver for the first time in situations which, though intended to represent abstract issues, were actually such as to provoke intense emotional participation, rather than cool and rational observation, in his readers. For the same reason Swift may not have seen how his erstwhile *persona* had become a character, and thus lost the element of distance from the reader, which is so essential to the *persona*'s ironic function: may not even have noticed how his puppet Lemuel had turned into a human being, and, just as he was being hustled off the stage, observed on his own behalf that irony could be cruel.

Ultimately, I suppose, the problem of the *persona* in relation to the individual-general dichotomy is connected with Swift's whole conception of irony as a weapon against the mob, which is after all a pejorative way of looking at man in general. But I have no time to pursue this, nor to consider whether there is not an ultimate contradiction between this steady animus against collectivities, and Swift's neo-classical preference for the general rather than the particular, of which the ironical mode is perhaps the central literary expression.

The tension between Gulliver as *persona* and Gulliver as individual character also looks forward. We can perhaps see in it how an age which did not find the lyric or dramatic modes wholly congenial was naturally tending towards a fuller realization of the individual character than either the ironic *persona,* or the neo-classical preference for the general as opposed to the individual, would allow: was tending, in fact, to the novel. This again, is too large a topic to be developed here; but one of its aspects—the problem of how the experiences of man individually considered could find literary expression in an age whose operative critical assumptions were towards general truth—cannot be avoided, since it is closely related to a new tendency in the ironic tradition which is characteristic of the succeeding period: the development, that is, of Romantic Irony.

IV

To a writer wholly given over to the cultivated complicity in human pettiness which the consciously ironic perspective requires, the subjective world of feeling, and even what Wordsworth called "the primary affections and duties"—these will seem meager and unimportant. Such a writer will tend to see himself and his affections ironically, and write—with Gibbon— "I sighed as a lover, I obeyed as a son." The abstractions, the conventional roles, the mighty framework for the eternal littleness of man—they surely damp our resolution to live our own lives. Mr. and Mrs. Gibbon, I fancy, found little more satisfaction in their son than Mademoiselle Susan Curchod in her lover. I observe in passing that the greatest eighteenth-century ironists—Swift, Pope, Hume, and Gibbon—were all bachelors.

We can, of course, pretend to make the best of the void, and take *Vive la Bagatelle* as our motto—*faute de mieux*. But, in Swift at least, we are aware that he has settled for long walks and dirty poems, not out of weakness, but out of an honest conviction that the possible alternative would be wrong, would be unworthy of a human being. Have no fear: I will proceed no further in speculative biography: my intention is only to suggest one explanation of Swift's attitude, and this only because I think it throws some light on the development of romantic irony.

The explanation, I think, lies in what I see as the basic schism in neo-classicism, the antithesis of reason and passion. Not, of course, that the opposition is by any means peculiar to it; but it became particularly influential when it was combined with the generalizing and antithetical mode of thought which is so characteristic of the Augustan period. The problem is a complex one, and particularly so in Swift: but the Fourth Part surely suggests that the later Swift accepted the reason-passion antithesis hook, line and sinker, especially sinker: all allowances made for the needs of dramatic heightening, there is surely nothing else in human thought which equals the violence and the starkness of the dichotomy of Yahoo and Houyhnhnm. There is a similar completeness and a barely less unconcealed violence in the opposition between Reason and Passion in one of the most familiar of Swift's "Thoughts on Religion":

Although Reason were intended by Providence to govern our Passions, yet it seems that, in two Points of the greatest Moment to the Being and Continuance of the World, God hath intended our Passions to prevail over Reason. The first is, the Propagation of our Species, since no wise Man ever married from the Dictates of Reason. The other is, the Love of Life, which, from Dictates of Reason, every Man would despise and wish at an End, or that it never had a Beginning.

The antithetical mode of thought made absolute excludes the mixed motives of actuality; the literal and absolute attitude to words dictates that "govern our Passions" should mean, not—as was traditional—adjudicate or balance or restrain them, but annihilate them: such are the logical confusions we must accept before we allow ourselves to be overwhelmed by the specious

finality of Swift's paradox. It would surely be better to apply
to the passage the words of the Russian poet Alexander Blok:
"In the vodka of irony the mocker drowns his hope along with
his despair." Poised between the squalors of passion and the
inoperancy of reason Swift sat so long on the fence that the irony
entered into his . . . soul.

After Swift the problem of how the writer should speak of
himself and deal with the life of the emotions came to the forefront of literary interest. There was, of course, Sentimentalism:
of which I will say nothing except that the reigning habit of
reifying abstractions and speaking of them with cool elegance
makes it difficult not to read the most ardent professions of love
or benevolence without smiling. Henry Brooke's *The Fool of
Quality,* and Mackenzie's *Man of Feeling,* to a modern reader
at least, overflow, not with tears, but with unconscious irony.

The great eighteenth-century novelists—of course—make the
individual and his feelings their central subject: and this, on
the whole, meant excluding the ironic *persona,* though not, of
course, irony. Here—until we get to Sterne—Fielding's *Jonathan Wild* is perhaps the most interesting work, because it is
so curious a mixture of genres: in the satirical part, about the
"Great Man" (no one in the eighteenth century seems to have
spoken about great men or heroes without irony), we find an
undeviating maintenance of the double role very similar to
that in Swift: but the sentimental part, centering on the Heart-
frees, seems to be open to objections very similar to those against
the sentimentalists proper: the abstract vocabulary makes the
whole thing unreal, especially when the reader carries over to
the pathetic part, as he cannot but do, the habit of ironical interpretation in which the satirical part has set him.

The two attitudes—sentiment and satirical irony—come together more convincingly in Sterne, and we get the new kind of
irony, romantic irony. There is neither time nor need to describe

the complexities of romantic irony: for, whether we are thinking of Byron or the German Romantics, and whether or not
we can follow Friedrich Schlegel, any conception of the idea
must include the two points which, I have been trying to argue,
the developing tradition of irony had brought to the forefront.
Romantic irony, that is, always involves the writer himself,
and his attitude both to the world and to his creation; and it is
subjective in another sense, because it usually involves the writer
in an internal counterpoint between his feeling and his reason:
"hot baths of sentiment followed by cold douches of irony,"
as Jean Paul said.

Sterne was accepted as a great forerunner of romantic irony
by Tieck, Schlegel and others; he is, of course, continuously
ironic about what he is writing. In itself, this is often only a
continuation of the "Cervantick manner," although of course
Sterne pays ironical lipservice to the Augustan impersonality
by pretending that it is not he, but Tristram, his character—or
is he no more than a *persona?*—who is addressing us. More
significant for our purposes is Sterne's treatment of sentiment,
the unrestrained expressions of feeling suddenly terminated
by a deft rational undermining: to take the most famous case—
Le Fever's death—we have:

> The pulse fluttered—stopp'd—went on—throb'd—
> stopp'd again—moved—stopp'd—shall I go on?—No.

It is interesting, I think, to see how this ironic mode was
foreshadowed. Something very like it is found in Swift's private
letters—especially in the *Journal to Stella,* with its playful yet
tender central relationship. The reason, I think, is obvious. The
private letter was largely free from the inhibitions on the expression of personal and emotional feelings which neo-classical
literary decorum, and the dichotomy of reason and passion, im-
posed on public discourse. Nevertheless, their effects were felt,
because, in the last analysis the inner life, unsupported by the

main orientations of eighteenth-century culture, seemed to lack any authorized standing; it was difficult to know how to assess its importance, and so its expression—even in letters to close personal friends—tended to be rounded off by a gesture of depreciation or apology, a closing obeisance to rationality.

Gray, for example, is habitually ironical about his own most real interests as a man and a poet. In one letter, to Thomas Warton the Younger, after giving vent to his enthusiasm for Ossian, he expresses the fear that "you will think I am grown mighty poetical of a sudden." In another somewhat similar passage we are given, in addition, an insight into the prosaic conception of prose, the sense that it was not the proper vehicle of feeling, which did so much to lead eighteenth-century writers into their ironical manner: Gray is ending a long description of the Kentish landscape to Norton Nicholls:

In the east the sea breaks in upon you, & mixes its white transient sails & glittering blew expanse with the deeper & brighter greens of the woods & corn. this last sentence is so fine I am quite ashamed. but no matter you must translate it into prose.

When Horace Walpole describes his enthusiasms there is usually a similarly ironical concluding evaluation of them: as when, for example, after revisiting Houghton after sixteen years, the thought of his father's death, and the dubious future of his great mansion, make him ask:

For what has he built Houghton? For his grandson to annihilate, or for his son to mourn over! If Lord Burleigh could rise and view his representative driving the Hatfield stage, he would feel as I feel now—poor little Strawberry! at least it will not be snipped to pieces by a descendant!—You will think all these fine meditations dictated by pride, not by philosophy—pray consider, through how many mediums philosophy must pass, before it is purified.

There is a more complex kind of ironic wisdom here, as indeed in many of Walpole's letters, and in those of several other writers of the period: but the point has by now been established that it is in the private writing of the eighteenth century that we get the most direct expression of personal feeling; and that even there it is frequently qualified by a persistent irony of tone, which brings it very close to what was later to be called romantic irony. Horace Walpole, indeed, almost foreshadowed the term itself when, after an enthusiastic description of the Grande Chartreuse to Richard West, he stopped short, fearing that he must sound "too bombast and too romantic."

V

I come, finally, to a great exception, as I believe, to much of what I have been saying: to Dr. Johnson. One may not think of him primarily as an ironist, but his pre-eminence among the eighteenth-century prose writers can perhaps be illuminated by a glance at his position in the tradition of irony.

In it, he and Swift, of course, are the mighty opposites, although they at least start from similar positions: from Christianity and a deep pessimism about human life. After a discussion of man's natural goodness, Lady Mcleod accused Dr. Johnson of being "worse than Swift"; and if in the *Tale of a Tub,* Swift had called happiness "the sublime and refined Point of Felicity, called *the Possession of being well deceived;* The Serene Peaceful State of being a Fool among Knaves," Johnson so little liked "any one who said they were happy" that when on one occasion his judgment was challenged, he thundered: "I tell you, the woman is ugly, and sickly, and foolish, and poor; and would it not make a man hang himself to hear such a creature say, it was happy?"

The tone of Johnson's retort points to the distinguishing feature of his irony: it usually operates through fairly conscious hyperbole, and this in itself humanizes it by breaking with the decorous impersonality which was so important a part of Augustan irony; Johnson brings himself—his own anger, not to say unhappiness—into the irony: he is not outside the ironic contradiction of attitudes but within it: he knows and relishes the folly of his own hyperbolic impatience, and this qualifies what might otherwise appear to be an assertion of his own superiority to the wishful deceptions of fallible humanity.

Bringing himself into the ironic contradiction of attitudes was easy enough for Johnson—was indeed inevitable—when he was merely being reported by Boswell, or, as in the present case, by Mrs. Thrale; but Johnson locates himself within his ironic vision almost as consistently in his writings for publication. The letter to Lord Chesterfield one might call half public; and there we notice how the brilliance of his ironies at Chesterfield's expense is qualified, humanized, by the confession of his own earlier personal humiliation: "no man is well pleased to have his all neglected, be it ever so little."

In Johnson's published works, in the *Lives of the Poets,* and *The Rambler,* for instance, we have the same refusal to locate himself permanently on the Parnassian eminence, above and beyond the mob, from which Swift and Pope had looked down. This I know is contrary to the opinions of those who see Johnson's magniloquence as arrogant and impersonal. It is, in a sense, both, but we may perhaps change T. S. Eliot's phrase about Donne and say that Johnson could be as personal as he pleased because he could be as impersonal as he pleased: he could introduce his own experience and his own mixed and fallible human nature into his public prose without any violation of classical decorum, because his perspective on himself and on the world was broad enough and impersonal enough to avoid any deflection of our attention from the subject to the personality involved in it.

As an example of this, perhaps the famous passage about Shenstone's gardening will serve:

Whether to plant a walk in undulating curves, and to place a bench at every turn where there is an object to catch the view; to make water run where it will be heard, and to stagnate where it will be seen; to leave intervals where the eye will be pleased, and to thicken the plantation where there is something to be hidden, demands any great powers of mind, I will not enquire; perhaps a sullen and surly speculator may think such performances rather the sport than the business of human reason. But it must be at least confessed, that to embellish the form of Nature is an innocent amusement; and some praise must be allowed by the most supercilious observer to him, who does best what such multitudes are contending to do well.

Johnson's wish to be just does not let him go so far as to allow us to envisage for a moment that he will ever turn into the man with a hoe. But he does refuse to range the full force of his mind against Shenstone and the multitudes who are contending in the sports of human reason. Those who mock must remind themselves that they may be sullen, surly or supercilious; and that to set the just bounds of speculation is not easy. Johnson does not see the situation in the general terms of an elite and a misguided mob, but rather in terms of a very specific contrast of particular and equally human attitudes: in the present case, a degree of folly on the part of the doers is at least free of the charge of malignity which might be leveled at the seers and judgers: and so Johnson "rejoices to concur with the common reader"—with the mob—as far as he honestly can.

The Shenstone passage illustrates many other distinguishing features of Johnson's irony. There is the Ciceronian amplitude and ornament which also makes its contribution to the humanization of the irony. The very complication of the syntax is necessary to enable Johnson to re-enact all the gradations of attitude in the judging mind, and to allow of such incidental ironic felicities as "stagnate where it will be seen," where the formidable analytic power is shown easily constrained to a suitably comic antithesis—"stagnate," incidentally, is calculated to enlist the rich variety of sensory connotations which Swift tends to avoid. Later we have the more outright jeer of "thicken the plantation where there is something to be hidden," archly prepared for by the earlier portion of the antithesis "to leave intervals where the eye will be pleased"—we're already primed to congratulate ourselves at the trickery whereby Shenstone avoids "displeasing" the eye. The whole conception of prose, indeed, allows for the complex organization of a wider range of feeling and attitude than that of Swift, and its final ironical surprise— the placing of Shenstone above the multitudes—is in the direction of magnanimous allowance rather than of direct climactic derision.

The passage can, perhaps, not unfairly be compared with an equally famous passage in Swift—the judgment of the King of Brobdingnag: "I cannot but conclude the Bulk of your Natives to be the most pernicious Race of little odious Vermin that Nature ever suffered to crawl upon the Surface of the Earth." Swift here allows himself more latitude than usual for adjectival qualification: but it is only for steadier bringing home of the single rational judgment: the taxonomist, at first baffled, has at last found proper words; man is pernicious—harmful, but harmful, not as lions or natural catastrophes are, but as cockroaches are, or bedbugs. No complication of the verdict is allowed. I must confess that I find something obtrusive about the consistent clarity, the intense delimitation of intention, in Swift's prose: the tone, the words, the syntax, the logic—all are aseptic; all bespeak what Johnson characteristically called Swift's "oriental scrupulosity" about his ablutions. Isn't Swift, in short, a cook who cares so much for cleanliness that all his dishes taste of soap?

Several other general points about Johnson's irony must be made very briefly. First, he was a true sceptic: "prodigies are always seen in proportion as they are expected" surely rivals Hume in its serene repudiation of popular credulity. In a sense Johnson was even more sceptical about reason than the romantic ironists; after all, they assumed in their heart of hearts that reason was truer than feeling, even if it wasn't so nice. Johnson made no such *a priori* assumptions, and therefore avoided letting the dichotomizing habit, whether in the Swiftian or the romantic way, become his master: "I hope . . . that I have lived long enough in the world, to prevent me from expecting to find any action of which both the original motive and all the parts were good." All is mixed; one cannot merely present a system of erroneous or inadequate ideas and leave the reader to elicit the truth by working out the opposite *per contrarium* in the obvious ironical manner; the universe is not logical; it is certainly not disposed in an endless series of exact linear contradictions; and so to discern what is false or foolish will not in itself give us any grip on reality. Johnson never forgot this: if he uses antithetical polarities their status is provisional, exploratory, pragmatic; and his irony in general is the product of a continually fresh attempt to perceive and express the total setting of any perception; perhaps we can call it an open irony, as opposed to the more predetermined and closed dichotomies within which Swift tends to work.

For this open irony Johnson had the full, indeed the unequalled, possession of a truly philosophical analytic power that could embody itself in the unexpected but logically convincing metaphor as easily as in the intricately appropriate abstraction. Consider, for the first, the famous epigram on Gray: "He has a kind of strutting dignity and is tall by walking on tiptoe"; and for the second—the manipulation of the intricately appropriate abstraction—the passage in the "Life" where Johnson considers Swift's treatment of his domestics: "That he was disposed to do his servants good on important occasions is no great mitigation; benefaction can be but rare, and tyrannick peevishness is perpetual." Johnson enlists the full weight of abstraction and impersonality in his wounding judgment; but there is— to use Bronson's fine phrase—a "yeast of insobriety" behind "tyrannick peevishness" which makes us marvel at the powers that could both observe the phenomenon and make the expression fit the crime. The judgment, of course, is contrary to the apparent, the commonly accepted scale of values; but its subversive paradox gains total authority from the fine balance of the phrasing: "benefaction can be but rare, and tyrannick peevishness is perpetual."

Here, perhaps, we have the major ironical characteristic of Johnson's style: the almost continual contrast between the poised, philosophical assurance of the manner, and the "yeast of insobriety" which informs the matter: while the grand generality of the manner functions as the hallmark of Johnson's public *persona,* the matter reveals a deep commitment to the particularities of a personal vision of reality; and somewhere within the dichotomy reason and passion are made one.

I cannot get any further in defining Johnson's irony. The *Life of Pope,* for example, does no more than set before us the infinite disparities and discontinuities of an individual life, and then place them in a larger context of generalization: but it is done so justly that we are continually moved to a rapture of assent. The irony, I suppose, is of the kind which has no special label but with which modern criticism has been most concerned: it demonstrates nothing, because it finds that it cannot truly do more than enlist all the resources of experience, understanding, and art, to create a dispassionate image of the endless incongruities which seem to be the condition of life in this vale of tears, and which are, I do not doubt, the most truly universal norms in what the eighteenth century called Nature.

IX

Defoe's Use of Irony

By MAXIMILLIAN E. NOVAK

I N AN INTRODUCTION to a recent anthology of Defoe's writings, Professor James T. Boulton argues that Defoe's style "makes no provision for irony" because Defoe expected that all readers of "normal intelligence should respond in the same manner with one another." Since Professor Boulton's comments are representative of a school of thought on Defoe, it is worth considering what he has to say on the subject. He continues:

To write ironically with success a writer needs to be alert to two audiences: those who will recognize the ironic intention and enjoy the joke, and those who are the object of the satire and are deceived by it. This implies that the ironist has ranged himself with those of his readers who share his superior values, intelligence and literary sensibility; together they look down on the benighted mob. This vantage point Defoe did not share. His Dissenting background engaged his sympathies with those who, on the political and social planes, were struggling to assert their rights, rather than with those whose struggle was to maintain an inherited position and traditional privileges. His education at Revd. Charles Morton's Dissenting Academy, with its emphasis on the vernacular and modern languages, mathematics, geography, and similar subjects with a practical, cash value, cut him off from the classical tradition instinctively assumed by the Tory satirists. . . . Defoe, then, wrote "to serve the World" not through any superior amusement shared with the Pharisee, but through informing, cajoling, and generally educating the Scribes.

In taking this attitude toward Defoe, Professor Boulton firmly aligns himself with John F. Ross, Ian Watt and Martin Price and against critics like Dorothy Van Ghent, Arnold Kettle and all of Defoe's biographers. Yet, several pages after the above pas-

189

sage, Professor Boulton refers to an "ironic remark" by Defoe. Surely there is a confusion here both in the nature of irony and in the character of Defoe.

Professor Boulton quotes Defoe's insistence on plainness, honesty and simplicity in writing, on convincing everyone by the truth of the subject framed in unadorned prose. He apparently believes that Defoe was basically a plain, sincere man, and though he remarks on Defoe's brilliant handling of rhetoric, he says little about the use to which this rhetoric was put.

I want in this paper to do three things: to take up the question of Defoe's character in relation to that of the ironist, to examine some examples of Defoe's irony, and to discriminate between techniques which are entirely ironic and those devices of fiction, paradox, parody and satire which may be part of an ironic work but which may also exist independently. What I would suggest is that the image of simple, honest Daniel Defoe, the plain speaker and stylist—an image which he frequently tried to palm off on his disbelieving contemporaries—should be replaced by that of Defoe the ironist.

Perhaps it would be best for this purpose to consider what Defoe's contemporaries thought of him, but first one might begin with a rather typical situation in Defoe's career. At the end of 1704 he began writing for a biweekly journal called *The London Post*. One of his first innovations was to introduce a dialogue between Truth and Honesty, somewhat in the manner of Bunyan. It was a rhetorical mask which Defoe must have found congenial, but in the issue of January 1, 1705, Honesty asks for a definition of Truth and receives the following reply from his companion: "Speaking *Truth* sometimes may do Mischief, concealing the Truth till a proper Occasion of telling it may be of great Advantage to the Cause of *Truth,* and telling of it before such a time may be of great Damage. But we ought to consider *Truth* in Opposition to *Falsehood,* the Particular Circumstances of the Case and the Necessity of Speaking the Truth." To this

Honesty replies by saying, "This is a meer Paradox." Yet Defoe had written almost the same thing to his patron, Robert Harley, a few months before:

Tho' This Part of Conduct is call'd Dissimulacion, I am Content it shall be Call'd what they will. But as a Lye does not Consist in the Indirect Position of Words, but in the Design by False Speaking, to Deciev and Injure my Neighbour, So Dissembling does not Consist in Putting a Different Face upon our Accons, but in the further Applying That Concealment to the Prejudice of the Person; for Example, I come into a persons Chamber, who on Surprize is apt to Fall into Dangerous Convulsions. I Come in Smiling and Pleasant and ask the Person to Rise and go abroad, or any other Such question, and Press him to it Till I Prevail. Whereas the Truth is I have Discovered the House to be on Fire, and I act this for Fear of frighting him. Will any Man Tax me with Hypocrisy and Dissimulacion?

The answer to Defoe's question was, as we shall see ... yes. And so, when accused of being a creation of the pen of Daniel Defoe, Truth and Honesty denied it vehemently, lamenting that anyone could believe such a lie. Every pamphlet, every paper that appears signed Truth and Honesty "must be the *Devil* or *Daniel De Foe.*" The choice presented no contradiction to Defoe's contemporaries, for so far from thinking Defoe the plain, simple, honest spokesman that he so often pretended to be, they often regarded him as a satanic imp, even more malicious than he was mischievous. They thought that if there was any fire in England's house, he would probably be the incendiary who lit it.

In a cartoon entitled *The Whig's Medly,* published in 1711, Defoe is shown with the Devil on one side and the Pope on the other; in his right hand he holds a seditious book. Surrounding the central picture is a portrait of Cromwell, a grotesque caricature of Defoe in the pillory, and two playing cards: the knaves of hearts and clubs. Underneath is the caption:

Here's Daniel, the Pope, and the Devil well match'd,
By whose Crafty Inventions all mischief is hatch'd:

> In Deceiving poor Creatures their chief Talent lies,
> Although to us Mortals they'd seem otherwise.
> From crafty deceivers, Good Lord, set us free,
> And keep us secure from the snares of these *Three*.

Though Defoe wrote one pamphlet in which he assumed the mask of the Pope, in his own time he was usually associated with the Devil, whose history he was to write in 1726. Of course, he was also accused of being a mercenary scribbler, a sophist and a Proteus. As one writer put it neatly: "His Papers contain malicious Insinuations, and false Suggestions, he is a Man of great Rashness and Impudence, a mear Mercenary Prostitute, a State Mountebank, an Hackney Tool, a scandalous Pen, a foul-Mouthed Mongrel, an Author who writes for Bread, and lives by Defamation...," but almost everyone felt there was an independent streak of pure evil in him beyond adherence to party or even money—a pleasure in sowing confusion in the forces of friend and enemy alike. One contemporary saw him as an arch-hypocrite:

> With up-lift Eyes, and with ambitious Heart,
> On England's Theatre to act his Part.
> How well he acted, witness ye that saw,
> How wrestling Gospel, and provoking Law!
> A true Malignant, Arrogant and Sour,
> And ever Snarling at establish'd Pow'r;
> More Famous for Ill-Nature than for Wit,
> And like a Bull-dog lik'd, because he bit.

The author of the *Female Critick* (1701) puzzled over Defoe's motivation in writing *The True-Born Englishman*. "But the Riddle is," she wrote, "Whom was this Poem calculated to please?... It can only please the Rakes of all Parties: They may dote on such a Champion against Religion and all good Manners, as also the Devil, their Instigator, to whose Protection I commit you."

After the appearance of *The Shortest Way with the Dissenters* at the end of 1702, the chorus of criticism grew. Defoe's real gift, remarked the writer of *The Shortest-Way with Whores and Rogues* (1703) was "a [matchless] Talent at Personal-Slandering." Defoe is an "Incendiary," cried another, and deserves a brutal punishment, the kind given to a "Man that makes it his Practices to stir up Divisions, and sow the seeds of Dissention." The Devil must have inspired him, wrote the author of *The Reformer Reformed,* while Mary Astell accused him of being a follower of Hobbes.

With the appearance of the *Review* in 1703, Defoe's critics found more to confirm their opinion. The author of *Remarks on the Review* (1706) launched upon a full interpretation of Defoe's satanic character:

There are some Spirits so Malignant, that to have done any thing conducive to Good, gives them the highest Chagrin; and they are never at rest, till by some Counter-act they return to their Aversion of Well-doing. I think Mr. *Review* to be a lively Instance of this Assertion ... No wonder that Lying spirit he possesseth should also Inspire him with so Inveterate a Rooted Malice against the Church, 'tis not enough for him to Sconce himself behind High Church like a Stalking-horse; for 'tis plain he has an Inbred Spleen against all Churches, by his Ridiculing all Preachers as Actors, and saying, that all Preaching is Theatrical, and a Trade for Money; and puts them on the same Foot with the Stage.

But for Defoe, "a Spirit Implacable, Turbulent and Devilish," he continues, it would be a time of peace and happiness, and he concludes by suggesting that Defoe will probably join with the "Pope or Turk," since he must be acting as an agent for one of them.

After the publication of *Jure Divino* (1706), Defoe's somewhat anarchistic attack upon the divine right of kings, there appeared *Jure Divino Toss'd in a Blanket,* associating Defoe

with those men "Of the first Rebel Lucifer's Black Stamp" who
support the mob:

> A hopeful Doctrine, drawn no doubt from Hell,
> To teach a stubborn People to Rebel;
> Which that there may be useful Rogues to prop,
> Such as *De Foe* the Devil conjures up.

One critic was at least charitable enough to assume that Defoe
might have been moved by the Devil unconsciously. *The Shortest Way with the Dissenters,* wrote the author of *The Review
and Observator Review'd* (1706) "hath in it self (I mean the
Design of it) the very Spirit of Lucifer, for no doubt but your
Intentions rambled far beyond your Pen, and in that Letter, as
we say of the Watermen, you look'd one way, and row'd another." But whatever the inspiration, he continued, it was "one
of the most devilish Designs that ever was heard of ... So you
begat an Imp upon Lucifer, and the Church of England must
have stood Father to it." The author of *The Moderation, Justice
and Manners of the Review* (1706) described him as one of those
writers "whose Throats are a burning Abyss, a Center of envious
Exhalations, set on fire of Hell."

As time passed, the idea that Defoe was a malicious spirit
began to be replaced by the image of a Proteus writing for all
sides; yet the author of *Remarks on the Letter to the Dissenters,*
written in 1714, repeated the older legend. Defoe, he wrote, was
set on "as 'tis said Conjurors set Devils to work. ... If he was but
an Honest Man," this writer remarked, "no matter whether or
no he was a Scholar; and if he wanted no Veracity, there is no
body you'd accuse him for his want of *Wit*. The Craft he so
much values himself upon might pass for it, were it not that
wicked Craft which deceiv'd our Mother Eve; and without
Redemption, wou'd have damn'd her whole Posterity."

The remark on Defoe's wit is significant, for although some
claimed he had a mere "Jack-Pudding Wit," others could not

understand why, given this wit, he should write the kind of
work which brought him into trouble:

> As Quacks for Pence, and Praises from the Mob,
> Their Legs and Arms with seeming Pleasure Stab;
> So how, (and yet I own thy Wit) D. F.—
> Such a ridiculous Animal art thou.
> Else why so fond, like Bessus in the Play
> To study thy own Kicking ev'ry Day?

If one did not accept the idea that Defoe was a malicious spirit,
the explanation of demagoguery and avarice seemed insufficient
to explain his efforts to stir up the country on political, social and
religious issues. Defoe's personality, then, was a puzzle to his
contemporaries. They did not regard him as a simple or an easy
writer, but as a man who revelled in paradox, deceit and uncom-
fortable truths. And Defoe did not always present himself as a
man of simple honesty or as a simple stylist. Even in the *Review,*
where he advocated putting "plain Things, in a plain Form," he
remarked that a good style must "touch the Reader, surprize his
Fancy, and fire his Imagination." In *The London Post,* Truth
and Honesty agreed that he was a far better writer than John
Tutchin of the rival *Observator:* "He does not directly Thunder,
Roar and Bellow, as t'other does, but he's damnable sly and Cut-
ting by the way of Innuendo, and Retort, calls as many Rogues
by Craft as t'other does in Courser Terms." Professor Boulton is
correct in arguing that Defoe did not belong to the Augustan
circle of wits who could feel superior to the masses by their learning, but Defoe had an answer to that. In his *Vindication of the
Press* (1718), he showed a singular lack of modesty about his
gifts. "The preference of Genius to Learning," wrote Defoe, "is
sufficiently Demonstrated in the Writings of the Author of The
True born English Man; (a Poem that has Sold beyond the best
Performance of any Ancient or Modern Poet of the greatest Ex-
cellency, and perhaps beyond any Poetry ever Printed in the

English Language) This Author is Characteriz'd as a Person
of little Learning, but of prodigious Natural Parts; and the immortal *Shakespear* had but a small share of Literature." Defoe's
irony proceeds from a "Self-conceit" which irritated many of
his contemporaries. One writer allowed himself some irony on
this subject:

> Let banter cease, and Poetasters yield,
> Since fam'd *De Foe* is Master of the Field.
> What none can comprehend, he understands:
> And what's not understood, his Fame Commands
> This Mighty Bard, more mighty in Invention,
> And most of all in humble Condescension.

Swift found Defoe's "mock authoritative Manner" irritating and
said that he was "so grave, sententious, dogmatical a rogue, that
there is no enduring him."

In the debate over the occasional conformity of Dissenters,
Defoe took up a minority position with full confidence. "He
that Opposes his own Judgment against the Current of the
Times," he wrote in his *Enquiry into Occasional Conformity*
(1702), "ought to be back'd with unanswerable Truths; and he
that has that Truth on his Side, is a Fool, as well as a Coward, if
he is afraid to own it, because of the Currency or Multitude of
other Men's Opinions: So to me 'tis every jot as wonderful to find
no Body of my Mind, and yet be Positively assured that I am in
the Right.... 'Tis hard for a Man to say, all the World is mistaken but himself; but if it be so, who can help it." It was all very
well for Defoe to dedicate his lengthy poem *Jure Divino* to the
Empress of Reason, but many of his contemporaries thought that
Defoe gave himself airs of being the only trueborn rational
citizen in her empire. Defoe probably deliberately dedicated his
poem to reason rather than to truth, for while he sometimes
vindicated himself as being ever on the side of truth, there were
occasions when he was hard put to defend this. But his gift for

creating a reasonable and convincing argument, even in a bad cause, he never denied.

Part of the problem lies with reading Defoe without considering whom he is addressing and why. In the *Review* and *The Compleat English Tradesman,* he defended clarity as the ideal for prose; in other places, he defended oblique methods of irony and fable. It seems to me that a mistake is also made about Defoe's audience. Pamphlets he wrote for the ministry or works like *The Secret History of the White Staff* (1714) were read by anyone interested in politics, just as *Robinson Crusoe* was read by Pope and Swift as well as by Charles Gildon's common denominator, the "old woman" who leaves it as an heirloom to her children. Even the *Review,* which was deliberately aimed at the Dissenters and those interested in trade, had a wide enough audience for Swift to complain that it "was grown a necessary part of coffee-house furniture." Swift also lamented the tendency of party writers to assume that "the common People understand *Raillery* or at least *Rhetorick;* and will not take *Hyperboles* in too literal a Sense." Such an attitude, he argued, "might prove a desperate Experiment." Defoe justified the repetitions in the *Review* by arguing that he wanted to reach even the "meanest Understanding," but he must have known that his ironic tracts would puzzle a large section of his readers. An optimist at heart, he probably underestimated the number.

In the case of *The Shortest Way with the Dissenters,* he turned directly against his audience and accused them of stupidity, mockingly regretting that he did not, like the proverbial bad Dutch artist, label his picture of a man and a bear: "This is the Man and This is the Bear." "I confess," he wrote, "I did not foresee an occasion for this, and having in Compliment to their Judgments shunn'd so sharp a Reflection upon their Senses, I left them at Liberty to treat me like one that put a Value upon their Penetration at the Expence of my own." And when he was jailed in 1713 for three ironic tracts, he argued that what he had done

was to use the most powerful of all rhetorical weapons to attack
the Pretender and his plans to assume the throne of England.
After noting the accusations against him, he defends his arguments as irony:

The Books I have written are as plain a Satyr upon the Pretender
and his Friends, as can be written, if they are view'd Impartially;
but being written Ironically, all the first Part, if taken asunder from
the last Part, will read, *as in all Ironical speaking must be,* just contrary: But taken complexly, taken Whole, and of a Piece, can leave
no room to doubt, but that they are written to Ridicule and expose
the very Notions of bringing in the Pretender....But if what I have
written be the strongest Irony, and consequently the greatest push
that I could make against the Pretender's Interest, then this Prosecution must be Malicious and Abominable. Nor is this Irony concealed,
as has been suggested formerly; but it is express'd plainly, and
explicitly, in words at length.

Irony, then, was "the greatest push" of rhetoric for making a
point, and Defoe, like his own Jonathan Wild, never allowed
the tools of his trade to grow rusty for want of use. Hardly a
year went by in which Defoe did not write a work of extended
irony, and, like Swift, he tended to drop ironic remarks with
surprising suddenness, though without the effectiveness of
Swift's bare style to give the irony added point. So far is *The
Shortest Way with the Dissenters* from being his only work of
irony, as some critics claim before dismissing it as fiction, that
one can observe Defoe employing different ironic effects
throughout his career and refusing to abandon the trope even
after being pilloried for it.

Defoe's intelligence ranged over a wide field of subjects,
where his mind found that kind of disparity between theory and
action, between ideals and practices, between reason and passion
that brought forth his ironies. In religion, he saw the High
Church practicing an unchristian persecution of the Dissenters,
and the Dissenters violating their own consciences by occasional

conformity in the Church of England. In politics, he saw a part
of the nation, which had asked King William to save them and
their country, pretend to regret the loss of James II and long
for his return—a country which had rebelled to assert the right
of parliament and the people to choose their own king and
which insisted on swearing oaths of absolute obedience to Queen
Anne and vowing her hereditary right to the throne. In social
and economic matters, he saw a society which starved the most
useful members (the poor laborers and sailors) and punished
the most enterprising of them (the thieves and pirates), when
many of the magistrates lived in vice and grew rich on a capital-
ism that seemed to Defoe less honest than robbery.

As Norman Knox has shown in his excellent *The Word Irony
and Its Contexts 1500–1755,* the term *irony* might indicate anything from simple deceit to the complex methods of dramatic
irony employed by Swift. The only rhetoricians Defoe quotes
are Quintilian and Gerardus Vossius, and it is to the latter that
we might turn to have some idea of what Defoe meant by irony.
Vossius admits that the word might be used to describe an attitude such as that assumed by Socrates, but he dismisses this as
having little to do with rhetoric; irony is not simple dissimula-
tion, nor mere trickery or sophistry. He quotes Fabius on the
point that "Irony is understood either by the tone of voice, or
by the character of the person speaking, or by the situation. For
if any of those is discordant with the words, it is apparent that
the meaning of the utterance is the opposite." After discussing
the difficulty of detecting irony and rehearsing various passages
in dispute, Vossius warns against seeing irony where none exists
or "where there is irony, taking the words literally" and notes
that "even the greatest men are deceived in this direction." He
finally settles for the only definition possible: "Irony is where
the opposite is understood to what is said."

Irony is evident in some of Defoe's early titles. *The True-Born
Englishman* turns on the irony of the English insulting William

by insisting that the army be composed entirely of "his Majesty's natural born subjects," and continually affronting the Dutch. Much of this poem is invective satire, but the overriding trope is irony, as in the following passage:

> The Civil Wars, the common Purgative,
> Which always use to make the Nation thrive,
> Made way for all that strolling Congregation,
> Which thronged in Pious Ch----s's Restoration.
> The Royal Refugee our Breed restores,
> With Foreign Courtiers, and with Foreign Whores:
> And Carefully repeopled us again,
> Throughout his Lazy, Long, Lascivious Reign;
> With such a blest and True-born English Fry,
> As much Illustrates our Nobility.

Defoe begins with a paradox of the kind that Mandeville was fond of. The metaphor is deliberately burlesque and the aim is to shock a nation which still went into national mourning every January 30 for the beheading of Charles I. Defoe then slips into irony through a series of deliberate religious comparisons with what he regarded as a group of foreign rakes and whores. Pious Charles is pictured as "carefully" contributing to the choice stock of the English by adding to the nobility his illegitimate children; heavy alliteration underscores the point skillfully. The anger which greeted Defoe's attack on Tutchin's *The Foreigners* was not merely directed against what was regarded as an insult to the ancestry of Englishmen. Defoe's political and social attitudes were anti-aristocratic and representative of the far left of the Whigs. Those who replied were sure that Defoe was a foreigner, perhaps Dutch, perhaps Irish, and one writer was sure that it was written by John Toland, a deist and republican.

During the following year, 1702, he experimented with irony in a number of pamphlets, and in *A New Test of the Church of*

England's Loyalty he based his irony on the kind of parallel which the High Church was fond of in its sermons. He compared the Church's rebellion against James with the puritans' against Charles I, using a parody of the argument of Edward Pelling that every bullet fired in the civil wars was an act of regicide. Defoe's account of the revolt against Charles is a good example of ironic understatement: "At last they took Arms, and when they did, they did it to purpose, carried all before them, subdued Monarchy, cut off their King's Head, and *all that.*" And assuming a pose of mock innocence, Defoe pretends to be shocked at the inconsistency of the Church to their principles:

But to find the Church of *England*-Men, whose Loyalty has been the Subject of a thousand Learned Authors, and numberless Sermons, whose Character and Mark of Distinction has been chosen more for her steady Adherence and Fidelity to her Prince than to God Almighty, whose Obedience to her Monarch has been declar'd to be inviolate and immoveable and who pretends to be Famous through the whole World for her Faithfulness to Kings; *for her,* as soon as ever the King did but, as it were, seem to aim at crushing her Authority, as soon as he did but begin to call her Clergy to an Account, and clap her *Golden Candlesticks* for Disobedience, for her to winck and kick, fly to Foreign Princes for Protection, and rise in Arms against her Prince, O Pelling! O Brady! O Sherlock! O Hominem! O Mores!

Thus Defoe swings from understatement to overstatement. The speaker seems to expect that having professed the impossible they would at least *try* to follow it. Defoe ends the pamphlet by urging the High Church to have "a little more Modesty" toward the Dissenters in matters of loyalty, since they are just as guilty in that respect "as your Neighbours."

In a work published in 1703, but probably written before *The Shortest Way,* Defoe experimented with irony through a fairly consistent persona. The speaker in *King William's Affection to the Church of England Examin'd,* like the persona in *The Shortest Way* is a High Churchman, less fanatical but equally sophistic. His task is to argue that there is no reason to be grateful to William III and that he was always an opponent of the Church of England. Like his greater pamphlet, the work is a series of fallacious arguments and absurd distortions of rational thought. The Churchman argues that there was no need for William to come over in 1688 and that James II was ruling well enough: " 'tis own'd there were some Infringements of the Law in the Reign of that unfortunate Monarch," he concedes. "But I presume the abus'd Nation is by this time convinced, that those were but trifling Bugbears, and that we might have rectified those magnified Mistakes, with out our paying so dear for *Dutch* Assistance, or Idolizing a Prince, who tho' he freed us from supposed Dangers, did afterwards bring our Church into real ones; and perhaps the State has not escaped without its scars." The speaker moves from simple concession on the point that William received the last rites of the Church of England to doubting the King's sincerity:

But when you have thoroughly consider'd K. W———'s Character, what deep Design and Fetches he always had in all his Actions; how little he discovered of his inward or real Sentiments, even to his most Familiar Friends; that Ambition or Interest was ever at the Bottom, whatever Face his outside Politicks wore; and that by thus speciously assuming Religion, he might even (to the last) hope to secure an Interest in the Clergy: I say, he that duly weighs all this, must own; that the Church is not indebted to him for such Hypocrisies...

The arguments become more and more strained until, two pages from the end, the mask is dropped and Defoe steps forward to attack the ingratitude of the Church.

In *The Shortest Way with the Dissenters* Defoe did much the same thing without dropping the mask. What is frequently said of this work, since Professor John F. Ross first offered the thesis in 1941, is that Defoe got carried away, identified with his High Church Hot Head and created a work of fiction rather than irony, that the arguments of the High Church were so extreme that Defoe merely imitated them. No one is more responsible for this view than Defoe himself, for he insisted that his work was "an *Irony not Unusual*," while claiming that he had said much the same thing as his opponents. It would be worth reading his statement carefully:

The Sermon Preach'd at *Oxford*, the *New Association*, the *Poetical Observator*, with numberless others; have said the same thing, in terms very little darker, and this book stands fair to let those Gentlemen know, that what they design can no farther take with mankind, than as their real meaning stands disguis'd by Artifice of words; but that when the Persecution and Destruction of the *Dissenters, the very thing they drive at,* is put into plain English, the whole Nation will start at the Notion, and Condemn the Author to be Hang'd for his Impudence.

The Author humbly hopes he shall find no harder Treatment for plain *English, without Design,* than those Gentlemen for their Plain Design in Duller and Darker *English.*

Defoe does not say that he imitated the statements of the High Church; what he says is that he translated their thoughts, hints, and biblical allusions into English. Now when Charles Leslie claimed that no one in the High Church had ever said anything like what appeared in *The Shortest Way* he was absolutely right; and to confirm it, all one has to do is read the sermons which Defoe burlesqued. Not the fiercest of the January 30th sermons of Edward Pelling, George Smalbridge or William Binckes ever approached Defoe's proposal for sending the dissenting preachers to the gallows and their congregations to the gallies if they did not join the Church immediately. Like Swift, in his *Modest Proposal,* Defoe works from animal imagery and a leap of logic. Once the speaker has reduced the Dissenters to "Ser-

pents, Toads, or Vipers," it is easy enough to argue, by analogy
with hunting such vermin, for the entire destruction of religious
dissent in England.

In addition to burlesque and fallacious argument, Defoe used
parody—specifically, parody of Henry Sacheverell's *Political
Union*. There are also echoes in language and statement of
William Binckes' infamous sermon of the preceding year, which
had been censured by Parliament and had narrowly escaped
condemnation as blasphemy. And there was also satire, satire
against the Dissenters, for Defoe had his spokesman quote John
How's statement that the difference between the Dissenters and
the Church was slight and conclude from this that after a little
force they would give in easily. Whereas How had replied in
the name of the majority of the Dissenters to Defoe's attack on
occasional conformity, Defoe was writing from his minority
position, that position which he described as unique within the
society. His satiric stance, then, was an appeal to the few intelligent men who could perceive how wrong the High Church
was in its failure of charity and yet see that the Dissenters were
providing their enemies with ammunition. Is there any wonder
that both sides were angry, that Defoe was accused of "setting
the nation together by the ears"? Defoe, as one critic remarked,
was "a very *Ironical* Gentleman all over."

Defoe's defense of his irony provoked some interesting replies
and explains why his contemporaries regarded him as a satanic
figure. He was accused of "invading the conscience" of the
reader to deceive him, of attempting to provoke the nation for
no reason whatsoever, of blaspheming and burlesquing Scripture, and of attacking the Queen—for though the Queen is
praised, who could say where the irony stopped? "Had he not
forgot his Farnaby, or read any rhetorick at all, instead of *Irony,*
he must have called it the most bitter Satyr or *Sarcasm,*" wrote
the author of *The Fox with His Fire-Brand Unkennel'd and
Insnar'd* (1703), "for Satyrs, tho' they have some humane shape

above, are known by their Tails or Cloven-feet below: And, if our Author had been bred a Scholar instead of a Hosier, he would have found another kind of Figure for making other Peoples Thoughts speak in his words. But, after all, his Brief Explanation falls very short of clearing him from Seditious Designs..." The High Church thought that Defoe wanted "by the villainous Insinuations of that pamphlet to have frightened the Dissenters into another Rebellion." The Dissenters were furious that he had attacked occasional conformity once more, and this time more effectively than he ever had at a time when an attempt was being made to outlaw the practice.

When Defoe was not attacking his audience for being unable to read irony, he was confessing that he had been an "ill-marks-man." But he later admitted that *The Shortest Way* was intended at least partially as a hoax or plot to trap sections of the audience. The High Church fanatics were to be tricked into approval, the naive Dissenters into alarm, and the intelligent reader was to be amused while recognizing the serious implications of a High Church persecution. In his *Present State of the Parties* (1712), he confessed that he might have provided marginal references to the passages he was parodying, but that then no one would have been tricked. To appreciate the irony fully, one must recognize the comic force lying underneath, perceive the absurdity of the arguments, and, preferably, know the persons being parodied well enough to enjoy the distortion and warping of the arguments. Defoe clearly underestimated both the number of those who would be taken in and the general anger which greeted the pamphlet, but he must have been aware that the work was seditious; and his excuse that he merely made explicit what the High Church concealed was the only plea he could make under the circumstances:

> My Satyr has the hardest Fate,
> Her Book's the Contradiction of the State.
> Riddle Aenigma double Speech,

> Dark Answers, doubtful Scriptures, which
> Puzzle the Poor, and pose the Rich:
> Are plain explicite things to these,
> Who punish Authors when the Subjects please.
> Nothing but this can such dark Steps explain;
> They like the Doctrine, *but they hate the Man.*

By the time he wrote his *Elegy on the . . . True-Born English-man,* he had regained some of his customary humor and attacked those who refused to help him:

> So I, by Whigs abandon'd, bear
> The Satyr's unjust Lash,
> Die with the Scandal of their Help,
> But never saw their Cash.

In *More Short Ways with the Dissenters* (1704), he ironically confessed that his error had been great indeed. It was "that he, like a too credulous Fool, gave any heed to such slight and cursory things as *Preaching,* and *Printing* of Books" and assumed that the threats against the Dissenters were really meant; but now, he says mockingly, he sees the light: "no, Good Men, it was far from their Thoughts. The Author therefore was most justly punish'd for his Folly, in believing any thing they said, and pretending to Alarm the Dissenters for the little insignificant Performances of the Pulpit or the Press."

After 1704, Defoe turned his irony in other directions. But in 1709, when Sacheverell once more startled England with a sermon, *The Perils of False Brethren,* arguing that the Church *"should be Terrible like an Army of Banners to our Enemies,"* Defoe wrote his *Letter to Mr. Bisset.* Using blame-by-praise irony, Defoe argued that Bisset should stop attacking Sacheverell, who had done something *"Seasonable, Useful* and *Profitable"* in revealing the designs of the High Church and that he ought to be thanked for his honesty. And in *Instructions from Rome, in Favor of the Pretender* (1710), Defoe assumed the mask of the Pope in order to give what Knox calls "ironic advice" to Sacheverell. This advice takes the form of demanding greater subtlety:

In the mean time let your Emissaries alter their Shapes; be one thing to Day, another to Morrow, now a Courtier, by and by a formal Cit, or a Soldier, sometimes a Tailor, other-times a Shoe-maker, or Valet-de-Chambre; a Beau among the Ladies; and Atheist among the Wits; or any other Variation or Transposition, agreeable to our Interest.

After this parody of Saint Paul, a parody which Defoe applied to himself in a letter to Harley concerning his spying activities in Scotland many years before, the Pope assures Sacheverell that he has nothing to fear and that "If they catch you—you won't suffer in the next world—any more than I."

Later in the same year, Defoe wrote one of his finest pieces of ironic argument, on the Addresses to the Queen, *A New Test of the Sence of the Nation,* in which he analyzed the kind of oaths sworn to princes, comparing those sent to James and those sent to Anne. What must be understood, he argued, is that words become customary and swearing an oath has now become what he calls the "No-meaning of Speech." So addressing in King James's time "was a customary Piece of Extravagance," and his mistake was in believing these professions of obedience literally, "whereas if truly asked if they would choose those men the King wanted they would say What! Does His Majesty think we are all Slaves!" To understand this, one has to understand the tyranny of custom over language: *"For Example,* a Man may *swear* to the Man he *fights against* and *fight* for the Man he *swears against:* And all this only by Custom stepping in, and legitimating the word *SWEARING,* and *JESTING,* to mean the Same thing in the *Sence of the Nation."* It is notable that Defoe adds a postscript to explain that what "has been said is Ironical, and the true Design of it all, is to let us see, that really this tumultuous Way of Mobbing our Governours by Addresses, has no Manner of Good in it . . ." He obviously wanted to make sure that at least some of his audience got the point.

The next year, he returned to the same subject with a mask work in Scotch dialect, *A Speech for Mr. D(unda)sse Younger of Arnistown* (1711), a mock defense of reasons for the Faculty of Advocates at Edinburgh accepting a medal with the face of the Pretender. Mr. Dundasse argues that having read the addresses to Anne proclaiming her hereditary right to the throne, he could only assume that a new revolution was brewing. "I might safely with the Whigs have believed the Lawfulness of Resistance in Cases of outter Necessity; that the Subversion of our Constitution by King *James* was sik a Case, and it was therfore lawful to resist him; that it will be alike lawful to resist ony of our footer Princes gif ever the sam Breeches of the Constitution sou'd be repeeted . . . ," but the Addresses, he says, convinced him he was wrong. This is typical of Defoe's irony. He is using the mask to attack the addresses and at the same time attacking the Jacobites, by the comic use of dialect and the positive arguments against them built in the work. At the same time he is moving toward a fuller development of individual character to give an added complexity to his irony.

In 1713, Defoe once more ran into trouble over three ironic pamphlets, *And What if the Queen Should Die?*, *Reasons Against the Succession of the House of Hanover,* and *What if the Pretender Should Come?* The situation is almost as interesting as that concerned with *The Shortest Way* ten years before. Defoe was once again attacking two points at once, the idea that anyone could think it was likely that the government would invite the Pretender back and the very idea of inviting him back when the succession was "UNALTERABLE!" He defended himself in the *Review* of April 16, 1713, pointing to the absurdity of the arguments presented:

Thus when I come at last to state the great Advantages of bringing in the Pretender, *what are they reckon'd up to be,* but easing the

People of the Trouble of chosing Parliaments, easing the Gentlemen
of the hazardous and expensive Journeys in the depth of Winter,
preventing the Rabbles and Tumults of Elections, the Pleasure and
Glory of Slavery, and being govern'd by a standing Army? What
have I recommended the Pretender for, but as Poyson administered
in Physick, which makes the Patient sick, causes him to vomit up
both the Physick and the Distemper: So the Pretender and Popery
being a Vomit to the Nation, would make us so sick that we should
vomit both up, and all our State Distempers with them.

The fact is that Defoe's choice of absurd arguments was not so
obvious and unsubtle as he would pretend.

In speaking of the benefits which might accrue by the dom-
ination of England by France, Defoe will clarify his irony by
using parentheses to break through the mask of his speaker, a
man in love with his own fallacious reasoning, but he depends
on a Whig view of French dominion which was not entirely
universal and which, at any rate, many people regarded as no
laughing matter:

What if they are what we foolishly call Slaves to the Absolute Will
of their Prince? That Slavery to them is meer Liberty; they entertain
no Notions of that foolish Thing Liberty, which we make so much
Noise about; nor have they any Occasion of it, or any Use for it if
they had it; they are as Industrious in Trade, as Vigorous in Pursuit
of their Affairs, go on with as much Courage, and are as well satisfied
when they have wrought hard 20 or 30 Years to get a little Money
for the King to take away, as we are to get it for our Wives and Children.... All the Business forsooth is this Trifle we call Liberty, which
rather than be plagued with so much Strife and Dissension about it
as we are, who would be troubled with it?

Many might have agreed that there can be no difference of
opinion between the King and his subjects; Defoe himself was
to argue in the *Mercator* that the trade with France was in favor
of the English balance of exports and that some control of the
press was necessary; and the argument of the difficulties of elec-

tions and traveling up to parliament found many echoes in the hearts of his readers. The point that Defoe was making was that political liberty involved a great deal of trouble—trouble which must be taken if liberty is to be guarded:

> But once set the Pretender upon the Throne . . . and all these Distempers will be cur'd as effectually as a Feaver is cur'd by cutting off the Head, or as a Halter cures the Bleeding at the Nose. How Infatuated then is the Nation, that they should so obstinately refuse a Prince, by the Nature of whose Circumstances, and the avowed Principles of whose Party, we are sure to obtain such Glorious Things, such Inestimable Advantages.

Here are all the devices of irony, parody of arguments, absurd analogies and questions, mock concern and concession, and sarcasms. He ends *And What if the Pretender Should Come?* by saying that James is actually a Protestant and a member of the Church of England "and that in a very Natural Primitive Sense of that Phrase as it was used by His Royal Predecessor, of Famous and Pious Memory, Charles II."

Reasons against the Succession of the House of Hanover is much less subtle, the main argument being that by bringing in the Pretender, England will so quickly come to realize its mistake that it would be but a short time before the Pretender and all thoughts of ever having him back would be ended once and for all. Yet Defoe was brought to trial, and he had to be rescued by a pardon from the Queen. The judge told him that "He might live to be hang'd, as much an Irony as he said it was." In 1732, a writer rehearsed the incident and found the excuse of irony a trivial pretext, and John Oldmixon, Defoe's contemporary, agreed. No one can deny that the attack on Defoe's irony has historical precedence, but Defoe was probably right in thinking this prosecution the work of his enemies.

It was about this time that Defoe began to work more fully in a jesuitical role of writing on both sides or for causes he could not possibly have supported fully. What attitude he took toward such performances is difficult to say, but it might have involved a private delight in deception. In *The Secret History of the Secret History of the White Staff,* Defoe presented himself as near death and therefore incapable of having written the three parts of *The Secret History of the White Staff,* an attempt to clear his old Patron Harley of Jacobite connections. A Quaker tells the writer of the pamphlet that he had a friend visit Defoe:

> It seems, he found the poor Man in a very Dangerous Condition, having had a Fit of an Apoplexy, and being very Weak, insomuch, that his Life was despair'd of; but, mentioning the said Books to him, and that the Town Charg'd him with being the Author of them, and that he had Written them by Direction of the said Lord Oxford, the said Person answer'd, that they did him a great deal of Wrong; neither did he believe, that the Lord *Oxford* was in any Way concern'd, directly or indirectly in the said Books, and that he believ'd his Lordship had never heard of them till they were publish'd. It was true, he said, that he happen'd to see some of the Copy, while it was at the Press, and that being desir'd to look upon it, he did Revise Two or Three Sheets of it, and mark'd some Things in them, which he dislik'd; but for the rest he could safely Swear he never saw them, or knew what was in them, till after they were printed, nor did he know whether the Things which he had mark'd (as above said) were alter'd in the Print, *Yea* or *No.*

The testimony is the more convincing, says the speaker, because "he could not question the Truth of what a Man, as it were stepping into the Grave, had so freely declar'd." The writer finally concludes that the accusations concerning the authorship of *The Secret History of the White Staff* was "popery in the most Jesuitical Branch of it, covering a Fraud with a greater Fraud." It might be worth keeping this in mind, for though there is deception intended in this pamphlet and Defoe was obviously writing as an ironist when he composed his picture of his deathbed, still this is far from being ironic in a rhetorical sense.

But Defoe did not abandon the rhetoric of irony. In 1715 he began his Quaker pamphlets, in which the parody of Quaker dialect allowed Defoe to slip into irony with ease. In *A Seasonable Expostulation with, and Friendly Reproof unto James Butler,* he verges from comic doubt about the Jacobite Duke of Ormond's intelligence ("for there are among us who say, that thy Attainments are small in those things, as well as thy Gifts") to a praise of the way the Duke of Ormond avoided fighting when he was commanding the English forces in Flanders, "because as thou knowest Friends approve of none of those Things; neither do we go out to Fight, or make War upon any Occasion whatsoever." Defoe was occasionally unironic in his Quaker mask, but he could also advise the Bishop of Bangor to join the Quakers after the Bishop had given his sermon suggesting a de-emphasis of Church power on the grounds that the kingdom of Christ was not of this world. One might argue that masks of this kind are almost inherently ironic, as was his mask of a Turk in *The Conduct of Christians Made the Sport of Infidels* (1717), in which Kara Selym tells his friend Muli Ibrahim Edad that the English would be better off if all turned Mohammedan. A similar exercise was his *Letter from the Jesuits to Father de la Pilloniere,* also written in 1717, in which the Jesuits counsel the ex-Jesuit Pilloniere to throw in his lot with the High Church and stop preaching reason or religion. "Your *Mistake,*" writes the representative of the Jesuits, "is owing to that lively Imagination you are often led away with: your fancy that the Light of Human Reason, like the *Heat* of the *Sun,* puts out the Eyes that Stare at it." Such a theory, he continues, will lead to the destruction of Catholicism in England.

During the last years of his life, most of Defoe's satire was turned against social and political evils in England. The ironic comparison between the statesman, stockjobber, avaricious merchant, overgrown tradesman and the thief appears throughout his pamphlets, criminal biographies and fiction. In 1722, he wrote *A Brief Debate Upon the Dissolving the Late Parliament,* a brilliant mock defense of the government which had brought about the South Sea Scandal, urging the electors to choose them once more:

What tho' in their abus'd Clemency they were pleas'd to consider some of the Poor Distracted People call'd Directors, and to grant them some small Pittances out of their Confiscated Estates. I say, small Pittances, such as 10000*l*, to a Man, and such as 20000, and even 50000 to one of them. What if Mr. *A.* above-mention'd has thrown him back all his Estate, which was so before he was dipt in the wicked Part, the House having contented themselves to strip him of his ill gotten part only, not to make the Thief restore four fold, according to Scripture Rule; I say, what if in their abounding Charity they did thus, and did not entirely give the Plunderers of the People to be given up to be plundered by the People? Can this guide us so far as to reject Men, who so accurately know their own Duty and so well perform it?

In his study of the robber Cartouche, he notes, "How fair an opportunity he had to leave off the trade ... as other wealthy merchants do," and passages of this kind are to be found throughout *Captain Singleton* and *Roxana*. In *The Life of Jonathan Wild* (1724), the hero-villain organizes the criminal world like a capitalist and absolute monarch. Such statements occasionally come closer to paradox than irony, but the reality of the world of the thief is allowed to show through to undercut what seems to be admiration for this extraordinary man:

But as *Jonathan* was a deep Studier of Nature, he knew that Mens Talents were different, and that he who had not Courage enough to bid a Man stand, upon the Road, might nevertheless make an excellent Pick-pocket; and he took care that no Man's Parts should be misapply'd: Nay, it is said that nothing pleas'd him more than to see a Child or Youth of a promising Genius, and that such never wanted his Encouragement; insomuch that a little Boy in a Crowd having at a certain time stole a Pair of silver Buckles out of a Man's Shoes, without being felt, his Mother, not a little proud of her Child's Ingenuity presented him to *Jonathan,* who gave him half a Crown, with this prophetick Saying, *My Life on't, he'll prove a great Man*— But I must observe, that *Jonathan's* Prophecy never was fulfill'd the Youth dying before he came to the Age of Manhood, for he was hang'd before he arriv'd at sixteen.

Defoe notes ironically how Wild fulfills Mandeville's criteria for contributing to the wealth of the nation by employing numerous hands as thieves or as artists to alter the appearance of stolen goods. His favorite proverb, *"that Honesty was the best Policy,"* and his admission that even in his profession there were occasional scoundrels, creates a character who stands as a worthy predecessor of the more brilliant renditions of Gay and Fielding.

Defoe's concept of the thieves' world as an ironic reflection of society appears most fully in 1728 with his *History of the Pirates,* in which various heroic figures are created to serve as a mirror for respectable society. At the end he abandons an oblique ironic method for direct satire. After praising the uprightness of Captain North, he finds the life of this pirate more moral than that of many men who pretend to live honestly. "If any thinks this Reflection severe, let him examine into the Number of Thousands who are perishing in Goals, by the Cruelty of Creditors, sensible of their inability to pay," wrote Defoe, probably thinking of difficulties with his own creditors. "Let him take a View of the Miseries which reigns in those Tombs of the Living, let him enquire into the Number of those who can, clear the English Laws, which allow a Creditor to punish an unfortunate Man, for his being so, with the most cruel of all Invented Deaths, that of Famine, let him I say, clear them from the Imputation of Barbarity."

The irony of his criminal biographies slips into his major works of fiction as well as into the pointed stories of works like *The Great Law of Subordination Consider'd* (1724) and *The Political History of the Devil* (1726). In the latter work, Defoe confronts his *alter ego* directly, treating him half ironically and half seriously. The central ironic point is that the devil is continually being surprised by the wickedness of human beings and learning new depths of evil from them. In 1728, Defoe produced his only work of fiction in which the narrator is consistently ironic about his life, *Street Robberies Consider'd*. The hero is born in Newgate, like Moll Flanders, but he treats his mother without even the little tenderness which Moll lavishes on her reformed parent. He begins the story of how he became the son of one of eight pirates by an account of his mother's arrest:

> ...my poor Mother going into a *Goldsmith*'s Shop to purchase a Ring, by an odd Sort of a Mistake, I don't know how, but it seems she walk'd off with a whole String of them: but the ill-natur'd Fellow had her pursu'd, took her up, and in short was very troublesome; for notwithstanding my Mother stood stiff in her Innocence, yet the malicious Wretch forc'd her to take up a new Lodging in *Newgate,* pretending this was not her first Offence; and not having her Health there, she was obliged to take the Air an Hour or two at the *Old-Baily;* and tho' she declar'd her Aversion for her new Lodging, yet they forc'd her there again, though with this Promise, that she should very shortly take a farther Tour for a little good Air; and because it would be difficult for a weak Person to walk up Holbourn Hill, she should be carry'd, with a suitable Attendance to her Quality. She told them her Inclinations would rather carry her some other Road. But *Willi nilli,* she was inform'd she should go that Way and no other.

His mother is able to escape this time by pleading her belly, but eventually she is caught and hanged at Tyburn, where, as her son says, "she made a very comfortable End."

This work differs from Defoe's earlier fictions, for social statement about thieves is left to a separate section at the end where Defoe's converted thief warns his readers how to guard against robbers and makes a compassionate appeal for the thief who is forced to steal because of poverty. Here an ironic fiction is allowed to lead in to the moral through an abrupt division, and this raises some questions about Defoe's art and its purpose. He always insisted on the utility of art, the purpose of which was to teach through delighting, but the didactic in his work has been overemphasized. In his *Pacificator* of 1702, Defoe entered the dispute between the moralists and the wits to support the former, but what he asked was a balance: wit tempered with morality. Defoe praises Blackmore's morality, but he has no illusions about his poetic gifts. For him, the great poets are Rochester, in spite of his immorality, for he had wit; Milton, in spite of his heresies, for he was a sublime poet; and Marvell, because he was a moralist and a wit. Few men expressed such contempt for bad prose style or the failure of artful rhetoric. He considered William Ridpath's inability to maintain a consistent point of view disgraceful.

When Defoe used all his rhetorical skill in a cause he could not support there is little sign of a failure of artistry. If he was ever carried away by his personas, it was because they delighted him as artistic creations. In *The Generous Projector* (1731), written at the end of his life, Defoe asked the reader to pardon the flow of ideas. "As I have but a short time to live," he wrote, "I would not waste my remaining Thread of Life in vain; having often lamented sundry publick Abuses, and many Schemes Occuring to my Fancy, which to me carried a face of Benefit; I was resolved to commit them to Paper before my Departure, and leave at least, a Testimony of my Good-will to my Fellow Creatures." I think that Defoe was unquestionably sincere in his dedication to reforming certain social ills. But he was also a professional writer, always in demand precisely because he entertained his audience, and Defoe was not a man to slight his talents.

Then there are the statements of his contemporaries who doubted his professions of honesty. One writer said that his object was "not to *amuse* but to *inflame a distracted Nation*," and another saw him as a Machiavel, working for the slippery

Robert Harley, obsessed by thwarted ambition, and complaining that he should have been prime minister:

> Why not? For it's possible to rise
> By crafty Projects and officious Lies;
> 'Tis plain, that I'm for any Station fit,
> For who can doubt my Cunning and my Wit,
> Since I am Courtier, Poet, Prophet, and a Cit?
> You know my Parts, for you have try'd 'em oft,
> I've been the Tool that rais'd you up aloft.

The fact is that Defoe did act to inflame the nation on occasions. In 1715 he wrote a number of anticlerical pamphlets. "For supposing 'em Ambassadors of Christ (tho' I never met with any of 'em yet could produce their Credentials)," he wrote in the manner of Voltaire on his death bed, "he never gave 'em Power to Dictate to, or Authority over the Consciences of Men." When an internal quarrel broke out in the Church over the Bishop of Bangor's sermon, Defoe leaped in with an attack on all sides. What was his intention? Making peace or creating confusion?

Kierkegaard argued that the true end of irony was not its utility but the private satisfaction of the ironist. "Should he wholly succeed in leading people astray, perhaps to be arrested as a suspicious character," he wrote, then the ironist has attained his wish." Much of Defoe's pleasure in irony lay in what must have been a private delight in deception. This is why so many of his works fall not under the rhetorical category of irony but rather under what Kierkegaard called "mere dissembling" or "Jesuitism." So one might describe the numerous prophecies which he published under the mask of a second-sighted Highlander as well as all those false memoirs which he wrote to confuse his contemporaries about the involvement of the ministry, particularly Harley, with the Pretender. Defoe could define the aims of history as an absolute adherence to truth in *The Storm* while writing fictions and hoaxes like the *Memoirs of John, Duke of Melfort* (1714) or *Memoirs of Monsieur Mesnager* (1717),

which Abel Boyer called one of "the most notorious and grossest
Pieces of Forgery that ever was fobb'd upon the Publick in any
civiliz'd Country."

Defoe could use parody with the same private satisfaction that
he found in fictional masks. How many of Defoe's readers
would have caught the parody of Pelling's arguments in his *New
Test of the Church of England's Loyalty,* or the parody of his
own gloomy predictions of the decline of English trade in *A
Brief Deduction of the Original, Progress and Immense Great-
ness of the British Woollen Manufacture* when it appeared a few
months later in his Whig journal, *The Citizen,* on October 9,
1727? Did anyone catch the parody of Sacheverell's style in *The
Shortest Way?* And, raised during a time when scepticism was
the dominant mode in philosophy, Defoe preferred paradox to
direct statement. "This, Sir, is an Age of Plot and Deceit," he
wrote in his *Letter to Mr. Bisset,* "of Contradiction and Paradox.
... It is very hard under all these Masks to see the true Countenance of any Man." For all his statements concerning plain
words, few men took such oblique approaches. He objected to
Bernard Mandeville's paradoxical concept of society with its acceptance of private vices as public benefits, but he was obviously
so delighted by Mandeville's paradoxes that it is sometimes
difficult to tell whether he is supporting or attacking his theories
of luxury and vice. One must not confuse hoaxes, parody, paradox, and fiction with irony itself. They are literary forms which
may be isolated from irony, and Defoe enjoyed them for their
own sakes. Yet it seems to me that irony almost always implies
some combination of these four elements.

Proving that Defoe had an ironic personality does not demonstrate his creation of ironic works, but, as I have tried to suggest,
these exist and are available to anyone willing to read them. The
point is that we must always expect irony of Defoe, whether in
Moll Flanders or in an ephemeral pamphlet. William Trent
regarded it as one of the identifiable features of his style. It is

part of his comic force which is too often ignored. Professor James Sutherland warned about this a long time ago: "There is a strong current of comedy running through his work," he wrote. "It appears most frequently in the form of a satirical comment, a *reductio ad absurdum,* a burlesque of some illogical position or dishonest idea. He had also a desperate gaiety in moments of crisis, a laughter from the depths of despair, which is peculiar to him ... his very laughter is often oddly serious. But he *can* laugh ... because he is detached from the immediate practical concerns of morality and religion and business; because for all his own obvious bias towards the practical, he does live in a world of ideas." The detachment of which Professor Sutherland speaks is what is frequently missed by those who know Defoe only through a few works of fiction.

Defoe's writings are rooted in the real and specific. He directed his irony against particular problems most of the time, and it takes some perspective to see that what is wrong with the speaker in *The Shortest Way with the Dissenters* is his total lack of Charity, that he is very much of a priest and nothing of a Christian. Only on rare occasions did Defoe write ironically about man as a whole, and *Mere Nature Delineated* (1726), in which he used the discovery of a wild boy to reflect on the entire civilized world, is not a notable success. He revelled in the minutiae which give to irony its exclusive quality, the thrill of recognition of individual parodies of arguments, styles and ideas which allows us to participate in the wit of the writer. It was for "miraculous Fancy and lively Invention in all his Writings, both verse and Prose" that Defoe once praised himself as well as for writing "up to the Test of moral Vertue," and these qualities are those which must enliven satire. As Professor Rosenheim points out: "Such satire continues to delight us largely by virtue of its literary excellence—by the satirist's success with plot and situation and character, by his humor, by his capacity to think and write metaphorically and colorfully, and, indeed, to exploit all the resources of diction, in short, by his employment of those skills which mark the successful imaginative writer rather than the tractarian or moralist." As long as Defoe is thought of only in terms of his desire to write "up to the Test of moral Vertue" rather than in terms of "miraculous Fancy and lively Imagination," he will be only partially understood.

Had I taken Professor Rosenheim's view that irony was at best a weak descriptive term, a minor division of satire, and spoken of Defoe's satire in general, this paper would be longer than it already is. But since the question of irony in Defoe is still an open one, I have chosen to mention only those works which were exclusively ironic. Defoe could and did expound upon the uses of satire at far greater length. "There are Crimes," he wrote, "which a lash of the Pen reach'd when a lash at the Cart's-tail would not; and a time when Men that have laugh'd at the Law, and ridiculed all its Powers, have yet been laughed out of their Crimes by a just Satyr, and brought to the necessity of hanging themselves for Shame, or reforming to prevent it." But this is another matter. The fact is that Defoe's irony may be his "strongest push" to express a didactic message, but it frequently proceeded from a sense of the comic or a delight in argument—a conviction that he alone perceived that the emperor was without clothes. The government pardoned him in 1713 but they could not have been very happy about works which stirred up the people against Jacobitism at a time when members of the ministry were in correspondence with the Pretender. Unlike some of his satires or lampoons, Defoe's irony did indeed proceed from detachment and involved a play of ideas, rhetoric and language which pleased no one so much as himself.

X

Swift's Use of Irony

By HERBERT DAVIS

To DESCRIBE *Gulliver's Travels* as Swift's deliberate retort to *Robinson Crusoe* would be unwarranted, but if we amuse ourselves by considering it as such, the result is as informative as it is entertaining. Moreover, we never see Swift more clearly than in relation to Defoe: each demands the presence of the other if we are to understand a battle, a Parliamentary conflict, a divided nation."

With these words, Nigel Dennis, in his brilliant little book on Swift, 1964, indicates some of the possibilities of such a discussion as we are engaged upon today. It might have been more entertaining if we had just talked about those two books, and played with the sharp contrasts—but Mr. Dennis has done that so admirably, that perhaps we were well advised to try and deal with one of the three things which he points out they had in common:

1) "They both took service under Harley"
2) "They were both passionately in favour of the education of women"
3) "They were both capable of satire"
and he notes particularly that Defoe's *Shortest Way with the Dissenters* anticipates exactly in tone and tendency Swift's *Modest Proposal;* though Defoe's irony is rather blunt, Swift's more refined.

I propose to examine some examples of Swift's different uses of irony, keeping in mind particularly the risk he took of being misunderstood; and not forgetting that some problems in the interpretation of irony may become more difficult with the passage of the centuries, as changing ways of life and standards of

221

behaviour sometimes throw into obscurity the original intentions of the writer.

Swift himself was aware of the danger of being misunderstood even by his first readers. In the Apology which he wrote for the fifth edition of *A Tale of a Tub,* in 1710, he admits that he had played some tricks, which might well have provoked some of his unsophisticated readers, but appealed to "the Men of Taste, who will observe and distinguish that there generally runs an Irony through the thread of the whole Book ... which will render some Objections that have been made, very weak and insignificant." I propose now that as readers "of Taste" we should "observe and distinguish" the irony that runs through the thread of all his work, for it is a way of writing which he seems almost to claim as his own special gift. In this art he was the great master and could brook no rival:

> Arbuthnot is no more my friend,
> Who dares to Irony pretend;
> Which I was born to introduce,
> Refin'd it first, and shew'd its Use.

But that is itself not to be taken too seriously. Swift might have forgotten the irony of Shakespeare which is often refined enough, but he would not have forgotten the claims of Socrates. And if pressed, he would probably have admitted that in the generation just before him, Andrew Marvell, whose work we know he admired, had shown some gift that way. He even anticipated that particular mixture of parody and irony which marks *A Tale of a Tub;* and Swift would have found it difficult to improve upon Marvell's parody of Charles II in his "Most Gracious Speech to Both Houses of Parliament":

If you give me the revenue I desire, I shall be able to do those things for your religion and liberty, that I have had long in my thoughts, but cannot effect them without a little more money to carry me through.

After explaining the kind of things he will do for them, he ends with this splendid irony:

> I desire you to believe me as you have found me; and I do solemnly promise you, that whatsoever you give me shall be especially managed with the same conduct, trust, sincerity and prudence, that I have ever practised since my happy restoration.

But this is still the simplest form of irony—to talk of the sincerity and prudence of Charles II, or to talk as Swift did of "the singular Humanity" of Dr. Bentley; it is what Puttenham had called "the drye mocke." And we must look for something more sustained as well as more refined, which runs through the thread of the whole *Tale*. Perhaps the chief cause of difficulty for modern readers is Swift's refinement of Marvell's mixture of parody and irony. In his parody of Dryden and L'Estrange, which he particularly draws to our attention so that we shall not miss the point, he adds a touch of contempt by assuming the role and the style of a Grub Street hack, who lives in a garret, and writes under the stimulus of hunger and want of money, and complains of the unfair competition of these two "junior start-up societies of Gresham and Will's," who have made "continual Efforts...to edify a Name and Reputation upon the Ruin of OURS." Here with one stroke he is able to reduce the Royal Society and the literary establishment who pay their court to Dryden at Will's Coffee-House to the Grub Street level. In his satire on the corruptions of the world of letters, Swift does not hesitate to use the extravagances and absurdities of tone and manner of the hack; and he makes the most of his role, to indulge in all kinds of follies and enjoys the freedoms and the privileges which are allowed to those who wear a mask. But recent critics like William Ewald and Ronald Paulson, in their attempts to analyse Swift's methods, seem to me in their emphasis on the use Swift makes of his disguise—of the language and tricks of Grub Street—to be in danger of confusing us so that the much more important element—the play of irony—is obscured. What I would contend is that here, just as with all his other later disguises, Swift simply makes use of a mask as it suits him; it is never permanently moulded over his face, and it always allows him to use his own voice. It is a mask which he holds in his hand, like a comedian, which may be withdrawn at any moment to show a sardonic grin or a humorous smile. Thus, when in his role of Grub Street hack he goes on to tell us of his literary plans, explaining that he has "neither a Talent nor an Inclination for Satyr" and is "so entirely satisfied with the whole present Procedure of human Things" that he has been "for some years preparing materials for '*A Panegyrick upon the World,*'" we can observe the very moment when parody turns into irony; and that satirical rogue—the real author—very conscious of the completeness of his own dissatisfaction with the whole world of religion and learning, removes the mask for a moment and indulges in the simplest form of irony. In fact, he never surrenders his pen into the hands of a Grub Street hack, whose manner and point of view are substituted for his own. He always remains himself in complete charge; he never becomes the sport of his own characters. Indeed, I cannot think of any writer who is at every moment in more complete and more conscious control. The puppets he is using are always being manipulated by his fingers, and their voices, however disguised, are always his voice.

I do not wish to be thought to suggest for a moment that there is not to be found in Ronald Paulson's study of *A Tale of a Tub* some excellent comments on Swift's irony. He has shown how often we ought to be reminded of such favourite books of Swift's as Erasmus' *Praise of Folly* and Cervantes' *Don Quixote,* how like his irony is to theirs, and his use of the fool and madman, to expose the world of reality underneath the world of illusion. The whole of the clothes imagery, whether applied to the universe—"a large suit of clothes, which invests everything"—or to the globe—"what is that which some call Land, but a fine coat faced with Green? or the Sea, but a Wastcoat of Water-Tabby?" or "the vegetable Beaux," or man himself, "a complete suit of Clothes with all its Trimmings"—is so inexhaustible in its possibilities that he can't let it alone. It may be used to frighten us with a vision of all these mirrors of illusion surrounding us; or it may finally be turned to account to be used at his own expense to remind us of the tricks he is playing upon us, all the finery he has put on for our amusement:

> Embroidery was sheer Wit; Gold Fringe was agreeable Conversation, Gold Lace was Repartee, a huge long periwig was Humor, and a Coat full of Powder was very good Raillery: All which required abundance of Finesse and Delicatesse to manage with Advantage, as well as a strict Observance of Times and Places.

In the digressions that interrupt the tale of the three brothers and their coats, he is concerned to expose the fakes and absurdities of the learned world—its criticism and its scholarship—and finally to strip off all the show and trappings of the professions and the world of rank and society and reveal the Bedlam which surrounds us.

Two of these digressions will provide us with opportunity to observe the "Thread of Irony"—the first, concerning critics, Section III, which begins with a grave apology for having got so far without having performed the usual politenesses expected by "my good Lords the Critics." He proposes to make up for this unpardonable omission by looking into the "Original and Pedigree of the word, and considering the ancient and present State thereof." He defends the critics against their detractors who say

> that a *True Critic* is a sort of Mechanick, set up at as little Expence as a *Taylor*.... On the contrary, nothing is more certain than that it requires greater Layings out, to be free of the Criticks Company, than of any other you can name. For, as to be a true Beggar, it will cost the richest Candidate every Groat he is worth; so, before one can com-

mence a *True Critick,* it will cost a Man all the good Qualities of his
Mind . . .

and he concludes with three maxims, which can be used to distinguish a true modern critic from a pretender. I will quote the
first, which shows alike the thread and the embroidery:

The first is, That Criticism, contrary to all other Faculties of the
Intellect, is ever held the truest and best, when it is the very first
Result of the Critick's Mind: As Fowlers reckon the first aim for the
surest, and seldom fail of missing the Mark, if they stay for a second.

Then, having brought his chapter to a successful conclusion, he
returns to the main story with the hope that "he has deserved so
well of their whole Body [the critics] as to meet with generous
and tender Usage at their Hands."

I do not find it very helpful to be told that the particular tone
of the raillery here is due to the fact that a Grub Street hack is
speaking; nor do I share Mr. Paulson's impression "that the
guiding hand of the satirist is not so evident as in the work of
Marvell or Eachard, because the gesturing Hack is all that is in
sight." I always hear the voice of Swift—the words are in fact
his own—and the tone seems to me to come directly from the
ironic intention of the author, when he refers, for instance, to
"our Noble *Moderns;* whose most edifying Volumes I turn
indefatigably over Night and Day, for the Improvement of my
Mind and the good of my Country."

But it is in the superb rhetoric of Section IX, the Digression on
Madness, that we recognize for the first time the peculiar intensity of Swiftian irony and realize that he had good reason to
claim this as the particular kingdom where he ruled alone. Dr.
Johnson must, I think, have had this particularly in mind when
he said that Swift exhibits in the *Tale* "a vehemence and rapidity
of mind, a copiousness of images, and vivacity of diction such
as he afterwards never possessed or never exerted." Yet I would
maintain that, in spite of all the exuberance and wit, the tricks

and gaieties of the book, we can find there also Swift's characteristic directness and concreteness, the liveliness of racy, living
speech: "when a Man's Fancy gets astride on his Reason, When
Imagination is at Cuffs with the Senses, and common Understanding as well as Common Sense is kickt out of doors; the first
Proselyte he makes is Himself."

Even when he moves to subtler and more abstract proposi-
tions, the language remains almost conversational in tone; it
never becomes academic or professional. The result is that the
calm surface of the prose allows us to perceive very clearly the
depth beneath; we are led on quietly and unsuspecting, and then
suddenly faced with the horror of the real situation:

> For, if we take an Examination of what is generally understood by
> *Happiness,* as it has Respect, either to the Understanding or the
> Senses, we shall find all its Properties and Adjuncts will herd under
> this short Definition: That, *it is a perpetual Possession of being well
> Deceived.* And first with relation to the Mind or Understanding; 'tis
> manifest, what mighty Advantages Fiction has over Truth; and the
> Reason is just at our Elbow; because Imagination can build nobler
> Scenes and produce more wonderful Revolutions than Fortune or
> Nature will be at Expence to furnish.

Then, after a couple of paragraphs, sparkling with wit full of
exuberance and the delight of the young man in the realization
of the splendid performance he was putting on, we are brought
back to this theme again, and the whole is resolved in those final
closing notes:

> He that can with Epicurus content his Ideas with the Films and
> Images that fly off upon his Senses from the Superficies of Things;
> Such a Man, truly wise, creams off Nature, leaving the Sower and the
> Dregs for Philosophy and Reason to lap up. This is the sublime and
> refined Point of Felicity, called, *the Possession of being well deceived;*
> The Serene Peaceful State of being a Fool among Knaves.

Swift's meaning here should be clear enough, as he points so triumphantly to the only way which could lead in this sorry world to any kind of felicity or serenity or peace.

I want to make quite clear what I think is the position of the writer here, for this passage, with its striking repetitions and underlinings, has always seemed to me to reveal very clearly something that we need to bear in mind in our interpretation of all Swift's work. The irony appears, I think we should agree, in such statements as refer to "the mighty advantages Fiction has over Truth" or to the wisdom of the man who "creams off Nature, content with the images that fly off from the superficies of things." But the whole argument is arranged to leave us with nothing but utter scepticism. There can be no happiness or felicity in this world except in the "perpetual Possession" of full and complete deception, no serenity or peace except for the fool who does not allow himself to be disturbed by the knaves. Lest we should be under any doubt about his position, Swift devotes the rest of the chapter to a very thorough examination of the world's knavery, and triumphantly proves its madness by taking us on a visit to Bedlam, and showing us there the talents and qualities essential for the highest success in all the professions, which "are here mislaid." He vividly describes the behaviour of the inmates—even adding a memorable illustration of the cells that were then open for the entertainment of the public—and explains his "high Esteem for that honourable Society, whereof I had some Time the Happiness to be an unworthy Member." He shows us some splendid examples of just those very qualities needed to command a regiment of dragoons, or required for success in Westminster Hall, the Court, or the City; and then he presses the irony a little further, by assuring us that it is not merely a matter of rescuing these talents now buried, "but all these would very much excel, and arrive at great Perfection in their several Kinds; which I think, is manifest from what I have already shewn..."

I am not myself aware that the conditions and circumstances

under which we now live have made Swift's *Tale of a Tub* out of
date or his irony difficult to interpret; but this may not be true
when we come to deal with that splendid piece of sustained
irony, in which he attempted to meet the attacks of the Deists
and the Whigs on the Established Church. He made sure that
they would read it by providing this alluring title: *An ARGU-
MENT to prove, That the abolishing of Christianity in ENG-
LAND, may, as things now stand, be attended with some In-
conveniences, and perhaps, not produce those many good Effects
proposed thereby.*

The attitude of the writer is exactly shown by the tone of this
statement. There will be parody as well as irony; for here is a
case to be argued, to be drawn up with all the care, the necessary
qualifications and detailed consideration of all objections, which
could possibly come into the minds of judge or jury, anticipating
every possibility that learned counsel on the other side might
bring forward—*in England, as things now stand,—and perhaps.*
He never forgets for a moment how difficult a case he has taken
on; he knows that he is reasoning against the general humour
and disposition of mankind. Yet, however absurd it may be and
whatever the consequences, he cannot but insist:

I do not yet see the absolute Necessity—in the present Posture of
our Affairs at home or abroad—of extirpating the Christian Religion
from among us.

This may appear too great a Paradox, even for our wise and paradoxical Age to endure: Therefore I shall handle it with all Tenderness, and with the utmost Deference to that great and profound
Majority, which is of another Sentiment.

Here I feel, in addressing a modern audience, under the very
different circumstances from those of 250 years ago in England,
it may be necessary to state that Swift is being ironical when he
speaks of "that great and profound Majority, which is of another
Sentiment." Then even the Tolands and the Tindals, the Deists

and the Freethinkers would have understood the irony; for they would only have claimed to be an advanced and enlightened minority, in their desire to overthrow the Established Church. Now, again, it may indeed be that there is no irony left at all in Swift's reminder that he had even heard it affirmed by some very old people that they could remember the time that "a Project for the Abolishing of Christianity would have appeared as singular as it would be at this time to write or discourse in its Defence." But I hope there is still a little sting left in that paragraph where he is careful to protect himself against any suspicion that he might be fool enough

> ... to stand up in the Defence of *real* Christianity; such as used in primitive Times (if we may believe the Authors of those Ages) to have an Influence upon Mens Belief and Actions: To offer at the Restoring of that, would indeed be a wild Project; it would dig up Foundations; to destroy at one Blow *all* the wit, and *half* the Learning of the Kingdom; to break the entire Frame and Constitution of Things; to ruin Trade, extinguish Arts and Sciences with the Professor of them; in short, to turn our Courts, Exchanges and Shops into Desarts.

And I am afraid there is still rather a grim irony in the objection he makes to doing away with the clergy: "Here are ten thousand Persons reduced by the wise Regulations of *Henry the Eighth,* to the Necessity of a low Diet, and moderate Exercise, who are the only great Restorers of our Breed."

A good many of his other points are rather outdated, depending as they do on such forgotten practices as assembling in churches and other forms of Sunday observance. But Swift was right in his forecast that abolishing Christianity would do nothing to extinguish parties among us; and his final warning has quite a familiar ring about it in introducing considerations which still seem to influence public policy:

> Whatever some may think of the great Advantages to Trade, by this favourite Scheme; I do very much apprehend, that in six months

Time, after the Act is past for the Extirpation of the Gospel, the Bank and the East-India Stock may fall, at least One per Cent. And since that is Fifty times more than ever the Wisdom of our Age thought fit to venture for the *Preservation* of Christianity, there is no reason we should be at so great a Loss, meerly for the Sake of *destroying* it.

We can perhaps be pretty sure of the objects of his attack in 1708, and therefore we are not likely to mistake the general intention beneath the irony. But if we probe further, hoping to discover exactly what sort of man the writer of the *Argument* was and, in particular, what was his own religious faith—what meaning did Christianity have for him—we may even here find ourselves baffled. To put it quite bluntly, when he talks about the *real* Christianity of primitive ages and shows that he is aware of its complete incompatibility with the whole structure of English society in his time—which side is he on? He is saying clearly enough that primitive Christianity would dig up the foundations, i.e., it would cause a revolution. When he goes on to say, "I hope no Reader imagines me so weak as to stand up in Defence of real Christianity," is that an ironical statement, which we have to turn upside down, so that it would mean that he is weak enough, fool enough nevertheless, to stand up for real Christianity?

But I must come to the more controversial questions, concerned with the interpretation of Swift's meaning and intentions in *Gulliver's Travels*. In the first book, the irony is sufficiently obvious. There can be no doubt of Swift's intentions when Gulliver gives his account of the intrigues of his great enemies at court and the barbarous proposals that they made for his destruction, and the final kindly suggestion merely to put out both his eyes, which he owed to his friend Reldresal: "he humbly conceived, that by this Expedient, Justice might in some measure be satisfied, and all the World would applaud the *Lenity* of the Emperor, as well as the fair and generous Proceedings of those who have the Honour to be his Counsellors." Gulliver's considerations on what he ought to do provide further opportunities for irony:

> ... as to myself, I must confess having never been designed for a Courtier either by my Birth or Education, I was so ill a Judge of Things, that I could not discover the Lenity or Favour of this Sentence; but conceived it (perhaps erroneously) rather to be rigorous than gentle ... if I had then known the Nature of Princes and Ministers, which I have since observed in many other Courts, and their Methods of treating Criminals less obnoxious than myself; I should with great Alacrity and Readiness have submitted to so easy a Punishment.

If we need an image which it would be useful always to have in mind to symbolize the relationship between Gulliver and his creator, we can find it in that dramatic moment so vividly described in the Second Book, when his gigantic Majesty the King of Brobdingnag, after listening to all of Gulliver's account of his own country, delivers his judgment. Here we get the full force of the dramatic irony, as Gulliver so honestly and so naively tells us what happened to him: "His Majesty ... taking me into his Hands, and stroking me gently, delivered himself in these Words, which I shall never forget, nor the Manner he spoke them in. ..." There is Gulliver, the little manikin, the very symbol of poor silly, stupid, wretched man, and Swift—his Creator— enlarged into this majestic figure who suddenly speaks with the authority of a mythical prophet-king. Not from a distant throne or like Zeus, thundering from the heavens; but he takes him into his hands and strokes him gently, and then, without irony, but with plain mercilesss invective and with the whole authority of the prophetic tradition behind him, he denounces the corruptions of that society Gulliver had described, and concludes the bulk of them "to be the most pernicious Race of little odious Vermin that Nature ever suffered to crawl upon the Surface of the Earth."

Swift continues to make use of Gulliver—the irony is at his expense in the next chapter, when he tries to explain that this king lives remotely from the rest of the world, and it would be hard "if so remote a Prince's Notions of Virtue and Vice were to be offered as a Standard for all Mankind." Then he gives an extraordinary example of the king's blindness, when the king refuses Gulliver's offer to provide him with artillery of a size proportionable to all other things in that kingdom:

> He was amazed how so impotent and grovelling an Insect as I (these were his Expressions) could entertain such inhuman Ideas and in so familiar a Manner as to appear wholly unmoved at all the Scenes of Blood and Desolation, which I had painted as the common Effects of those destructive Machines.

But Gulliver continues to give himself away, chattering about the defectiveness of the Brobdingnagians' learning and their legal system and their ignorance of the whole art of government.

There is no difficulty here in the interpretation of Swift's meaning. No one could mistake his intention that we are to accept the values of the Brobdingnagians; Gulliver's views are quite clearly not those of Swift. Swift has picked him up and is looking at him with pity and amusement.

In the Third Book, where it has often been noticed that Gulliver is not given such a prominent role, he is again made use of, on one occasion where he adds to the effect of horrible surprise at the revelation of the Struldbruggs by describing his "inexpressible delight" when he first heard of this race of Immortals:

> Happy Nation, where every Child hath at least a Chance for being Immortal! Happy People, who enjoy so many living examples of great Virtue. ... But happiest beyond all Comparison ... those excellent Struldbruggs ...

He notices that his companions are amused by his enthusiasm, and they lure him on to tell them what schemes of living he would have formed, if he had chanced to have been born a Struldbrugg. They then tell him the truth and afterwards he saw five or six of different ages—"the most mortifying sight I ever beheld." But Gulliver learns from his experience and confesses: "my keen Appetite for Perpetuity of Life was much abated. I grew heartily ashamed of the pleasing Visions I had formed . . ."

Here there is no doubt that Gulliver's education has been successful, and he is allowed to express the moral which Swift intends us to draw from this particular adventure. But in the last book, we are faced with real difficulties, since in the last twenty or thirty years we have been offered entirely new interpretations of Swift's meaning. We have been told that the dramatic irony has been entirely overlooked, and that Swift's intentions have been entirely mistaken. We should have realized that Gulliver was a dramatic character in the story, and that the last voyage to the country of the Houynhynms and the Yahoos is really an account of his final folly in his admiration for this rationalist society and his worship of "his Master and Lady," as he calls those gifted horses who were his hosts, whom he finally had to leave—"mine Eyes flowing with Tears, and my Heart quite sunk with Grief." How else are we to understand Gulliver's ridiculous behaviour when he takes his final leave before getting into his boat:

> As I was going to prostrate myself to kiss his Hoof, he did me the Honour to raise it gently to my Mouth. I am not ignorant how much I have been censured for mentioning this last Particular. Detractors are pleased to think it improbable, that so illustrious a Person should descend to give so great a Mark of Distinction to a Creature so inferior as I.

How else are we to explain his absurd behaviour, when found by the Portuguese seamen who were astonished that this strangely dressed creature answered them in their own language, but at the same time fell alaughing at his strange tone in speaking like the neighing of a horse? In spite of all the kindness of Don

Pedro, the Portuguese captain, Gulliver continues to behave like a madman, and when he finally gets back to his wife and family, his behaviour is so atrocious that it is obviously Swift's intention to alienate our sympathy for Gulliver entirely, and use him as a symbol of the fate of those who cannot accept the human compromise, but give themselves up to strange ideals of purely rationalist existence untouched by folly and evil passions. For he tells us that the sight of his family filled him with disgust and contempt:

...my Memory and Imaginations were perpetually filled with the Virtues and Ideas of those exalted Houyhnhnms. And when I began to consider, that by copulating with one of the Yahoo-species, I had become a Parent of more; it struck me with the utmost Shame, Confusion and Horror.

It is certainly true that—whatever his purpose—Swift was careful to leave us in no doubt about Gulliver's feelings after his unfortunate exile from the Houyhnhnm country:

As soon as I entered the House, my Wife took me in her Arms, and kissed me; at which, having not been used to the Touch of that odious Animal for so many years, I fell in a Swoon for almost an Hour. At the Time I am writing, it is five Years since my last Return to England: During the first Year I could not endure my Wife or Children in my Presence, the very Smell of them was intolerable; much less could I suffer them to eat in the same Room. To this Hour they dare not presume to touch my Bread, or drink out of the same Cup...

I do not think it would have been possible for any Anglican priest to use such words unconsciously, and such a one as Swift must have been willing to allow these overtones to remain—the bread and the cup; and even the word *presume,* from the opening phrase of the prayer before the act of communion; even the phrase *suffer them,* of the children's eating in the same room; even the tone ringing so clearly in the phrase *to this hour.* There is here,it seems to me,evidence enough of Swift's intention to emphasize Gulliver's complete estrangement from the human race, his inability to live any longer in communion with his own kind.

But the question at issue is what conclusion did he wish his readers to draw from Gulliver's behaviour. It has been in recent years the subject of lively debate—particularly in the United States, where if you go into any paperback-book shop you will almost certainly find two volumes entirely devoted to a discussion of the subject. It is largely concerned with the use of irony. One view is that Gulliver in this last voyage and final adventure in the land of the Houynhnhnms must be seen as the victim himself of Swift's irony. Swift has allowed him to become more and more fascinated by this rationalist society only to expose his folly and madness in accepting their values, which we ought to recognize as those of the Deists and Freethinkers—the modern rationalist faith of the enlightment. We are reminded that Swift was an orthodox clergyman, who had spent his life in attacking the views of the Deists and Freethinkers, and that his purpose in the Fourth Book could only have been to use it as a dramatic parable to uphold the doctrines of Augustinian Christianity. In short, to quote from one of the most recent pronouncements on the subject; "When placed in their proper historical and ideological context, the horses are in every important respect like the Deists," or, to quote from another, "as symbols of Swift's religious irony, the horses could only represent Deists."

It is perhaps fair to point out that this is to challenge the interpretation of Swift's meaning which was accepted unchallenged for two hundred years. It also seems to me to ignore Swift's manifest intention in revising *Gulliver's Travels* for the Dublin edition of his *Works* in 1735, to restore certain long passages which the printer of the London edition had been afraid to include because they so ruthlessly exposed the vices of human nature and the horrible corruptions of human society, as Gulliver tries so helplessly to explain them to the innocent mind of his Houynhnhnm master. Can there be any doubt what is the intention of Swift as Gulliver speaks of war, and politics, and the scandals of the law? Can we possibly forget the likeness of his position to that he had held in the land of Brobdingnag, when in one of these conversations he tells us:

> I was going on to more Particulars, when my Master commanded me Silence. He said, whoever understood the Nature of Yahoos might easily believe it possible for so vile an Animal, to be capable of every Action I had named, if their Strength and Cunning equalled their Malice. But, as my Discourse had increased his Abhorrence of the whole Species, so he found it gave him a Disturbance in his Mind, to which he was wholly a Stranger before.... when a Creature pretending to Reason, could be capable of such Enormities, he dreaded lest the Corruption of that Faculty might be worse than Brutality itself. He seemed therefore confident, that instead of reason, we were only possessed of some Quality fitted to increase our natural Vices; as the Reflection from a troubled Stream returns the Image of an ill-shapen Body, not only *larger,* but more *distorted.*

Can anyone who reads that—without preconceived notions—doubt on which side Swift himself stood at this moment, and that what he wanted to do was to make his readers feel the horror that had caused this "disturbance in the mind" of this innocent, truthful horse. The spell that he casts over us, the power of the narrative, the parody of the traveller's tale, make us almost forget that it was his imagination that had created this scene, forcing Gulliver to give us away so badly, and his mind that found the dread words which fall from the lips of Gulliver's master. But if we do forget him, we are likely to be made maddeningly aware of the power of his presence, as he embroiders the thread of his irony with that last striking image of the reflection of an ill-shapen body, as it appears not only *larger,* but more *distorted* in a troubled stream.

When Gulliver goes on to describe the virtues of the Houynhnhnms, we are given a picture of calm beauty, of classical virtue —of friendship and benevolence, of decency and civility—something which is as remote as possible from everything that Swift ever said or wrote about the Deists, whom he does, in fact, in one of his doggerel verses, describe as Yahoos. And in the tenth chapter, just before Gulliver is told that he must depart, he gives an account of his little economy, which is indeed a Swiftian parody of Utopia. The only irony here is that the poor fellow does not yet know that he is about to have to give it all up—and return into this sorry world. Finally, Swift brings Gulliver to the point where he can no longer bear to have any communion with humanity. I am not sure that it is a mistake to think that he never allowed Gulliver to represent his own view.

In the last chapter of the book, Gulliver concludes the story by giving some account of his design in publishing the work for the public good; and finally, I think, Swift allows himself to emerge and make a little ironical speech of his own. For his real intentions were not, I think, without malice; indeed he confessed privately that he had written with one intention—"to vex the world." And perhaps that is just what he means, if we understand the irony, when he says:

> I am not a little pleased that this Work of mine can possibly meet with no Censurers ... I meddle not the least with any Party, but write without Passion, Prejudice, or Ill-will against any Man or Number of Men whatsoever. I write for the noblest End, to inform and instruct Mankind, over whom I may, without Breach of Modesty, pretend to some Superiority, from the Advantages I received by conversing so long among the most accomplished Houynhnhnms. I write without any View towards Profit or Praise. I never suffer a Word to pass that may look like Reflection, or possibly give the least Offence even to those who are most ready to take it. So that, I hope, I may with Justice pronounce myself an Author perfectly blameless ...

There is no difficulty in interpreting another work which he planned for the public good; for it is, I suppose, the most completely sustained and unbroken irony that he or anyone else ever wrote. He did not live to finish it, but what he had done was printed shortly after his death under the title *Directions to Servants*. I am afraid the topic is one that has no longer much relevance today, and this remains one of his works which only has a sort of historical appeal. It was planned to give proper directions for the performance of every single detail in the duties of a very large staff, such as was required to run a great house in Swift's time; and though he had a wide experience of English society, I rather think it is particularly coloured by his intimate knowledge of the ways of the servants' hall in the houses of his Irish friends. It is what he called a "perfection of folly," and the irony that runs through the whole is quite simple and direct. Like *Polite Conversation,* an amusement of his leisure, which he kept long by him, it shows the very habit of his mind—his constant tendency to play with parody and irony. But thus kept in exercise, it could be turned to dangerous purpose when required, and could reveal how deeply Swift continued to be engaged in public affairs in the years which followed his final return to Ireland after the success of *Gulliver's Travels.*

From time to time, there appeared a number of small pamphlets printed at the same press and looking very much like the Drapier's Letters, but with no other indication of authorship on the title page. The first was called *A short View of the State of Ireland,* where he allows himself to describe the delightful progress the Commissioners from England might make through the country, wondering at the improvement of the land, the thriving towns and villages, the vast numbers of ships in the harbours, and carriers crowding the roads, laden with rich manufactures. Suddenly he breaks off and gives up—"my heart is too heavy to continue this Irony longer." Two years later, however, in 1729, when he has come to find all his proposals utterly useless in the face of both English exploitation and the discouragement and misery of the people of Ireland, the only satisfaction that was left for him was to indulge in the savage irony of *A Modest Proposal,* which I am inclined to regard as the most perfect piece of writing that ever came from his pen. He made no mistake here. There could hardly be any doubt of his meaning, or of the completeness of his scepticism, as he contemplates the face of Ireland with utter despair. Yet, he must still lift up his voice in a last protest, parodying the proposals of the economists in this imaginative discovery of his, the only possibility left, this plan which he presents with irony and wit and humour.

Here his attack is mainly against the people of Ireland— "I desire the Reader will observe, that I calculate my Remedy *for this one individual Kingdom* of Ireland, *and for no other that ever was, is, or I think ever can be upon Earth"*—and then he goes on to list all the things that might have been done and that have often been suggested, and charges them with being unwilling ever to try and put them in practice. But he does not forget the crimes of the absentee landlords—"I grant this Food will be somewhat dear, and therefore very *proper for Landlords;* who, as they have already devoured most of the Parents, seem to have the best Title to the Children"—nor fail to include among the advantages of his proposal the fact that it is one "whereby we can incur no Danger of *disobliging* ENGLAND":

For this kind of Commodity will not bear Exportation; the Flesh being of too tender a Consistence, to admit a long Continuance in Salt; *although, perhaps, I could name a Country, which would be glad to eat up our whole Nation without it.*

There is a strange intensity throughout, an imaginative fire which leaps from one point to another devouring everything it can reach. There would be so many advantages in this scheme to fatten healthy infants to be sold as meat at twelve months old:

It would increase the care and tenderness of mothers towards their children.

Men would become as fond of their wives during the time of pregnancy, as they are now of their Mares in foal.

It would make a fitting dish for *merry meetings* particularly weddings and christenings.

He admits that it would not deal with the problem of that vast number of people, who are aged, diseased, or maimed, "But I am not in the least Pain upon that Matter; because it is well known, that they are every Day *dying,* and *rotting,* by *Cold* and *Famine,* and *Filth* and *Vermin,* as fast as can be reasonably expected." Here the force of the irony depends upon the violence of the impact of the words—the horrible excess of the added phrase *and rotting* and the repetition of it again in the words *filth* and *vermin.*

Swift continued for several years in various ways to concern himself with the miseries of Ireland, the corruptions and enormities of the city of Dublin, and even produced another "Proposal to pay off the National Debt without raising any taxes," which was included in his *Works* with this warning note at the head of the page: "The Reader will perceive the following Treatise to be altogether Ironical." But in none of his other papers do we find the perfection, the completeness, which must, one feels, have been enough even to satisfy Swift himself. He could hardly have done better in his attempt to go on "vexing the world," forcing his readers at least to recognize his revulsion, and to understand the cause of his despair. Here is his last challenge. Having made his proposal, he bursts out, "Therefore, let no Man talk to me of other expedients," and adds, "Therefore I repeat, let no Man talk to me of these and the like Expedients; till he hath, at least, a Glimpse of Hope, that there will ever be some hearty and sincere Attempt to put *them in Practice.*" It is the same despair, the same pessimism, as he had expressed in the Letter of Captain Gulliver to his cousin Sympson, complaining that there had been no sign of any reformation anywhere since the publication of his travels:

And it must be owned, that seven Months were a sufficient Time to correct every Vice and Folly to which the Yahoos are subject; if their Natures had been capable of the least Disposition to Virtue or Wisdom:...I must confess, since my last Return, some Corruptions of my Yahoo Nature have revived in me...; else I should never have attempted so absurd a Project as that of reforming the Yahoo race in this Kingdom; but, I have now done with all such visionary Schemes for ever.

I must confess that I find a remarkable similarity between the attitude of Captain Gulliver and the author of *A Modest Proposal*. The quality of the irony, the very ring of the words they use—their tendency to despair because of the Yahoo nature of man. Did then, you may ask me, this orthodox Anglican dean give up all Christian hope, and have to content himself with the foolishness of doing little charitable deeds, such as making small loans to poor craftsmen who were willing to work? Or was he perhaps driven by the very depth of his despair back to the Christian faith?

I recently found a comment of his on the creed of the Christian church which I should like to know the meaning of. It is written clearly in his own hand on the margin of a page towards the end of the seventh volume of Baronius' *Ecclesiastical History* (which he notes that he finished reading in 1729, the same year as *A Modest Proposal*). In the appendix to that volume, Baronius prints the document accepted by the Russian Church as the statement of the Christian Faith when they were received into communion with the Church of Rome. This included the *Credo* text of the Nicene Creed in Latin, exactly as it is translated in the English prayer book, then in use at the cathedral of St. Patrick's. Over against the opening words Swift has written:

> *Confessio fidei*
> *barbaris digna*

which I suppose must be translated, "A creed worthy of the barbarians," or, perhaps, "fit for the Russians."

Does this mean that, after all, Swift had become a creature of the Enlightenment, a real contemporary of Voltaire, or at least so much an Augustan as to find the source of his morality in Republican Rome rather than among the Christian barbarians? This, I suppose, would be easily acceptable to many of Swift's modern readers, probably to all of his admirers in Russia and in Asia. But might there be another remote possibility, that he was here indulging himself for a moment in a sort of Pauline irony, where he admits that having had to give up all hope of the world—that Augustan civilized world his friends still believed in (he separates himself from them in that phrase in a letter to Pope—*vous autres*)—nothing now was left for him but the faith of the barbarians, that primitive Christianity which he had once said it would indeed be a wild project to offer to restore?

XI

Letters of Advice to Young Spinsters

By IRVIN EHRENPREIS

MOST GREAT moral issues have no history. They loom up in new forms at different periods, but they fail to develop themselves fundamentally. Old positions are reaffirmed after centuries of discussion. Research and analysis move nobody from one side of the argument to the other. Among such issues, none is more bleakly persistent that the proper relation of men to women. From the courts of love to the *mariages de convenance,* from vestal virgins to lady commissars, philosophy has fought with custom over the balance of power between the sexes. Always and everywhere gross inequality has been the rule; and yet the exceptions tell us more than does the common practice.

I count Jonathan Swift as being in a modest way one of those exceptions. So I hope to define some of his peculiar views and to show how his character as an author illustrates them. But instead of surveying the whole range of entries that might belong under the heading of relations between the sexes, I shall deal with only two, the education of females and the status of unmarried women. My reason is that on these topics Swift shows remarkable independence.

I shall compare Swift with other English writers—making a grand leap from the age of humanism to the Victorian age—in order to bring out some implications of his position. But I do not mean to hint that any evolution or progressive development will be visible in my accounts of these outlooks. On the contrary, the odd differences and likenesses ought to suggest a depressingly ambiguous conclusion. Finally, the bulk of my reflections will be given to a number of familiar letters written by Swift, Esther Johnson, and Esther Vanhomrigh. In these we can see how deeply his genius as an author is connected with, or derived from, his attitude toward women.

Now let me throw a panoramic glance at the sixteenth century. It may have been providential that Henry VIII's children and successors included two females. The example of Queen Elizabeth and other learned princesses on the continent had a powerful exemplary effect during the age of humanism. Even before her birth, Sir Thomas More delivered a classical statement on the intellectual training of ladies (*c.* 1518); and More was one of Swift's heroes, just as Elizabeth was one of his heroines.

Nor do I think that it affects the harvest, that a man or woman has sown the seed. If they are worthy of being ranked with the human race, if they are distinguished by reason from beasts; that learning, by which the reason is cultivated, is equally suitable to both. . . . But if the female soil be in its nature stubborn, and more productive of weeds than fruits, it ought, in my opinion, to be more diligently cultivated with learning and good instruction . . .[1]

More's admiring contemporary, the learned Luis Vives, taught the same doctrine, denouncing the foolish notion that scholarly studies inclined women toward evil manners: a mind set upon learning, said Vives, will abhor lust and light pleasures.[2] Thomas Elyot and Roger Ascham also backed this line of argument,[3] and the great educator Richard Mulcaster said God would never have given women "their own towardness" if it was to be left idle and unused.[4] Even during the reign of Gloriana such voices were a minority. But they were not muted; and Spenser's celebration of his sovereign's virtues paid tribute to her intellectual powers.

The Puritans undermined such ideals with their own picture of women as, at best, obedient wives, sober mothers, and efficient housekeepers. Among Christian and non-Christian thinkers alike the view that women are, as Castiglione said, imperfect creatures, incapable of the same virtues as men, has always been commonplace.⁵ But the normal Protestant identification of good women with chaste matrons tightened the chains on women, and the Puritans made this identification peculiarly heavy. By insisting on one standard of morality for both sexes, the Puritans did strengthen the integrity of the family.⁶ But they simultaneously demolished the dignity of spinsters and bachelors. Above all, the Puritan clergy felt pressed to display their destestation of popish doctrine by embracing matrimony as a holy rule. A few might be supposed to enjoy the blessing of continence, but, otherwise, none was allowed to escape the duties of a husband. One scholar says, "This dedication of the Puritan clerical caste to conjugal life was hardly less important in its effects than that of courtly poets to the worship of feminine beauty."⁷ Inevitably, women found their place defined by such teachings. "Who can be ignorant," cries Milton, "that woman was created for man, and not man for woman?"⁸ Adam's relation to Eve in *Paradise Lost* embodies the principle: Eve is described as "inferiour, in the mind / and inward faculties" (VIII, 540-42). Adam is her "guide and head," without whom she has no purpose (IV, 442-43), and at her best she sees how her own beauty is excelled by his "manly grace and wisdom" (IV, 490-91).⁹

Two hundred years after *Paradise Lost,* John Stuart Mill— a widower like Milton, though not remarried—published a classic work on the social position of women. Mill had written a sketch of his principles as a very young man, and he could hardly have sounded more furiously opposed to those of the epic poet. In this early essay, Mill had denounced the customary enchainment of women to a matrimonial doom. "It is not law,"

248
 Advice to Young Spinsters

he had said, "but education and custom which make the difference."

Women are so brought up, as not to be able to subsist in the mere physical sense, without a man to keep them: they are so brought up as not to be able to protect themselves against injury or insult, without some man on whom they have a special claim, to protect them: they are so brought up, as to have no vocation or useful office to fulfil in the world, remaining single; for all women who are educated to *be* married, & what little they are taught deserving the name useful, is chiefly what in the ordinary course of things will not come into actual use, unless nor until they are married. A single woman therefore is felt both by herself & others as a kind of excrescence on the surface of society, having no use or function or office there. She is not indeed precluded from useful & honorable exertion of various kinds: but a married woman is *presumed* to be a useful member of society unless there is evidence to the contrary; a single woman must establish what very few either women or men ever do establish, an *individual* claim.[10]

Like several Renaissance thinkers,[11] Mill pleaded that the relation between the sexes ought to be one of perfect equality. In *The Subjection of Women* (1869)—published a few years before his death—he admitted "no power or privilege on the one side, nor disability on the other."[12] In his *Autobiography* (1873) he said that among the earliest and most persistent of his convictions was the principle that "complete equality in all legal, political, social and domestic relations" ought to hold between men and women.

To these celebrated declarations Mill's contemporary James Fitzjames Stephen replied, "Men are stronger than women in every shape. They have greater muscular and nervous force, greater intellectual force, greater vigour of character."[13] If marriage is to be permanent, said Stephen, "the government of the family must be put by law and by morals in the hands of the husband."[14] A disobedient wife, he said, shows "a base, unworthy, mutinous disposition—a disposition utterly subversive of all that is most worth having in life."[15] Mill's one-time friend Carlyle also saw, in the notion of an equality of the sexes, a transgression of a law of nature. He told his fiancée, " 'The man should bear rule in the house, and not the woman.' This is an eternal axiom, the law of nature, which no man departs from unpunished."[16]

Midway between the humanists and the Victorians lies the Augustan age, and here I return to Swift. I shall not claim the Dean possessed a deep philosophical view of woman's nature, or that he was so radical a thinker as Mill. But I shall argue that he represents a fascinating mixture of the eternal opposites in the still unsettled controversy, and that his letters to Esther Johnson and Esther Vanhomrigh illustrate the fact. I shall further argue that in the rhetoric and prose style of his own letters and those of Mrs. Vanhomrigh we can trace the effect of their opposed conceptions of womanly character.

We may begin with Swift's least eccentric statements. In the essay *A Letter to a Young Lady,* he employs a definition of the marriage yoke that was quite normal—the female being subordinate to the male and obliged to please him. Addressing the bride, Swift says, "The grand affair of your life will be to gain and preserve the friendship and esteem of your husband."[17] But one must not suppose he left things at that. What sets Swift apart from his simpler contemporaries is a pair of assumptions. First, whether or not a woman married, Swift believed that her intellectual and moral character should be developed as fully as possible. In a utopian passage of *Gulliver's Travels* he described the Lilliputians as educating girls like boys: "Neither did I perceive any difference in their education, made by their difference of sex, only that the exercises of the females were not altogether so robust; and that some rules were given them relating to domestick life, and a smaller compass of learning was enjoyned them." In Houyhnhnmland, Gulliver's master thought it monstrous of mankind "to give the females a different kind of education from the males, except in some articles of domestick management."[18] Even in the *Letter to a Young Lady*, Swift wrote, "I am ignorant of any one quality that is amiable in a man, which is not equally so in a woman . . . so there is no quality whereby women endeavour to distinguish themselves from men, for which they are not just so much the worse."[19]

The second assumption setting Swift apart from most of his contemporaries is that women who never marry remain complete human beings and require no special justification for their state. Writing to a man who wished to marry his own beloved Esther Johnson, Swift said, "Nor shall any consideration of my own misfortune of losing so good a friend and companion as her, prevail on me, against her interest and settlement in the world, since it is held so necessary and convenient a thing for ladies to marry; and that time takes off from the lustre of virgins in all other eyes but mine."[20] Hating the Puritans as venomously as Swift did, it is no wonder that he felt satisfied to remain a celibate priest. He may remind us of Tertullian and Jerome when he extolls the crown of virginity. But he deserves some credit for respecting the character of independent single ladies. Mary Astell, whose *Essay in Defence of the Female Sex* came out thirty years before *Gulliver's Travels*, had argued that women were equal to men. In soul, body, intellect, and morals, she declared, men had no essential advantage over her own sex. "Nothing but disencouragement, or an idle uncurious humour," she said, "can hinder us from rivalling most men in knowledge of great variety of things."[21] Yet she did not propose that the two sexes be educated alike, and she did not raise the question of matrimonial or spinsterly status. Lady Mary Wortley Montagu belongs to the generation following Swift's, and she ardently recommended the intellectual cultivation of women. But when she heard of a rich, unattached widow, she shuddered. "Learning," she wrote, "is necessary to the happiness of women, and ignorance the common foundation of their errors."[22] But to be a young, wealthy widow, said Lady Mary, was to "walk blindfold upon stilts amidst precipices."[23] There was, she said, only one way for a woman to establish herself in secure good fortune; and that was through a prudent marriage.[24]

About fifteen years after these bleak remarks we meet a fair approximation of Swift's views in *The Man of Feeling*. Here a temporary mouthpiece of Mackenzie's harangues the protagonist of the novel:

> Nor are your females trained to any ... useful purpose: they are taught, by the very rewards which their nurses propose for good behaviour, by the first thing like a jest which they hear from every male visitor of the family, that a young woman is a creature to be married; and when they are grown somewhat older, are instructed, that it is the purpose of marriage to have the enjoyment of pin-money and the expectation of a jointure.[25]

Maybe it is more than a coincidence that Mackenzie assigns these scornful sentiments to a misanthropic bachelor.

Unlike Mackenzie's misanthrope, Swift understood the painful implications of his own doctrine. In some of his poems he makes the consequences explicit and arrives at a pessimistic paradox: viz., that if a woman does rise to his standards, no eligible man will appreciate her, and she will never find a husband;[26] and if a man is the sort Swift admires, he is unlikely to meet a suitable wife.[27] The honorific connotations for spinsterhood and bachelordom are obvious.

Swift's letters to Esther Johnson—today commonly known as Stella—are one-sided. None remains of the many she wrote to him. But almost seventy remain of his to her, practically all dating from the triennium 1710–1713. Besides, there are what amount to public letters in verse, i.e., the dozen poems he addressed to her from 1719 to 1727. The series of sixty-five diary letters in less than three years, we know misleadingly as the

Journal to Stella. These are the most self-revelatory compositions Swift ever produced; they are important sources for the history of England under Queen Anne; they were used by Herbert Davis as the foundation of his little book on Mrs. Johnson;[28] and they have been examined by Professor Mackie Jarrell and Professor Frederik Smith as examples of Swift's literary art.[29]

The letters involving Esther Vanhomrigh—known today as Vanessa—are two-sided and cover a period of ten and a half years. Besides preserving twenty-seven of Swift's letters to herself, Mrs. Vanhomrigh kept drafts of seventeen she wrote to him. Yet the materials of this correspondence are so private and personal that they have been read almost wholly as biographical documents.

There can be no question of dealing with such a miscellany as two distinct correspondences. Rather we have the opposed characters of two women embodied in the brilliant familiar letters of their common friend. What emerges from a comparison is the fact that Swift tried to force both into the same pattern and succeeded only with Stella, the elder of the two. His best letters represent one kind of rhetoric; Vanessa's represent another. The style of his letters has one relation to his purpose; the style of Vanessa's has another. But I am going to dwell on the fact that both of these gifted writers have left us not merely documents of the deepest psychological interest but also works of epistolary art, fine specimens of a genre seldom handled in literary terms. Character, motive, mode, style, and tone are what we have to consider.

Let me start with my unkindest cut. In May 1719—in his fifty-second year—Swift assured Mrs. Vanhomrigh in bad French that she possessed honor, good sense, wit, grace, and firmness of spirit; compared with her, he said, all other women were beasts in skirts.[30] A couple of months later Swift assured Mrs. Johnson in verse that no two women combined could supply her charms:

> Oh, would it please the gods to split
> Thy beauty, size, and years, and wit,
> No age could furnish out a pair
> Of nymphs so gracefull, wise and fair
> With half the lustre of your eyes,
> With half your wit, your years and size . . ."[31]

Spenser, calling on the muses to help him "blaze / Her worthy praise, / Which in her sexe doth all excell"[32] could hardly have gone further. But in the fall of the following year Swift insisted to Mrs. Vanhomrigh that she still excited his unalterable admiration: "I have the same respect, esteem and kindness for you I ever professed to have and shall ever preserve, because you always merit the utmost that can be given you . . ."[33] About the same time, he paid another versified tribute to Mrs. Johnson's merit:

> Pallas observing Stella's wit
> Was more than for her sex was fit;
> And that her beauty, soon or late,
> Might breed confusion in the state,
> In high concern for human kind,
> Fixt *honour* in her infant mind.
>
> • • •
>
> Her hearers are amaz'd from whence
> Proceeds that fund of wit and sense;
> Which though her modesty would shroud,
> Breaks like the sun behind a cloud,
> While gracefulness its art conceals,
> And yet through ev'ry motion steals.[34]

The monotony of the compliments reveals not the kinship of the subjects or the duplicity of the admirer but the sameness of the model he set before them. The two women's differences are historically visible. The fixed routines long established with Esther Johnson, her public acceptance by Swift's circle, the steadiness of her domestic life, assign her to the part of the motherly wife. When Swift reproached her, it was not for imprudence but for angry stubbornness.[35] Mrs. Johnson had only a small fortune and the humblest parents. Esther Vanhomrigh was not only younger and more exciting than Mrs. Johnson; she was rich and came from a family with a high, secure place in Dublin society. When Swift scolded Vanessa, it was for her melancholy and her failures to be discreet. He visited her as secretly as possible, giving her the role of daughter-mistress.

The extant letters from Esther Vanhomrigh to Swift begin at an earlier date and end at a later than those he wrote to Esther Johnson. For coherence of structure, intensity of expression, and modernity of style they are superior to those written by Swift to either lady. The feature that distinguishes and dominates them is passion. Possibly the letters actually sent were more restrained than the drafts the lonely spinster preserved for us. But these drafts maintain the directness and singlemindedness typical of love letters. She has two subjects: Swift and herself. External events can only frame this relationship:

I firmly believe could I know your thoughts (which no humane creature is capable of geussing at because never any one liveing thought like you) I should find you have often in a rage wished me religious hopeing then I should have paid my devotions to heaven but that would not spair you for was I an enthusiast still you'd be the deity I should worship. What markes are there of a deity but what you are to be known by? You are present every where. Your dear image is before my eyes. Some times you strike me with that prodigious awe I tremble with fear; at other times a charming compassion shines through your countynance, which revives my soul. Is it not more reasonable to adore a radiant forme one has seen than one only described?[36]

Anecdotes are rare and vague in Mrs. Vanhomrigh's letters; she has few characterizations of interesting persons; she supplies little news or gossip. In other words, she lacks the substantive quality to be found in typically good letters of the eighteenth century—say the letters of Lady Mary or Horace Walpole. But the immediacy and impetuosity of her style are hardly ever relaxed; the confessional exposure of the heights and depths of her emotions is continuous but varied. Besides these prehensile gifts she has wit, and uses it in the way that her particular correspondent will appreciate. In doing so, she illustrates a critical principle, that the form of a letter is dictated by the relation between the writer and the recipient. Thus, complaining, as usual, of Swift's failure to write to her, she says,

> ...you must needs be extreamly happy where you are to forgett your absent friends and I believe you have formed a new system and think there is no more of this world passing your sensible horizon. If this be your notion I must excuse you; if not you can plead no other excuse, and if it be so I must reckon my self of another world. Butt I shall have much a do to be persuaded till you send me some convincing arguments of it, dont dally in a thing of this consequence but demonstrate that tis possible to keep up a correspondence between friends thô in different worlds...[37]

The wit here is good enough for Dorothy Osborne writing to William Temple. But it is cut to fit Vanessa's very different correspondent. When Mrs. Vanhomrigh mocks at philosophical systems, she conciously mirrors Swift's own attitudes; and the spontaneity with which she gives her conceit a series of graceful turns suggests his own manner of gallantry. When she explicitly considers the foundation of their friendship, she (oddly enough) sees it as rational; yet the rational aspect is precisely what her style ignores. In fact, her accomplishment as an epistolary author depends on the fixity of her passion, which gives, over the years, a lyric pathos to her yearning for an inactive, absentee lover. Perhaps the most famous and effective passage in all her writing is the least rational:

O — — — how have you forgott me. You indeavour by severities to force me from you, nor can I blame you, for with the utmost distress and confusion I behold my self the cause of uneasie reflections to you. Yet I can not comfort you but here declair that tis not in the power of arte time or accident to lessen the unexpressible passion which I have for — — —. Put my passion under the utmost restraint, send me as distant from you as the earth will alow, yet you can not banish those charming idaea's which will ever stick by me whilst I have the use of memory. Nor is the love I beare you only seated in my soul, for there is not a single atome of my frame that is not blended with it. Therefor don't flatter your self that separation will ever change my sentiments, for I find myself unquiet in the midst of silence and my heart is at once pierced with sorrow and love...[38]

The nature of Vanessa's genius can be clarified by two references, one to John Locke, the other (and, of course, more important) to Swift. Locke had a bluestocking admirer a quarter-century younger than himself. She was Damaris, daughter of the Cambridge Platonist Ralph Cudworth, who in turn had tutored Sir William Temple at Emmanuel College. Locke and Damaris Cudworth exchanged superfine *billets doux* over the pseudonyms of Philander and Philoclea; and the junior correspondent wrote a vile poem in tetrameter couplets eerily foreshadowing *Cadenus and Vanessa;* in this she told how she had offered Locke her love and he had replied with a promise of friendship. Two sentences from one of her letters will be a measure of Vanessa's powers:

Be it under whatever pretence you please that you have sent me a letter you ought not to fear that it should be ill taken, since nothing can be liable to a misinterpretation that you say, who, as I believe, you could not really deceive, so perhaps should you design it, you might not find it very easy, there being something necessary besides wit to make one succeed in it. You might therefore without any apprehension have written to me all that you pleased.[39]

The static dignity of this empty and affected style brings out the drama of Vanessa's. Swift's replies to his suffering satellite bring

out another quality. He could be *galant* and *sympathique* and
précieux. But he could also achieve bathos with incongruous
appeals to reason:

> We differ prodigiously in one point, I fly from the spleen to the
> worlds end, you run out of your way to meet it. I doubt the bad
> weather has hinderd you much from the diversions of your country
> house; and put you upon thinking in your chamber. The use I have
> made of it was to read I know not how many diverting books of
> history and travells. I wish you would get your self a horse, and have
> always two servants to attend you, and visit your neighbors, the
> worse the better.⁴⁰

Many of Swift's letters to Esther Vanhomrigh are unusually
coherent. He concentrates on the themes of her character and
its relation to his own. But he also brings in a miscellany of
names and events. Often he reports on his recent trips or pastimes; he tells what other people are doing around him; he
gives Vanessa advice about her health. Into the closeted air of
her own letters Swift brings scenes of the great and petty world.
Yet his are seldom excellent letters. The finest passages often
deal with facts he could tell anyone. The most conventional
phrases are usually in the passages devoted to his panting admirer, and suggest the tradition of *lettres galantes*. Here, for
example, is Swift's description of a visit to a humble parsonage
in Berkshire. It is pleasant, but more like Gray than Swift.
Notice how hard it would be to decide from the language how
well he knew the recipient of the letter or what sort of connection there was between that person and himself:

> I am at a clergyman's house, an old friend and acquaintance,
> whom I love very well, but he is such a melancholy thoughtfull man
> partly from nature, and partly by a solitary life that I shall soon
> catch the spleen from him. Out of ease and complaisance, I desire
> him not to alter any of his methods for me; so, we dine exactly
> between twelve and one, at eight we have some bread and butter,

and a glass of ale, and at ten he goes to bed. Wine is a stranger, except a little I sent him, of which one evening in two, we have a pint between us. His wife has been this month twenty miles off at her fathers, and will not return this ten days, I never saw her, and perhaps the house will be worse when she comes. I read all day or walk, and do not speak as many words as I have now writt, in three days."[41]

Apart from the evasiveness of the style—the reluctance to name places and persons—the letter might be directed to a father, a brother, or an old friend not seen for ten years. It hardly sounds like a message to a woman in love with the writer. Here is a passage from the very last of Swift's extant letters to Vanessa:

When you are melancholy, read diverting or amusing books; it is my receit, and seldom fails. Health, good humor and fortune are all that is valuable in this life; and the last contributes to the two former.[42]

I have not quoted the many piquant or touching sentences from Swift's letters to Vanessa because they would misrepresent the general effect of a man straining to transform a romantic obsession into a placid acquaintanceship. In his best prose, it is normal for Swift to play style against meaning, to sound casual when he says something shocking. It is normal for Vanessa to make style and meaning congruent, as Swift does in poetry. Vanessa's prose suggests the manner we think of as Romantic; she exerts herself to sound pathetic and sincere. But Swift leans the other way. As his relation to the person he addresses grows more emotional, he feels committed to making his manner more formal, to impose the distance the other person is trying to bridge. The truly irrational foundation of the tie between the Dean and his correspondent compels him not only to use private codes and foreign languages but also to express himself with a reserve that compensates for her extravagance. He remains Swift, and cannot write badly; but the less she accepts the role of a satisfied spinster—fond of books, improving conversation, and normal society—the more caution he must display.

A contemporary of John Stuart Mill's once described the kind of woman whom Swift found it easiest to write to:

I speculate much on the existence of unmarried and never-to-be married women now-a-days, and I have already got to the point of considering that there is no more respectable character on this earth than an unmarried woman who makes her own way through life quietly, preservingly, without support of husband or mother, and who, having attained the age of forty-five or upwards, retains in her possession a well-regulated mind, a disposition to enjoy simple pleasures, fortitude to support inevitable pains, sympathy with the sufferings of others, and willingness to relieve want as far as her means extend.[43]

The role described here by Charlotte Brontë (a year before *Jane Eyre* came out). fell not to Mrs. Vanhomrigh but to Mrs. Johnson. In a verse epistle to Swift, Stella thanks him for saving her from the desolation of women who rely for their appeal on beauty alone:

> Stella to you, her tutor, owes
> That she has ne'er resembled those;
> Nor was a burthen to mankind
> With half her course of years behind.
> You taught how I might youth prolong
> By knowing what was right and wrong.[44]

This poem is the nearest thing we have to a letter from her to Swift. It bears out his praise, in the memoranda on her death, of Mrs. Johnson's intelligence, humility, and charity. It also gives modest support to her character as a humanist lady, able to write couplets as well as read them. Because the relation between this pair of friends was straightforward and rational, his letters to her could be as erratic as he pleased—unpredictable, full of life. In structure and conventional rhetoric the letters to Vanessa are superior; those to Esther Johnson are fragmentary and dramatic, either beyond rhetoric or making a mockery of rhetoric. On so firm a groundwork of mutual understanding as they possessed, he could play the kind of games with identity that are essential to his literary genius; mimicry, parody, sudden hops from plain speech to irony. The journal letters Swift wrote to Mrs. Johnson are his chief contribution to history and to epistolary art. This is careful praise, because Swift wished to be a great historian and was a great letter-writer. Like Mme. de Sévigné and Lady Mary Wortley Montagu writing to their daughters, Swift drew amazingly varied inspiration from the remoteness of a beloved, appreciative reader.

One of the recurrent features of the letters to Mrs. Johnson is Swift's tendency to treat her as an equal, making few chivalric allowances for her femininity and trusting her to follow his leaps of thought and mood. He sends her pamphlets[45] and discusses politics with her as he would with a man of the world.[46] Only too often Swift alludes to Mrs. Johnson's lack of learning, but with steady regret—and he tries continually to fill the gaps. One recalls the warning he delivered in *A Letter to a Young Lady on Her Marriage*. There he urged that the new bride make up for her lack of formal education through private study; and in so doing, he lamented, "after all the pains you may be at, you can never arrive, in point of learning, to the perfection of a school-boy."[47] When Esther Johnson died, Swift praised her for knowing Greek and Roman history, for speaking French, for understanding Platonic and Epicurean philosophy, and for grasping the nature of government.[48] Like Colin Clout's great mistress—it seems—she did "in sciences abound."[49] But in the letters Swift sent during her early thirties, he sounds less assured. Exhorting her to read, he teases her for neglecting books: "From the very time you first went to Ireland," he says to Mrs. Johnson, "I have been always plying you to walk and read."[50]

He corrects her spelling remorselessly: "Ppt has made twenty false spellings in her writing; I'll send them to you all back again on the other side of this letter, to mend them."[51] He makes no concession to her virginity but deals with birth, copulation, and death as if she had a Wife of Bath's familiarity with the whole range of domestic experience. Here he is, reporting the details of a loathsome illness:

> On Thursday morning appeared great red spots in all those places where my pain was, and the violence of the pain was confined to my neck behind a little on the left side; which was so violent that I [had] not a minutes ease nor hardly a minutes sleep in three days and nights. The spots encreasd every day and had little pimples which are now grown white and full of corruption [tho'] small. The red still continues too, and most prodigious hott and inflamed. The disease is the shingles.[52]

Often he uses masculine forms of address to Mrs. Johnson and her friend Rebecca Dingley, calling them "boys" and "sirrahs." His anti-Puritanical leanings go so far that he shares with Mrs. Johnson pleasantries one would hardly expect a clergyman to share with anyone:

> When Mr. St. John was turned out from being secretary at war, three years ago, he retired to the country: there he was talking of something he would have written over his *summer-house,* and a gentleman gave him these verses:

> > From business and the noisy world retir'd,
> > Nor vex'd by love, nor by ambition fir'd;
> > Gently I wait the call of Charon's boat,
> > Still drinking like a fish, and [?swiving] like a stoat.
> ... I think the three grave lines do introduce the last well enough.[53]

I shall provide a further example to show the several factors working together: Swift's wish that Mrs. Johnson should be well-informed, his awareness that her education is incomplete, his indifference to her spinsterhood, and his confidence that she will not mistake his coarseness for disrespect:

The doctors tell me, that if poor Collonell Disney does not get some sleep tonight he must dye. What care you; ah but I do care; he is one of our Society, a fellow of abundance of humor, an old battered rake, but very honest, not an old man but an old rake. It was he that said of Jinny Kingdom the maid of honor, who is a little old, that since she could not get a husband the Qu—— should give her a brevet to act as a married woman: You don't understand this. They give brevets to majors and captains to act as collonells in the army; brevets are commissions...[54]

The relation that makes the framework of Swift's letters to Esther Johnson is as confidential and free as any that Swift ever formed. He was not afraid of being misinterpreted by the closest friend he had. Thanks to this emotional security, he could ignore the epistolary forms of the humanists, whose letters to ladies exemplified their training in classical rhetoric. He could ignore the demands of the French *lettres galantes*—the mannered wit of Guez de Balzac, Vincent Voiture, and Bussy Rabutin—though this was the style he aimed at in his letters to ladies of fashion and to Esther Vanhomrigh. He could fall back on his literary instincts and produce repeatedly the contrast between syntax and meaning that Swift infused into his masterpieces of ironic prose.

A simple example is the opposition between a relaxed, spontaneous order of words and a shocking sentiment; for example, on Swift's prospect of being godfather if their friend Mrs. Walls should give birth to a boy:

No truly, I will not be godfather to goody Walls this bout, and I hope she'll have no more. There will be no quiet nor cards for this child. I hope it will die the day after the christening.[55]

To us the heartlessness sounds unforgivable, because there is no sign of deliberation in the colloquial syntax: we seem to hear precisely what Swift means just as he happens on the words. To Mrs. Johnson the intention is clearer: Swift knows she agrees with him that Mrs. Walls shows no dedication to motherhood and already has a bigger family than she can look after. If Swift had pretended to feel cheerful upon seeing another ill-discharged responsibility added to Archdeacon Walls' load, he would have been hypocritical; so Swift inverts the usual sentiments and produces a language of pseudo-misanthropy. If we are to digest the wit, we must take it inside the epistolary frame provided by Mrs. Johnson's intimacy with her oldest friend.

The opposite of this effect takes place when Swift allows elementary feelings to subdue the ironic manner. Mrs. Johnson writes from Dublin to tell him that the mother of his friend Lord Shelburne has just died. Swift, in London, adopts his pose of worldliness and assumes the son will be pleased by the consequent advantage to his fortune. So he drily writes, "At four I went to congratulate with Lord Shelburn, for the death of poor Lady Shelburn dowager; he was at his country house; and returned while I was there, and had not heard of it, and he took it very well."[56] But at the end of the paragraph, just before going to bed, Swift lets his own fondness for the dead lady peep out from a curtain of small talk. He knows Mrs. Johnson has been dining and card-playing with Dean Stearne, Mrs. Walls, and other friends: "What had the Dean for supper? How much did Mrs. Walls win? Poor Lady Shelburn ..."[57] Here Swift is not talking to himself, with us eavesdropping. He is asking Mrs. Johnson to join him in his sadness, carefully understated, over the loss of an acquaintance he will miss.[58] We can understand the tone only as it emerges from the exchange between the letter-writer and a friend who, like himself, is content to live without a family but not without friends, and who, like himself, has made peace with the ways of the world.

Thanks to this community of sensibility, the letters to Esther Johnson give Swift openings for anecdotes and reflections that deal repeatedly with the same persons and themes, as these develop over a long, dramatic period in his own life and in English political history. The element of sequential narrative is remarkable, therefore, whether as the story of the Oxford ministry or the career of Jonathan Swift. With the signing of the Treaty of Utrecht and Swift's appointment to a deanery, this element finds its climax, peripety, and denouement; the letters reach an end quite naturally, then, with Swift's departure for Dublin, to be installed in his deanery.

This large narrative element in the letters to Mrs. Johnson is well known, and I shall not discuss it further. Instead, I shall call attention to smaller and more Swiftian surprises. The pseudo-cynical contrast between style and meaning is a kind of mimicry: Swift pretends to be indifferent to suffering, or he imitates the tone of a rake. Straight mimicry also appears in these letters; and the success of such little acts depends on the lady recipient's wit. She must have the kind of ear that easily distinguishes her friend's nuances of humor.

This aspect of Mrs. Johnson's literary culture Swift explicitly praised: "It was observed by all her acquaintance, that she never failed in company to say the best thing that was said."[59] And he assembled a little, disappointing collection of her *bons mots.*[60] Similarly, he singled out her "true taste of wit and good sense, both in poetry and prose."[61] These are powers the humanistic ladies valued themselves on, from Queen Elizabeth to Lady Mary Wortley Montagu; they permeate the letters of Dorothy Osborne to Swift's master, Sir William Temple; they are what Ménage taught Mme. de Sévigné. Swift confidently relies on them in a passage like the following, when he makes believe he has been watching Mrs. Johnson lose money at the game of ombre:

Why, the reason you lost four and eight-pence last night but one at Manley's, was because you played bad games: I took notice of six that you had ten to one against you. Would any but a mad lady go

out twice upon Manilio, Basto, and two small diamonds? Then in
that game of spades, you blundered when you had ten-ace; I never
saw the like of you: and now you are in a huff because I tell you this.
Well, here's two and eight-pence half-penny towards your loss.[62]

My concluding quotation is the most elaborate specimen.
Swift mimics both Mrs. Johnson and himself in a hoax. She has
not written for three weeks. He pretends the reason is that Mrs.
Walls has had a bad lying-in and that Mrs. Johnson and her
companion Mrs. Dingley have had to spend all their time with
her. The Archdeacon mentioned is Walls, the prolific father;
the Dean is their friend, John Stearne; Pdfr is Swift. Mrs. Stoyte
is a married friend; Catherine is an unmarried friend. First of
all, Swift speaks, reproaching Mrs. Johnson for her long silence.
Next he replies in her voice, giving the imaginary reason. Then
Swift mimics Mrs. Johnson's scolding him for putting wrong
words in her mouth; and finally he returns to his own voice
and comments on a detail of the made-up story:

> Three weeks and three days since my last letter from MD, rare
> doings: why truly we were so busy with poor Mrs. Walls, that indeed,
> Pdfr, we could not write, we were afraid the poor woman would have
> died; and it pitied us to see the archdeacon, how concerned he was.
> The dean never came to see her but once; but now she is up again,
> and we go and sit with her in the evenings. The child died the next
> day after it was born, and I believe, between friends, she is not very
> sorry for it. —Indeed, Pdfr, you are plaguy silly to-night, and han't
> guest one word right; for she and the child are both well, and it is
> a fine girl, likely to live; and the dean was godfather, and Mrs.
> Catherine and I were godmothers; I was going to say Stoite, but I
> think I have heard they don't put maids and married women to-
> gether; though I know not why I think so, nor I don't care; what
> care I? but I must prate...[63]

The woman who read that passage correctly needed more than
learning; she had to have come to terms with permanent spin-

sterhood; and she probably had to be able to write excellent letters. The descent from Spenser's Gloriana to Swift's Stella is immense; yet the thread of connection is dimly visible.

Notes

1. *Correspondence,* ed. E. F. Rogers (Princeton, 1947), no. 63, as quoted in Ruth Kelso, *Doctrine for the Lady of the Renaissance* (Urbana, Ill., 1956), p. 62.

2. *De institutione feminae Christianae,* I, iv, as quoted in Kelso, loc. cit. See also Carroll Camden, *The Elizabethan Woman* (Houston, 1952), pp. 47–48.

3. Kelso, p. 74; Camden, pp. 48, 56.

4. *Positions Wherin Those Primitive Circumstances Be Examined . . . for the Training Up of Children* (1581), pp. 166–74, as quoted in Camden, p. 47.

5. *The Courtier,* trans. T. Hoby (Everyman's Library), p. 196.

6. Louis B. Wright, *Middle-Class Culture in Elizabethan England* (Chapel Hill, N.C., 1935), p. 218.

7. W. R. and M. Haller, "The Puritan Art of Love," *Huntington Library Quarterly,* V (1942), 238.

8. *The Doctrine and Discipline of Divorce,* Bk. II, chap. xv.

9. Cf. Spenser, *Faerie Queene,* V, v, 25:

> But vertuous women wisely understand
> That they were borne to base humilitie,
> Unless the heavens them lift to lawfull soveraintie.

10. F. A. Hayek, *John Stuart Mill and Harriet Taylor* (London, 1951), p. 63.

11. See Kelso, pp. 18–21.

12. Chap. I, para. 1.

13. *Liberty Equality, Fraternity* (1873), ed. R. J. White (Cambridge, England, 1967), p. 194.

14. *Ibid.,* p. 196.

15. *Ibid.,* p. 197.

16. J. A. Froude, *Thomas Carlyle* (London, 1882), I, 346.

17. *Prose Works,* ed. H. Davis (Oxford, 1939–68), IX, 89. Here, as in all my quotations from Swift, Esther Johnson, and Esther Vanhomrigh, I ignore the original capitals, italics, and abbreviations except where they agree with modern usage.

18. *Prose Works,* XI, 46, 253.

19. *Ibid.,* IX, 93.

267

20. *Correspondence,* ed. H. Williams (Oxford, 1963–65), I, 45–46.

21. *An essay in defence of the female sex* (London, 1696), p. 54.

22. *Complete Letters,* ed. R. Halsband (Oxford, 1965–67), III, 83. I follow the modern usage in capitals.

23. *Ibid.,* p. 80; cf. p. 99.

24. *Ibid.,* p. 83.

25. *The Man of Feeling,* ed. B. Vickers (Oxford, 1967), p. 40.

26. See *Cadenus and Vanessa.*

27. *To Lord Harley,* ll, 23–32, in *Poems,* 2nd ed., ed. H. Williams (Oxford, 1958), I, 177.

28. *Stella: a Gentlewoman of the Eighteenth Century* (New York, 1942).

29. Mackie L. Jarrell, "Swift's Peculiar Vein of Humor" (unpublished dissertation, University of Texas, 1954); Frederik N. Smith, "Dramatic Elements in Swift's *Journal to Stella,*" *Eighteenth-Century Studies,* I (June, 1968), 332–52.

30. *Correspondence,* II, 325–26.

31. *Poems,* II, 722.

32. *The Shepheardes Calender,* "Aprill," ll. 43–54.

33. *Correspondence,* II, 360.

34. *Poems,* II, 723, 726.

35. *Ibid.,* pp. 730–32.

36. *Correspondence,* II, 364. I have expanded contractions, added capitals at the beginnings of sentences and periods at the end, and other punctuation medially. This passage may show the influence of Pope's *Eloisa to Abelard.* "Religious" may mean "a nun."

37. *Correspondence,* I, 309. I suppose there is an allusion to Berkeley's immaterialism.

38. *Ibid.,* II, 363. The dashes stand for tender expressions, probably "dear, dear Cadenus." There may again be echoes of *Eloisa to Abelard.*

39. Maurice Cranston, *John Locke* (New York, 1957), p. 219.

40. *Correspondence,* II, 429–30. I have expanded contractions, etc.

41. *Ibid.,* p. 26.

42. *Ibid.* pp. 432–33.

43. Letter of 30 Jan. 1846 to Margaret Wooler.

44. *Poems,* II, 737. I accept the attribution to Esther Johnson.

45. *Journal to Stella,* ed. H. Williams (Oxford, 1948), II, 519.

46. *Ibid.,* I, 159, for example.

47. *Prose Works,* IX, 92.

48. *Ibid.,* V, 231.

49. Spenser, *Colin Clouts Come Home Againe,* l. 745.

50. *Journal,* II, 403.

51. *Ibid.,* p. 388; cf. pp. 392–93.

52. *Ibid.,* p. 528.

53. *Ibid.,* I, 164. The bracketed word is conjectural; in the original there is only a dash, which may be the editor's; but the word must have been some slang term for copulating.

54. *Journal,* II, 639.

55. *Ibid.,* I, 129.

56. *Ibid.,* I, 132.

57. *Loc. cit.*

58. Cf. *ibid.,* I, 141.

59. *Prose Works,* V, 237.

60. *Ibid.,* pp. 237–38.

61. *Ibid.,* p. 231.

62. *Journal to Stella,* I, 43.

63. *Ibid.,* pp. 202–3.

XII.

Ladies of Letters in the Eighteenth Century

By ROBERT HALSBAND

ONE VANTAGE point from which to observe ladies of letters in eighteenth-century England is the clash in 1733 between two of that period's most vivid literary characters, Lady Mary Wortley Montagu and Alexander Pope. In that year, with the first of his brilliant imitations of Horace's satires, the poet attacked the lady he had once adored. Not poisoning or hanging can one expect (he writes):

> From furious *Sappho* scarce a milder Fate,
> P-x'd by her Love, or libell'd by her Hate.

London's literary and Court circles evidently identified Lady Mary as the Sappho of the couplet: she was, after all, the patron saint of smallpox inoculation as well as a notorious wit. And so she called on Pope's friend Lord Peterborough and asked him to intercede. He would not involve himself in the affair, Peterborough told her; but he then sent her a letter saying that

[Pope] wondered how the town could apply those lines to any but some noted common woman, that he should yet be more surprised if you should take them to yourself. He named to me four remarkable poetesses and scribblers, Mrs. Centlivre, Mrs. Haywood, Mrs. Manley, and Mrs. Behn, ladies famous indeed in their generation, and some of them esteemed to have given very unfortunate favors to their friends, assuring me that such only were the objects of his satire.

271

Who were these "remarkable poetesses and scribblers"? Aphra Behn, long since dead, wrote plays and prose romances— *Oroonoko,* her most famous; and she achieved burial in the cloister of Westminster Abbey without redeeming her reputation for immorality. Susannah Centlivre, who began her career as an actress, wrote verse and published many plays—nineteen in number, of which fifteen were staged. Pope taunted her in print for being a cook's wife: her husband, to be sure, held the post of Yeoman of the Mouth to Queen Anne. Of the women listed, Mary de la Rivière Manley was highest in the social scale, the daughter of a Cavalier knight; she wrote plays, a few political pamphlets, and popular *romans à clef* to expose contemporary scandal. Eliza Haywood, the only one of the four still alive, busily continued her scribbling career until 1756, with a voluminous output of plays, verse, periodical essays, and fiction. However varied these Sapphos were in their social origins, careers, and literary works, they had one trait in common: they wrote to earn money. How enthusiastically would they have emended Dr. Johnson's dictum to read: No woman but a blockhead ever wrote except for money!

This profile of women writers in the earlier years of the eighteenth century is only one side of the coin. What is depicted on the other is quite different—as we can see in the stately quarto volume published in 1752 by George Ballard of Magdalen College, Oxford: *Memoirs of Several Ladies of Great Britain, Who Have Been Celebrated for Their Writings or Skill in the Learned Languages, Arts and Sciences.* "It is pretty certain," he oraculates in his preface, "that England hath produced more women famous for literary accomplishments, than any other nation in Europe." Beginning with Juliana the Anchoret of Norwich, who died in 1443, Ballard sketches the careers of sixty-four ladies. No raffish poetesses like Pope's Sapphos win a place in his literary pantheon; for our period he treats such worthies as the feminist Mary Astell and the poet Lady Winchilsea. Although he disdains to include Mrs. Manley, he considered her pseudo-fictional romances reliable enough to quote a long passage from the *New Atlantis* for one of his biographical sketches. All his ladies have one trait in common besides their respectability: they did not write for money. Could there have been any connection between respectability and profit?

In the development of the "Female Pen"—a phrase used by Aphra Behn and Mrs. Centlivre—Mrs. Behn is generally credited with being the first to earn her living by her writings. Despised in her own time by what we would today call the literary Establishment, she was fortunate enough after more than two centuries to be praised by no less a champion than Virginia Woolf. "With Mrs. Behn we turn a very important corner on the road," writes Mrs. Woolf. "We leave behind, shut up in their parks among their folios, those solitary great ladies who wrote without audience or criticism, for their own delight alone." Elsewhere in her essay—whose main theme is that "a woman must have money and a room of her own if she is to write fiction"—Mrs. Woolf enunciates her pecuniary bias: "Money dignifies what is frivolous if unpaid for." If the pursuit of money distinguishes the dilettante amateur from the dedicated professional, why must a woman writer have a modest private income? Mrs. Woolf's generalization may apply to women of her own time but how does it fit those of the eighteenth century?

Apart from Lady Mary and the writers invoked by Pope, what other women published their writings in the first half of the century? If we scan the standard bibliography of the period we find not many of Mrs. Woolf's "solitary great ladies"—the Countess of Winchilsea and Lady Chudleigh. The other women listed as poets are Mary Barber, Mary Chandler, Mary Masters, and Elizabeth Rowe; as playwrights, Mary Pix and Catherine Trotter; and as writers of fiction, about ten, ending with Sarah Fielding. In her preface to *David Simple* (in 1744) Miss Fielding apologizes for her presumption: "Perhaps the best Excuse that can be made for a Woman's venturing to write at all, is that which really produced this Book; Distress in her Circumstances: which she could not so well remove by any other Means in her Power." Whether inspired by the Muse or by distressed circumstances, how many of these women's names—let alone their writings—have survived their own day?

In Lady Mary we see a woman who defies the categories, or better still, combines them. Her reputation, soiled by Pope and by Horace Walpole, approaches that of the disreputable Sapphos; yet she is still an aristocratic lady, daughter of a duke and mother-in-law of a Prime Minister. She had considerably more than £500 a year to live on; and as for a room of her own: in England she had a town mansion and a country house, and when she lived in Italy one or two spacious *palazzi*. She did not write for money, but neither did she write "without audience or criticism." She applied herself to the writer's craft with an intensity and dedication that should have won Mrs. Woolf's admiration.

Before dealing with Lady Mary's ideas on women we must be aware of her contradictions and complexities. As a young woman she was like Oscar Wilde's Gwendolen Fairfax; gay, paradoxical, unrestrained by the rigidities of her social rank. Then, as she grew older and her social arteries hardened, she occasionally sounds like Gwendolen's mother, Lady Bracknell, appalled by the restless lower classes. She had once hobnobbed with Pope and Johnny Gay; as an old woman, she considered Pope an upstart whose birth and hereditary fortune entitled him to be a footman. Contradictions also appear because her opinions are not developed in a deliberate, reasoned treatise but in spontaneous, unrehearsed letters; and these, like most informal letters, are the resultant of three forces—the writer, the occasion, and the recipient. During the final decades of her life her main correspondent was her daughter Lady Bute, a proto-

Victorian of impeccable respectability; and Lady Mary tried to accommodate herself to the notions of her beloved child.

Her opinion of women's capabilities, a topic close to feminism, underwent a contrary change—conservative when she was young, radical when she was old. As a young lady, she sent her translation of Epictetus to Bishop Burnet, and along with it a letter in defence of learning for women; she then continues: "I am not now arguing for an Equality for the 2 Sexes; I do not doubt God and Nature has thrown us into an Inferior Rank. We are a lower part of the Creation; we owe Obedience and Submission to the Superior Sex; and any Woman who suffers her Vanity and folly to deny this, Rebells against the Law of the Creator and indisputable Order of Nature." But in her sixties, she was inclined "to think (if I dare say it) that Nature has not plac'd us in an inferior Rank to Men, no more than the Females of other Animals, where we see no distinction of capacity." She may not have dared to utter this revolutionary thought in her younger days, but she had clearly implied it in her remarks about women's education and, in fact, had exemplified it in her own self-education and energetic career as a writer.

In no part of the world are women treated with so much contempt as in England, she writes; the greatest injustice is to deprive them of the opportunity for education, as though the "same Studies which raise the character of a Man should hurt that of a Woman. We are educated in the grossest ignorance, and no art omitted to stiffle [*sic*] our natural reason." Elsewhere she summed up her philosophy of women's education with admirable succinctness: "Learning is necessary to the Happiness of Women, and ignorance the common foundation of their Errors both in Morals and Conduct." In her education, a woman should "conceal whatever Learning she attains, with as much solicitude as she would hide crookedness or lameness." Womanly modesty is all-important; and girls, while encouraged to read, should not expect or desire any applause from it. In a simi-

lar vein, Lord Chesterfield praised Lady Hervey as being well
bred and polite, and with all the reading that a woman should
have, and more than any need have, for she understood Latin
perfectly well, though she wisely concealed it.

In her own education Lady Mary received the traditional
training of a girl of her social class, but on her own initiative
she went far beyond it. To begin with, her governess taught her
to write a hand that was clear and regular, while her own personality added a masculine boldness. Since she was the oldest
daughter in a motherless household, it was her duty to carve at
her father's dinners, and so a carving-master came three times
a week to instruct her in that craft. She was taught needlework
and drawing but apparently no musical instrument; French, of
course, and Italian as well. She read with abandon in English
and French poetry, drama, and romances, evidently to her
father's satisfaction. "My obsolete Education was aplauded
when I should have been whipp'd," she recalled in her old age.

She went far beyond this obsolete education, and with the
aid of dictionaries and grammars she studied Latin—five to six
hours a day for two years, she told Joseph Spence. As an adolescent, she translated Ovid, her favorite Latin poet; and by the
time she was twenty-one she could send Bishop Burnet her
translation (from the Latin) of Epictetus's *Enchiridion*. Although Hannah Woolley, in *The Gentlewoman's Companion*
of 1675, had advised studying Latin as well as French and
Italian, few gentlewomen took that hard advice. Too many
parents were fearful that if their daughters understood any
learned language or were conversant with books they might
not find husbands.

When Lady Mary, as a young wife, attended the court of
George the First soon after his arrival from Hanover, she set
about learning German. She would learn a foreign language
not only to win a king's attention but to enjoy a literary work.
Many years later she refused to read *Don Quixote* in transla-

tion, explaining to her daughter: "thô I am a meer pidler in the Spanish Language, I had rather take pains to understand him in the Original than sleep over a stupid Translation." When she had accompanied her husband on his embassy to Constantinople she learned Turkish *en route;* and on her voyage home she copied inscriptions from Greek monuments in Asia Minor. No doubt she was a "meer pidler" in these linguistic and antiquarian pursuits, but they show how boundless her intellectual horizon was. In her own words, she was born not with an inclination but with a passion for learning. Although she set no limits on her knowledge, she always believed "the reputation of learning a misfortune to a woman."

She expresses a parallel aristocratic attitude toward writing: as demeaning if done for publication, and disgraceful if for profit. But here she was bravely inconsistent. "When I print, I submit to be answer'd and criticised," she tells her daughter, "but as I never did, 'tis hard to be abus'd for other people's Follys." She forgot this pose once when she exclaimed in vexation: "I have seen things I have wrote so mangle'd and falsify'd I have scarce known them. I have seen Poems I never read publish'd with my Name at length, and others that were truly and singly wrote by me, printed under the names of others." Still, she insisted that she had never aimed at "the Vanity of popular Applause."

In writing to Sir James Steuart, she revealed her literary obsession: she was "haunted . . . by the Daemon of Poesie"; she then implores him to have indulgence for her "as for a sister of the quill." But then she apologizes: "Do not be offended at the word Poet; it slip'd out unawares. I know that you scorn it, tho' it has been dignify'd by Lord Sommers, Lord Godolphin, and Dr. Atterbury." What a strange trio of poets to invoke!— a Lord Chancellor, who wrote some slight verses on classical themes; a Lord High Treasurer, who wrote three verse fables; and a Bishop (she overlooks his Jacobite taint), who wrote Latin verse. This antithesis of Grub Street is the *reductio ad absurdum* of Lady Mary's aristocratic standard of literature.

In contrast to these are writers who write "meerly to get money"; they are corrupted, she says, because they are forced to "fall into the notions that are most acceptable to the present Taste." Her cousin Henry Fielding, she recalls, would "have approach'd nearer to his excellencies if not forc'd by necessity to publish without correction, and throw many productions into the World he would have thrown into the Fire if meat could have been got without money, or money without Scribbling." And then she proclaims her lofty principle: "The Greatest Virtue, Justice, and the most distinguishing prerogative of Mankind, writeing, when duly executed do Honor to Human nature, but when degenerated into Trades are the most contemptible ways of getting Bread." This implies a choice between Grub Street and the Temple of Apollo. When compared with Mrs. Woolf's generalization, this paradox emerges: the pecuniary motive that is in Lady Mary's view destructive of literary value is precisely what, in Mrs. Woolf's, dignifies the writing of women.

In her own multifarious career as a writer, one wonders, did Lady Mary satisfy her elevated aspirations? For her essential dilemma was this: how to write for the public yet maintain her aristocratic decorum and fulfill what she believed to be the noble aims of literature. A glance at her career will help answer those questions, and will, besides, throw some light on publishing practices and on women writers of her day.

Her writings can be classified in three ways: those that remained unpublished in her lifetime; those printed without her authority; and finally, those whose publication she arranged.

Still among her unpublished manuscripts are her juvenilia: poems, translations, a pastoral in prose and verse, a brief epistolary romance. These typical effusions of a young lady with literary tastes and ample leisure raised no problems of publication, of commercialism, or, if truth be told, of literary distinction.

A more puzzling form of nonpublication is her critique of Joseph Addison's tragedy, *Cato.* Her husband, a close friend of its author, let her read the play in manuscript before it was staged in 1713. She then composed her critical essay, which Addison read carefully enough to follow a few of her suggested changes. Whether she intended her essay to be printed or merely circulated among her friends is not clear. She headed it: "Wrote at the desire of Mr. Wortley; suppressed at the desire of Mr. Addison." It was probably Addison's "excessive jealousy of his reputation" (as a contemporary observed) that made him suppress the essay.

Still another of Lady Mary's equivocal nonpublications was a dramatic work. Marivaux's vivacious comedy entitled *The Game of Love and Chance* had been produced in Paris in 1730, and in London at the Haymarket Theatre in 1734. Lady Mary got hold of a copy, and adapted it into a three-act comedy; her version, entitled *Simplicity* and only recently discovered, is remarkably naturalized—as English as roast beef and Yorkshire pudding. Yet it was neither staged nor published. Did she intend it for the theatre? Or merely as a private exercise to demonstrate her versatility?

A lady ambitious for literary reputation within her own social circle could allow her writings to be passed about among her friends. Although a great admirer of La Rochefoucauld, Lady Mary once tested her wit against his when she wrote a long essay in French to refute one of his maxims: her startling theme is that marriages can be delightful as well as convenient. She let her friends read it and, if they wished, take copies. Such "publication" was proper; it brought the author neither vulgar applause nor money but the admiration of her social peers.

The Court and upper-class circles were a spawning ground for all sorts of verse—squibs, ballads, epigrams, imitations, songs, epistles. From Pope and Swift down to barely literate coxcombs, everybody (it seemed) wrote them. "Poets encrease and multiply to that Stupendous degree," Lady Mary remarks to her sister (in 1723), "you see 'em at every turn, even in Embroidier'd Coats and pink colour'd Top knots. Makeing verses is allmost as common as takeing snuff, and God can tell what miserable stuff people carry about in their pockets and offer to all their Acquaintance . . ." Even as late as the 1770's this kind of "publication" was neatly caught in Sheridan's *School for Scandal,* when Lady Sneerwell wonders why Sir Benjamin Backbite never publishes anything, and he replies: "To say truth, ma'am, 'tis very vulgar to print; and as my little productions are mostly satires and lampoons on particular people, I find they circulate more by giving copies in confidence to the friends of the parties."

Exactly such an episode occurred in 1715 with Lady Mary's *Town Eclogues,* clever imitations of Virgil's bucolics, dealing with persons and scandals of the *beau monde.* And with piratical printers and Grub Street scavengers hungry for titbits like these, three of the eclogues fell into the hands of Edmund Curll, who published them with a teasing preface. Unauthorized publication was an affliction visited upon other writers— notably Pope and Swift, who also suffered from the Unspeakable Curll. His *Miscellanea* in 1726 was the direct cause of Pope's and Swift's determination to issue their own *Miscellanies in Prose and Verse.*

Admirers and friends could also be a source of unauthorized publication. When Lady Mary met the uncharitable Horace Walpole in Florence she let him transcribe her six town eclogues, which he later gave to Dodsley to print—without her permission. Similarly, a letter she sent from Constantinople to a friend in Paris was printed there, and another was printed in London after her return. What could she do about these? Had she wanted to win popular applause she could have issued a corrected, authorized edition. (This is what Pope had done with his letters, after having arranged for an unauthorized edition to be published first.)

When she wrote for publication she did so anonymously. Her first published piece appeared in the *Spectator,* an essay in the form of a letter in which she assumes the feminist role of the president of a widows' club. Her authorship of this piece has only recently been discovered, giving her the honor (250 years later) of being the only woman who contributed to that periodical.

Her belletristic essay is gentle compared to the strident one she sent to a newspaper, *The Flying Post,* during the controversy about smallpox inoculation in 1722. She called her piece "A Plain Account of the Inoculating of the Small Pox by a Turkey Merchant." Before printing it, the newspaper editor toned down its sarcasms about physicians and their College. Lady Mary's propaganda for inoculation thrust her into the arena of controversy, though anonymously, because of her passionate belief in a public benefit.

She moved closer to public affairs when (in 1737) she wrote a series of essays on political and social questions, partly in defense of Sir Robert Walpole's ministry. Her friendship with Walpole's mistress, who became his wife, probably impelled her to defend him. She called her periodical *The Nonsense of Common-Sense*—to refute the Opposition paper *Common Sense*—and flippantly headed each issue: "To be continued as long as the Author thinks fit, and the Publick likes it." Its most eloquent essay advocates women's right to be respected and honored. Besides its persuasive arguments, the most striking proof of its feminist power could not be divulged by the author; namely, that the essays were written by a woman. With its ninth issue the paper ended its run, an unusual (if not unique) example of a political periodical written by a woman.

On the literary scene of that decade Pope was the center of controversy, bombarded by pamphlets shot by his enemies. From one of them came (in 1733) the anonymous *Verses to the Imitator of Horace,* one of the crudest and cruellest of the war. As to its authorship, Pope believed that both Lady Mary and Lord Hervey "had a share in it, but which was uppermost, I know not. I pretend not to determine the exact method of this witty fornication." (In all probability, Lady Mary wrote it and Hervey arranged for its publication.) Two different but almost identical editions were published on successive days. The title of one of them states that the *Verses* were "By a Lady," and few readers could have been ignorant of the lady's identity; in self-defense, Lady Mary was willing to reveal her authorship. Of the fighters in the Popeian war only one besides Lady Mary was a woman—Elizabeth Thomas, who attacked him for the *Dunciad;* but few if any of all these pamphleteers could match Lady Mary in ferocity or effectiveness.

She attacked Pope for revenge; for a less personal reason, she launched a pamphlet at his friend Swift. Two years after Swift published *The Lady's Dressing Room* there appeared a handsomely printed pamphlet entitled *The Dean's Provocation for Writing the Lady's Dressing Room.* Very cleverly imitating his verse form and ribald diction, it belabors him for his alleged misogyny. Why Lady Mary was provoked to write and publish this pamphlet—which has only now been identified as being by her—is uncertain: the satisfaction of defending women, of scoring off Pope's friend and a man she detested, of pushing her way forward as a woman who (anonymously) could take on the formidable author of *Gulliver's Travels.*

Her third pamphlet was relatively benign, though not without a moral message. James Hammond, a young protégé of Lord Chesterfield's, had addressed an amorous poem to Catherine Dashwood, a lady who was "inexorably cruel" to him. Lady Mary in an *Answer,* published anonymously with Hammond's poem, advises him to desist since he cannot offer marriage with financial safeguards. Courtship, marriage, and gal-

lantry (in the ungallant eighteenth-century sense) were topics
that always interested Lady Mary. Her pamphlet and her other
two verse satires were all issued within one year, and show that
on occasion she did seek vulgar applause by putting her work
in print.

All her writings so far discussed—unpublished, or circulated
privately in manuscript or publicly in print—do not include her
letters, the literary form on which her reputation rests today.
"The familiar letter was the chosen medium of the age," Chaun-
cey Tinker has stated, naming as its leading practitioners three
men—and one woman, Lady Mary. Is there any connection between her activities as a letter-writer and as a woman-of-letters?

The Sapphos who inhabited Grub Street in the earlier part
of the century must have written personal letters, but where are
they now? Scattered to the four winds. Many of Lady Mary's
private letters survive because she and her correspondents and
their descendants carefully saved them. Her informal letters
were private, not to be divulged to the world for reasons of
propriety if not discretion. This is not distinctly an eighteenth-
century attitude, for I doubt that any of us would let strangers
read the letters we send to intimate friends. Lady Mary's letters
to her sister in the 1720's are easily her most scintillating correspondence, full of gay scandal and witty comment. Yet in one
of them, after saying that she had read the recently published
letters of Madame de Sévigné, she continues: "very pretty they
are, but I assert without the least vanity that mine will be full
as entertaining 40 years hence." Her prediction—that as a letter-
writer she would perhaps become a woman-of-letters—was not
mere bravado, for during these very years she compiled a work
to serve her in that coveted ambition.

During the two years when she accompanied her husband
on his embassy to Turkey she had kept copies (fifty-two in number) of many of the letters sent to her friends and relations.
She adapted them slightly before copying them into two al-

bums. Soon after her return to England she lent the albums to
interested friends—to Lord Pembroke, the antiquarian collector,
who was impressed by her copy of classical inscriptions, and to
Mary Astell. Miss Astell, who welcomed it as a proof of feminist power, enthusiastically wrote out a preface in verse and
prose: "I once had the Vanity to hope I might acquaint the Public that it ow'd this invaluable Treasure to my Importunitys,"
Miss Astell writes, "But alas! The most Ingenious Author has
condemn'd it to obscurity during her Life . . ." In other words,
Lady Mary was pleased to let her friends read the Turkish
Embassy Letters, circulating them in manuscript, but refused
to let them be printed for the public at large. This, at any rate,
was true in 1725, when Miss Astell lamented her decision. I
shall return to the Turkish Embassy Letters later, for their ultimate fate—in the second half of the century—very neatly rounds
out Lady Mary's literary career.

As we have seen, there are no literary women comparable to
Lady Mary in the first half of the century, but in the latter half
women won a place in the world of literature with dignity,
even with profit as well. Elizabeth Montagu, most famous as a
founding mother of the Bluestockings, is sometimes confused
with Lady Mary; she was married to a cousin of Lady Mary's
husband. While she immersed herself in literature and the conversation of the learned for sixty years, she published only two
slight works: three dialogues printed in Lord Lyttelton's *Dialogues of the Dead,* and an *Essay on Shakespeare,* a well-mean-
ing but shallow book intended to refute Voltaire's critical "mis-
representations." Although these were issued anonymously their
authorship was no secret; a lady whose works enhanced a peer's
book and who defended England's greatest poet suffered no
disgrace for appearing in print. She also wrote letters of astonishing profusion and prolixity—possibly as many as ten thousand survive. Her correspondence, whatever its literary quality,
at least satisfied her rage for writing, but none of it was pub-

lished until the next century: her only readers were the recipients and their friends.

The two Montagus are also comparable as patronesses, a role they played by wielding influence, bestowing rewards, and extending sympathy to the writers they befriended. At the beginning of her literary career Lady Mary had enjoyed a poetic camaraderie with Pope and Gay; she read plays that Edward Young and Henry Fielding submitted to her, and rewarded them with suggestions as well as influence; and she gave cash presents to writers who dedicated their books to her, Richard Savage among them. Mrs. Montagu patronized writers as worthy as James Beattie, and as unworthy as Ann Yearsley, the milkwoman of Bristol; and she could be so silly as to take up the cause of James Macpherson, who instituted the feast of shells at her house, when they drank out of a nautilus to the immortal memory of Ossian.

Perhaps it is too easy to ridicule Mrs. Montagu. Here is how a young contemporary summed up her influence as a popular hostess: "Together with a superabundance of vanity ... she had quick parts, great vivacity, no small share of wit, a competent portion of learning, considerable fame as a writer, a large fortune, a fine house, and an excellent cook. Observe the climax, for it is not unintentional: the cook may perhaps be the only one of the powers I have enumerated who could carry on the war single-handed." (That contemporary, incidentally, was Lady Louisa Stuart, youngest granddaughter of Lady Mary.) And in our own day Mrs. Montagu has been dubbed by Bonamy Dobrée the Queen of the Bluestockings and the Grand Duchess of the Bores.

Yet she cannot be disregarded. She and her circle constitute a distinct and unique phenomenon in English literary history and point up (by contrast) the position of literary women in the earlier part of the century. In Lady Mary's day, where could a woman go to meet others, men and women, who shared her literary interests? The men had their coffee-houses, taverns, and clubs. From the quasi-fictitious clubs of the *Spectator* papers to the Literary Club of Dr. Johnson's circle, men could enjoy these enclaves of social and intellectual fellowship.

In France, the *salon,* with a powerful and viable tradition, flourished throughout the century under a succession of hostesses —Madame de Tencin, Madame Geoffrin, Madame du Deffand (best known in English letters through her desperate friendship with Horace Walpole), and Mademoiselle de Lespinasse. Both men and women took equal part in these *salons.*

Could Lady Mary have founded a *salon* in London? In the opinion of Professor Tinker, who posed the question, although she had a wide acquaintance among the authors of her day, a genuine interest in literature, and very remarkable powers, she "repelled men as much by her insolent cleverness as by her slovenly manners." Aside from his reliance on Pope and Walpole for characterizing Lady Mary, I think Professor Tinker has oversimplified. No woman by herself, however genial her cleverness or fastidious her manners, could have founded a social institution. Mrs. Montagu's friends and allies included other energetic Bluestockings—Mrs. Vesey, Mrs. Boscawen, Mrs. Delany, Mrs. Chapone, Miss Carter, and Hannah More. By the time Mrs. Montagu queened it over the Bluestockings and conducted what was at least parallel to the French *salon,* the status of women had radically changed. They had the advantage of more education, and swelled the ranks of the growing reading public. They even outwrote the men in one literary genre: the majority of eighteenth-century novels (as Ian Watt estimates) were written by women.

The Bluestocking circle, when formed, was not intended to be pretentiously learned (as the word has come to mean in its pejorative sense). Hannah More published a poem in 1786 called *Bas Bleu,* and subtitled "Conversation." In her preface she explains that the Bluestockings were "little Societies ... composed of persons distinguished, in general, for their rank, talents, or respectable character" who met "for the sole purpose of conversation, and were different in no respect from other parties, but that the company did not play at cards." In the poem Miss More dissociates her Bluestocking conversation from that of French *salons,* which (she maintains) encouraged a strained, artificial wit and ridiculous preciosity.

The English Bluestocking assemblies did not perpetuate themselves, as the French *salons* did, but died out with their founders. While they flourished they at least provided a milieu where women could mingle with their intellectual peers of both sexes. They also bridged the gap between genteel amateurism and respectable professionalism by welcoming women who earned their living by their writings—provided, of course, that they remained respectable.

Elizabeth Carter was one of the earliest of these ladies. The daughter of a clergyman, she was prodigiously learned: to Latin, Greek, and Hebrew she added French, Italian, Spanish, and German, and, in her later years, Portuguese and Arabic. Dr. Johnson's tribute to her is often quoted: she "could make a pudding as well as translate Epictetus from the Greek, and work a handkerchief as well as compose a poem." Her first poem had appeared in the *Gentleman's Magazine* in 1734, when she was seventeen; and after anonymous translations from French and Italian (which brought her renown), she issued her Epictetus by subscription in 1758, thus earning by it almost £1,000. Her collected poems went into three editions. Besides these profits, she prospered with annuities from Mrs. Montagu (£100) and from General Pulteney (£150).

Hannah More, a generation younger, was as earnest a Bluestocking, and even more successful. Her tragedy *Percy,* staged by Garrick, ran for twenty-one nights, bringing to her almost £600, and its first edition of four thousand copies was sold out in a fortnight. Her collected works, published in her lifetime, fill nineteen volumes, and she died worth £30,000. Financial success and moral respectability could go no higher. An anonymous pamphleteer in 1743 had defended on religious grounds the right of women to publish; Hannah More's main reputation for her voluminous writings is that of a religious writer: here is an indication of the shift in the status of women.

Less affluent but equally blameless women plied their busy pens. Charlotte Lennox had to struggle to earn her living, writing plays .(only one of them staged), poems, and—more successfully—seven novels. Fanny Burney achieved remarkable and precocious *éclat* as a novelist, at first anonymously, but it was her old-fashioned father who discouraged her from pursuing a career as a writer; and so to please him she endured palatial servitude as Second Keeper of the Robes to Queen Charlotte.

The irrepressible Mrs. Thrale illustrates still another aspect of the woman of letters in the second half of the century. As she herself explains, when her husband, a wealthy brewer, ordered her not to think of the kitchen she was "driven" to literature as her sole resource. Like the Bluestockings and other literary ladies, she was a profuse letter-writer, often with a self-conciousness born of the belief that posterity would appreciate her private communications. But Mrs. Thrale violated convention by publishing her private letters in her own lifetime. Encouraged by the success of her anecdotes of Dr. Johnson (in 1786), she issued *Letters to and from Samuel Johnson* two years later. Since Johnson had by then been dead four years, her breach of decorum was less serious; the letters of the leading writer of the time were, in a sense, public property, and a greater writer than Mrs. Thrale was soon to issue a biography containing many of his private letters.

Apart from the Bluestockings, two literary women who were contemporary show a zeal and dedication that is thoroughly professional.

Catherine Macaulay, a vigorous radical and republican, was

the first woman to attempt the writing of history on a large
scale. The eight massive volumes of her *History of England
from James I to the Hanoverians* created something of a stir. If
it is forgotten today, she lives on in the pages of Boswell's *Life
of Johnson,* in the episode when Johnson dined at her house
and, pretending to be a convert to her egalitarianism, asked her
to allow the footman to sit down with them. He later told Boswell, "Sir, your levellers wish to level *down* as far as themselves;
but they cannot bear levelling *up* to themselves." And near the
close of the century Mary Wollstonecraft published her *Vindication of the Rights of Women* (in 1792), an extensive and closely
reasoned treatise that pleads the cause of women. Most of the
feminist propaganda of the past had been written by men. Now,
a woman summoned up the passion to vindicate—and to advo-
cate—the rights of her own sex.

Among dedicated feminist champions, Mary Wollstonecraft
had been preceded by Mary Astell at the beginning of the century. And, as will be recalled, Miss Astell had paid tribute to
Lady Mary's Turkish Embassy Letters as proof that a woman
could excel in the world of literature. Lady Mary kept the two
albums of letters with her (along with her other manuscripts
and her library) during her sojourn of twenty-two years on the
Continent. In 1761 she started on her way home to England.
While detained in Rotterdam by winter weather, she presented
the albums to a sympathetic clergyman, with an inscription stating that she was giving them to him "to be dispos'd of as he
thinks proper." What lies behind this cryptic testament? Had
she wanted the albums to be inherited by her daughter, along
with all her other manuscripts, books, and possessions, she
would not have handed them over to the clergyman. The dis-
posal she clearly intended must have been publication.

Although she was willing to sacrifice her decorum (posthu-
mously), the clergyman felt that he must maintain his. When
Lady Mary died, eight months after making her bizarre gift,

he wrote to her daughter informing her of it, whereupon Lady Bute demanded that he surrender the two albums. At first he refused, but after six months and the offer of a large sum of money he agreed. Lady Bute, of course, had no intention of publishing the letters, and it seemed then that Lady Mary's final and grandest ambition for literary glory would be frustrated. By a fortunate accident, however, the letters had somehow been copied out of the albums. Ironically, their previous circulation in manuscript now prevented their suppression by Lady Bute. One year after Lady Mary's death the letters were published, and with such striking and widespread success that they established her solid reputation as a great letter-writer. Mary Astell's preface to the albums, printed with the letters, predicted that *"Male-Authors* with an envious eye [would] Praise coldly, that they may the more decry"; but she was wrong: Gibbon, Voltaire, Johnson, among others, praised them enthusiastically.

Did Lady Mary's literary career, we may wonder, fulfill her professed concept of authorship? Writing can be one of man's noblest prerogatives, she states, but when practiced solely to earn money it is easily corrupted. Her most intense and dramatic attempt to seize literary fame—through the posthumous publication of her Turkish Embassy Letters—could not have been mercenary in motive. Or lacking in decorum, for that matter. These letters are her public testament, the brilliantly polished record of the observations and thoughts of an enlightened, emancipated woman whose view goes beyond insular England to embrace all of Europe and the realm of Islam. The letters are Lady Mary's credentials as simultaneously a *bel esprit* and (by precept and example) a feminist champion. Through being a great letter-writer she achieved her ambition of being a woman-of-letters.

Her career, with its span over the mid-century, bridges the gap between, on the one side, women writers as tawdry Sapphos *or* stately ladies, and, on the other side, women writers as professional *and* respectable members of the republic of letters. And what lies on the horizon in the next century? Ladies of letters whose work gave them a stature comparable to men's: Maria Edgeworth, Jane Austen, the Brontës, George Eliot, Elizabeth Barrett Browning. It is inconceivable that they could have emerged if their century had followed the seventeenth; the eighteenth had prepared the way.

Index